Faith and Doubt

[The] Man of Letters . . . must be regarded as our most important modern person . . . Men of Letters are a perpetual Priesthood, from age to age, teaching all men that a God is still present in their life . . . there is no class comparable for importance to the Priesthood of the Writers of Books.

Carlyle, *Heroes, Hero-Worship and the Heroic in History,*
Lecture on 'The Hero as Man of Letters'.

It is our lay writers who are moulding the character and forming the opinions of the age [and taking the place of] the clergy in the direction of the thought of England.

W. E. H. Lecky, *The Religious Tendencies of the Age.*

FAITH AND DOUBT

RELIGION AND SECULARIZATION
IN LITERATURE FROM
WORDSWORTH TO LARKIN

R. L. Brett

MERCER UNIVERSITY PRESS

James Clarke & Co
Cambridge

James Clarke & Co
P.O. Box 60
Cambridge
CB1 2NT

Mercer University Press
6316 Peake Road
Macon
Georgia 31210-39601

ISBN 0 2276 7941 5

ISBN 0 86554 544 8

British Library Cataloguing in Publication Data:
A catalogue record is available from the British Library.

First published in the UK by The Lutterworth Press, 1997
First published in the USA by Mercer University Press, 1997

Printed in Great Britain by Hillman Printers (Frome) Ltd.

CONTENTS

FOREWORD   vii

PREFACE   ix

INTRODUCTION   1

I   Wordsworth and Coleridge   6

         Wordsworth   21

         Coleridge   37

II   Carlyle and Arnold   54

III George Eliot and Dickens   84

IV   Tennyson and Browning   125

V   Yeats and Eliot   161

VI   Auden and Larkin   205

     NOTES   240

     BIBLIOGRAPHY   247

     INDEX   256

FOREWORD

Raymond Brett died before the publication of this book, before even the proofs were ready for inspection. This was especially sad, since of all his books it is the one which shows most fully his remarkable range of knowledge and understanding in literature, philosophy and theology. His scholarship and critical acumen, his characteristic lucidity, impartiality, and humanity are all in evidence here in the work for which, I feel sure, he would most wish to be remembered.

'Much from him I profess I won,
And more, and more, I should have done'.

Tom McAlindon
University of Hull
May 1997

PREFACE

A list of all those to whom I am indebted in writing this book would be too long and disproportionate to its importance. I hope my debt is sufficiently acknowledged in the Bibliography. Two exceptions must be made to this. I am especially grateful to my friend Professor T. McAlindon and the Computer Centre at Hull University, who while I was in hospital, made clean copies for the publisher of my rather disorganised computer discs. Above all, as with all my previous publications, my largest debt is to my wife, whose encouragement and advice were invaluable; she has always been my 'sternest critic but the best'. Any faults that remain are my sole responsibility.

INTRODUCTION

The approach of this book is impenitently biographical and historical. In this and some other respects it runs counter to much contemporary theory and practice, but as I hope to show, this approach is intrinsic to its subject matter. The American New Critics, the Jungians, the structuralists and post-structuralists, the deconstructionists and the Marxists have all conspired to dismiss the author from critical discussion, but there are welcome signs that this is now changing.

The argument of the American New Critics, that one cannot discover the author's intentions, certainly diminishes the importance of the author. This was reinforced by the concern of the structuralists not with the author but with the universal truths they discerned underlying works of literature in different ages by different writers. In this they were at one with some Jungians and their archetypes. The Marxists, too, treat the author not as in Wordsworth's phrase, 'a man speaking to men' but as the mouthpiece of the historical forces revealed by the theory of dialectical materialism. Moreover, all of them marginalised not only the author but the individual text.

Northrop Frye in *The Archetypes of Literature* describes the poet as delivering the poem 'in as uninjured a state as possible, and if the poem is alive, it is equally anxious to get rid of him and screams to be let loose from his private memories and associations'. But Frye recognises, as all parents do, that their offspring are never finally off their hands, and he accepts that a study of the author's psychology may throw light on the work itself. A more radical account was elaborated by Roland Barthes in *The Death of the Author*, but like the report of Mark Twain's death, this was greatly exaggerated. A work may achieve a degree of independence from its creator, but often a knowledge of its origins may throw useful light on our understanding of it. Knowing that the child Wordsworth addresses in his sonnet, 'It is a beauteous evening, calm and free', is his own illegitimate daughter whom he is seeing for the first time, increases our understanding of the poem. On a larger scale the biographical studies by Lyndall Gordon increase our appreciation of Eliot's work.

When they had finished dancing on the supposed grave of the

author the theorists were faced with questions about the literary object and the principles that govern criticism. One of the most influential of the theorists was Barthes whose 'Criticism as Language' first appeared in a special issue of *The Times Literary Supplement* in 1963. Barthes argued that criticism was a meta-language, concerned only with language and therefore tautologous and having nothing to do with the truth. It is possible to argue that literature itself because it is fictional has nothing to do with the truth and is non-referential. But one cannot apply this to criticism, for as Wittgenstein maintained, all aesthetic judgements are descriptive of the object.

Barthes added to the confusion with his rhetorical question, 'How can anyone believe that a given work is an object independent of the psyche and personal history of the critic studying it, with regard to which he enjoys a sort of extra-territorial status?' This reinforced the notion that the perception of a work changes from age to age and leaves the work with no permanent or objective status. As far back as 1949 René Wellek anticipated this view in the chapter he contributed to his and Austin Warren's *Theory of Literature* which still remains a standard work. In the chapter, entitled 'The Analysis of the Literary Work of Art' he advances the following definition:

> The work of art, then, appears as an object of knowledge *sui generis* which has a special ontological status. It is neither real (like a statue) nor mental (like the experience of light or pain) nor ideal (like a triangle). It is a system of norms of ideal concepts which are inter-subjective. They must be assumed to exist in collective ideology, changing with it, accessible only through individual mental experiences.

It would have been more accurate to speak of 'physical' rather than 'real' in describing a statue, and 'private' rather than 'mental' in writing about the experience of light or pain. Both of these wrongly imply that what is mental cannot be real.

Literary objects are produced by the mind but are real and open to public inspection. They belong to what Sir Karl Popper designated World 3 objects. In his 'Knowledge: Subjective versus Objective' Popper distinguishes between an objective world of material things (which he calls World 1), a subjective world of minds (World 2) and a world of objects which are the products of minds, but once produced, are independent (World 3). World 3 objects comprise ideas, scientific theories, works of art, language; all that makes up our cultural inheritance. Wellek suggests that the literary work exists only in the minds of critics, changing from generation to generation and realising itself fully only in 'collective ideology'. But is this Hegelian kind of explanation satisfactory? It is true, of course, that no amount of conceptual analysis will exhaust the meaning of a work of literature, but this is not to say that the readers create the work, only that they appreciate it in different ways. The discussions that occupy the following chapters are about works that have a historical reality. Knowledge of their authors may help us to understand them better but their meaning is not indeterminate or subjective.

A common belief of many modern literary theorists is that the literary work is simply a linguistic object. Certainly words are the tools the writer uses to make the work, but the work is more than words. The writer creates a story, an action (this is true even of lyric poetry), a plot, a set of characters, all of which come to life by means of language, but all of which remain non-verbal. Certainly novelists such as George Eliot and Dickens create characters with a life of their own who cannot be described fully by linguistic analysis or stylistics. There are deconstructionists who deny this and treat the work not only as a linguistic fact, but speak of language in the manner of Heidegger, as the master rather than the tool of the writer. One of these, Paul de Man, in his 'Shelley Disfigured'[2] maintains that 'we are the product rather than the agent of language' and it is not the writer who speaks the language, but the language who 'speaks' the writer.

This argument diminishes not only the writer but also his work and Barthes extends the process of deconstruction to the reader as well. In *S/Z* he writes, ' "I" is not an innocent subject, anterior to the text, one which will subsequently deal with the text as it would an object to dismantle or a site to occupy. This "I" which approaches the text is already itself a plurality of other texts, of codes which are infinite'. This scepticism goes even further with Derrida's belief that logic itself is unreliable.

Scepticism about the author, the text, and even the reader, leaves the critic free to interpret the text as he wishes. Behind this, however, there are two dogmatic approaches which are hard to reconcile with it. These descend from Hegel and Marx. The title Karl Popper gave to his book, *The Poverty of Historicism*, indicates the intellectual damage their notion of inexorable historical forces leads to; both undervalue literature and the arts.

Hegel did not accept the creativity of the writer who, in his view, is the instrument of the zeitgeist; his work is dictated by the Spirit who controls all things. There is no reciprocity between the writer and his work and he lacks any real freedom.

Marx, as is well known, turned Hegel upside down; the artist for him is not the instrument of the Spirit but of the material and economic forces that govern history. This is clearly illustrated in the writings of Terry Eagleton. In a Foreword he contributed to Daniel Cotton's *Social Figures: George Eliot, Social History, and Literary Representation* he writes:

> What we witness in 'George Eliot'– the name can be presented thus to signify one major instantiation of this liberal humanist – is the strenuous consolidation of an impressive power, depth, range, and intricacy whose hour has now come.

In this acknowledgement of her achievement we have lost the flesh and blood woman whose writings were the product of her spiritual and intellectual struggles and whose fictional characters love, rejoice, suffer, and mourn. In his *Marxism and Literary Criticism* Eagleton declares that

> The difference between science and art is not that they deal with different objects, but that they deal with the same objects in different ways. Science gives us conceptual knowledge of a situation; art gives us the experience of that situation, which is equivalent to ideology. But by doing this, it . . . begins to move us towards that full understanding of ideology which is scientific knowledge.

This is to make art an inferior kind of activity when compared with science; something that can be left behind when real knowledge is obtained.

It is not true that literature and science deal with the same objects. Science is concerned with theories that are falsifiable, but there are things in life that go beyond this and are best left to art. Literature represents human experience in all its richness and complexity. It is not concerned with abstraction, but with the wonder of life and its concrete variety. In this it comes close to religion; we see this especially in the writers treated here.

They all lived in a period of great changes. Wordsworth and Coleridge witnessed a sharp break with the past; they lived through the French Revolution and were the heirs of the new philosophy, described by Kant as 'a Copernican Revolution' in men's thinking. They faced the attacks on miracles by Hume and on the church by Gibbon. Those who followed them saw the beginnings of the Industrial Revolution, the new criticism of the Bible coming out of Germany, later still the challenge of Darwinism, and throughout the nineteenth century, German Idealism coloured men's thinking even when they were unaware of it. The Communist Manifesto was published in 1847, but Marxism was not influential until well into this century; then it brought about changes as great as those produced by two world wars.

These writers were shaped, as we all are, by the times in which they lived, but they were not determined by them. They met the issues of their times by a process of give and take; all agreeing with Carlyle, whose secularisation of Christianity nevertheless led him to declare that 'a man's religion is the chief fact with regard to him'. They took seriously questions of faith and doubt, but not all of them made the journey to a new or renewed religious faith. Some never started the journey, others became agnostic on the way or replaced their faith with a substitute religion. But their writings all reveal the changes in religion they encountered and the part they played in bringing them about.

I

Wordsworth and Coleridge

In January 1801, on the publication of the second edition of *Lyrical Ballads*, Wordsworth sent William Wilberforce a copy of the new and expanded collection of the poems which he and Coleridge had first published in 1798. The two volumes were accompanied by a letter, signed by Wordsworth but drafted by Coleridge.[1] For most people *Lyrical Ballads* represents no more than a radical break with poetic convention, a desire to establish a new style and diction, and it may seem surprising that Wordsworth and Coleridge should send their poems to a leading Evangelical, especially when we know that Wordsworth had a marked dislike of the Evangelicals. But the dislike was modified here, for Wilberforce was admired by both men, and not only for his campaign against slavery. Their letter suggests that their poems share a common purpose with Wilberforce's *A Practical View of the Prevailing Religious System of Professed Christians* and compares the superficiality of so much religion and the insincerity of contemporary poetry:

> In your religious treatise these truths are developed, & applied to the present state of our religion; I have acted on them in a less awful department, but not I trust with less serious convictions.

Wilberforce's *Practical View* was published in April 1797. There was little demand for religious works at the time and the publisher advised an edition of only 500 copies, but it sold out almost immediately and soon became a best-seller. Coleridge probably read it while he was writing the 'Ancient Mariner' and Wordsworth before composing 'Tintern Abbey', the two major poems in the 1798 edition of *Lyrical Ballads*. One can discern in both these poems the same pattern of religious experience that is central to Wilberforce's account of religious faith. Wilberforce declares that a Christianity which is more than nominal must be characterised by a sense of sin and guilt, of a consciousness of forgiveness, and the awareness of rebirth to a new life. All these are features of the spiritual crises related in these poems and both poets would have recognised this, but to understand how this came about we need to trace the development of their beliefs during the previous years.

Both men grew to manhood at a time when the French Revolution threatened fundamental changes in Western society. Both supported the revolutionary cause and at Cambridge had become 'democrats', what today would be called members of the revolutionary Left. Coleridge had been an undergraduate at Jesus College, which was a centre of left-wing politics, and while there had come under the influence of William Frend, a Fellow of Jesus, who abandoned his Anglican orders to embrace Unitarianism. At this time Unitarianism was part of a wide sweep of ideas which included not only dissent from the established church, but freedom of conscience, electoral reform, and republicanism. Many on the left looked back on the preceding one and a half centuries as a long revolutionary struggle which had started with the English Civil War, continued through the American War of Independence, and reached its consummation in the French Revolution. In 1795 Coleridge had given a course of lectures in Bristol on politics and religion in which he looked back on those figures who had been in the van of this struggle, the 'Sages and patriots that being dead do yet speak to us, spirits of Milton, Locke, Sidney, Harrington.'[2]

Although the two men made profound changes in their opinions in the intervening years, Wordsworth could still in 1802 invoke many of the same names in the sonnet he included in 'Poems Dedicated to National Independence and Liberty':

Great men have been among us; hands that penned
And tongues that uttered wisdom – better none:
The later Sidney, Marvel, Harrington,
Young Vane, and others who called Milton friend.
These moralists could act and comprehend.

For both of them Milton was the great exemplar in religion, politics, and poetry. Inspired by him and those round him, there ran through this dissenting and radical movement a strain of millennialism, a belief that the kingdom of Christ would be established on earth in the near future and that its coming would be achieved by political action. Many saw the portents of this in Biblical prophecy and believed that contemporary events foreshadowed the apocalyptic vision of the 'Book of Revelation'. Milton in many of his prose works viewed the Civil War as a version of Armageddon and identified Charles I as the Antichrist. That the prophecy remained unfulfilled proved no deterrence to the believers; for them it was only postponed.

In 1793 and 1794 the distinguished Unitarian, Joseph Priestley, preached two famous sermons which identified the events of the Revolution in France with the earthquakes described in Revelation. The other great Unitarian preacher of the day, Richard Price, also welcomed the French Revolution with apocalyptic fervour and saw it as the realization of his millennarian hopes. In his 'Discourse on the Love of our Country', delivered at the Meeting House in the Old Jewry in London in January 1789, he spoke of the struggles of the seventeenth century and the demand for American independence, and declared, 'And now methinks, I see the ardour for liberty catching and spreading; a general amendment beginning in human affairs; the dominion of kings changed for the dominion of laws, and the dominion of priests giving way to the dominion of reason and conscience'. Hazlitt, who belonged to a younger generation, describes in his essay 'On the Feeling of Immortality in Youth' how he grew up in these exciting days.

> For my part, I set out in life with the French Revolution, and that event had considerable influence on my early feelings, as on those of others. Youth then was doubly such. It was the dawn of a new era, a new impulse had been given to men's minds, and the sun of Liberty rose upon the sun of Life in the same day, and both were proud to run their race together.

But it proved to be a false dawn. Hazlitt goes on to describe the disillusionment that followed:

> Little did I dream, while my first hopes and wishes went hand in hand with those of the human race, that long before my eyes should close, that dawn would be overcast, and set once more in the night of despotism.

This path of disillusionment with revolutionary hopes was one Wordsworth and Coleridge also trod.

The first meeting of the two men was not in Cambridge (for Wordsworth had left the university in 1790, a year before Coleridge took up residence) but in Bristol. Already in 1793 Coleridge had heard Wordsworth's poetry read aloud at a meeting of a literary society in Exeter and felt that he was listening to an important and original poetic voice, but it was not until two years later that they met. Wordsworth had gone to Bristol to visit his friends the Pinneys, who were rich sugar merchants there. Coleridge was already in Bristol where he had gone to join forces with Southey, a native of the city, to make plans for a Pantisocratic community in America. This was to be a break with the old and corrupt societies of Europe and would be a self-governing community in which all would have equal rights, all would contribute according to their means, and all would share equally in the fruits of their labours. It would consist at first of six young couples who would share in the farming, the maintenance of the property, and in educating their children. Although the scheme never advanced beyond the planning stage because of differences between its founders, it had one decisive effect. This was Coleridge's marriage to Sara Fricker, Southey's sister-in-law; a step that was to change his life in ways he could not have foreseen.

Instead of journeying to the New World, Coleridge and his wife moved in December 1796, to Nether Stowey in the Quantocks where his friend, Thomas Poole, had secured them a cottage. Wordsworth and his sister Dorothy were living nearby at Racedown in Dorset where the Pinneys had lent them their country house. The two men had corresponded with each other since their meeting in Bristol and their friendship now became intimate. Forty years later Wordsworth still remembered in vivid detail Coleridge's visit to Racedown. He and his sister, he wrote, both had a distinct memory of how Coleridge 'did not keep to the high road, but leaped over a gate and bounded down a pathless field by which he cut off an angle.'[3] Coleridge's visit lasted three weeks and he was soon back again with a chaise to take them to Nether Stowey. A fortnight later the Wordsworths moved to Alfoxden and became Coleridge's neighbours. The period of their friendship and collaboration had begun.

In 1796 Coleridge had brought out *Poems on Various Subjects* which contained 'Religious Musings', a poem he had begun in 1794. He must have given a copy to Wordsworth for in a letter to his friend John Thelwall, an atheist and republican, who had disapproved of the poem, he wrote:

> A very dear friend of mine, who is in my opinion, the best poet of the age . . . thinks that the lines from 364 to 375 and from 403 to 428 the best in the Volume, – indeed worth all the rest – and this man is a Republican, and at least a Semi-atheist.[4]

This reveals not only Coleridge's admiration for Wordsworth's poetry but something of their religious and political opinions. Both the passages referred to (and the second must be lines 403-418 for that is where the poem ends) describe the Last Day and the coming of Christ's kingdom on earth. In the first passage 'Milton's trump' heralds the appearance of 'Adoring Newton', David Hartley, 'he first who marked the ideal tribes/Up the fine fibres through the sentient brain', and Joseph Priestley, 'patriot, and saint and sage', all three of whom played an important part in the development of Coleridge's thought. Newton whose account of the physical universe laid the foundations of eighteenth-century empiricism, like Milton, was an Arian. Priestley began life as a Calvinist, but became in succession, as Coleridge later described him in *Table Talk* in 1834, 'Presbyterian, Arian, Socinian, and last, Unitarian'. Like Coleridge, but many years earlier, Hartley had gone up to Jesus College, Cambridge, intending to become ordained, but had found he could not subscribe to all of the 39 Articles, though in spite of his reservations, he remained in the Church of England. Coleridge's admiration for him can be seen in his choice of the name Hartley for his eldest son, born in the year in which 'Religious Musings' was published.

When he abandoned the ministry Hartley turned to medicine and practised as a physician. His medical training and an interest in philosophy led to the publication of his *Observations on Man* (1749), popularised in a shorter version by Priestley, with the title, *Hartley's Theory of the Human Mind*. Hartley's account of the mind turned on two main principles. The first, which he called the Doctrine of Vibrations, argued that the body and mind form one physical system which operates by means of vibrations that run along the nerves as particles from the sense organs to the brain, and then in reverse from the brain to the muscles. More influential than this dubious physiology was his other theory, the Association of Ideas. Hartley did not originate this and the term itself was coined by Locke, but he applied it more radically than any of his predecessors.

In December 1794, Coleridge had written to Southey about the attractions of these theories and declared, 'but I go farther than Hartley, and believe the corporeality of thought – namely, that it is motion.'[5] Although he was still a disciple of Hartley as late as 1796, there were changes in his thinking and this is already seen in 'Religious Musings', which makes a brief reference to Berkeley, whose philosophy, especially in its later and more Platonic form, marked a significant movement away from the empiricist tradition of the past. Again Coleridge acknowledged his intellectual allegiance by giving his second son, born in 1798, the name of Berkeley. But the changes in the thinking of both Coleridge and Wordsworth between 1796 and 1798 were brought about not only by their reading, but by their own experience, and this was even truer of Wordsworth than Coleridge.

When he met Coleridge, Wordsworth was going through a momentous period in his life. Both men had been active in politics. As well as giving lectures in Bristol against the government and its policy towards France, in 1796 Coleridge had started *The Watchman*, a journal which gave his views a wider circulation. But Wordsworth's involvement with the events in France were more personal. He had first visited France when he left Cambridge in 1790 and set out with his college friend Robert Jones on a three-month walking tour through France and across the Alps into Switzerland. France was *en fête* for the Bastille had been stormed in the previous year and a constitutional monarchy established. Wordsworth was swept off his feet by the success of the Revolution and in the following year he returned to France and it was then that he met and fell in love with Annette Vallon, who in December 1792, bore him a daughter, Caroline.

Annette came from a family that supported the Royalists, but it was not political differences that parted the lovers. There were obvious obstacles in the way of a marriage, the chief being Wordsworth's financial dependence on relatives who wished him to be ordained as an Anglican parson. This would have given him financial independence but a French Roman Catholic wife would have made it difficult and he himself was lukewarm about the plan. *The Prelude* gives some account of the emotional stresses he suffered at this time and the conflicting loyalties that pulled in different directions, although no mention is made directly of Annette.

In October 1792 Wordsworth left Orleans for Paris where the Jacobin extremists were about to seize power. It is probable that he would have stayed in Paris, for shaken as he was by the excesses of mob rule, his belief in the Revolution remained firm. He tells us in *The Prelude* that it was shortage of money which forced his return to England, but looking back in the 1850, revised version of the poem, he also added that it was a merciful deliverance:

Dragged by a chain of harsh necessity,
So seemed it, – now I thankfully acknowledge,
Forced by the gracious providence of Heaven, –
To England I returned. (X, 222-5)

This may refer to the danger of being imprisoned in France, as some Englishmen were when the Terror took over the Revolution, but more probably it recognises that his whole life and poetic career would have been disastrously different if he had thrown in his lot with the new order in France as he had once planned.

On returning to England, Wordsworth at once associated with revolutionary circles in London. It was a time of a mounting crisis in his affairs. Little is known of his movements, but in June 1793 he spent a month in the Isle of Wight with his friend William Calvert, who generously paid both their expenses. Here Wordsworth could see the English fleet as it lay off Spithead ready for the war which Britain declared against France; a declaration which came as a terrible blow to his hopes and made a return to France virtually impossible. *The Prelude* again throws light on his state of mind and the profound depth of his feeling. It records his 'ghastly visions' of despair and the nightmares in which he pleaded:

> Before unjust tribunals – with a voice
> Labouring, a brain confounded, and a sense,
> Death-like, of treacherous desertion, felt
> In the last place of refuge – my own soul. (X, 412-15)

The 'ghastly visions' came to him when he separated from William Calvert at Salisbury, after leaving the Isle of Wight, and travelled alone on foot across Salisbury Plain to stay with his friend Robert Jones in Wales. The solitary journey included two or three days on the Plain where he had almost hallucinatory images of the primitive inhabitants waging war against each other. His route took him to the Wye valley and five years later when he re-visited the Wye he recounted in 'Tintern Abbey' how he had come earlier as:

> more like a man
> Flying from something that he dreads than one
> Who sought the thing he loved.

'Salisbury Plain' which had its origin in this episode was begun almost immediately, but he revised it at Racedown and later still gave it the title 'Guilt and Sorrow'. It is a poem full of gloom and foreboding, bitterly radical and anti-war in its sentiments.

A leading figure in the circles Wordsworth frequented at this time was William Godwin whose *Political Justice* was published in 1793, the year in which Wordsworth returned to England. Godwin modified some of his views in later editions of his work, but the first version advanced a theory of human perfectibility which caught the imaginations of those who had enthusiastically welcomed the French Revolution. Godwin saw man as self-sufficient, capable of throwing off the shackles of government, the law, property rights, and marriage. Society was to be based entirely on the exercise of reason. The extremes to which Godwin pushed his doctrines is seen in the famous argument that given the choice between rescuing one's mother or Fenelon from a fire, we should choose the philosopher, since he would be of greater use to society. This was probably levelled at Burke, who had argued that society is based upon an extension of the ties of family and friendship, whereas for Godwin government and society are necessarily corrupt if they are subject to vested interests whether of family, class, or nationality.

Although the example of the fire employs the utilitarian argument that the test of a right action is whether it benefits mankind, it was difficult for Godwin to write in terms of 'right' or 'wrong', since he also preached a doctrine of necessity or determinism, which entailed that guilt was a meaningless concept. The notion that marriage was an irrational institution probably helped Wordsworth cope with his feelings about Annette, but more than this, his teaching suggested that calm of mind could be achieved by rational control. Wordsworth's revulsion at the violence which had broken out in France welcomed an argument for reform based on reason and the control of the passions; the idea that education and not violence could be the agent of change attracted him and other revolutionaries. Wordsworth later described in Book XI of *The Prelude* (1805) how he and his friends adopted these notions:

This was the time, when all things tending fast
To depravation, speculative schemes –
That promised to abstract the hopes of Man
Out of his feelings, to be fixed thenceforth
For ever in a purer element –
Found ready welcome.

But by this time he had found that the feelings are not so easily controlled and he continues:

Tempting region that
For Zeal to enter and refresh herself,
Where passions had the privilege to work,
And never hear the sound of their own names.

With hindsight he now regards Godwin's theories as unrealistic:

the dream
Flattered the young, pleased with extremes, nor least
With that which makes our Reason's naked self
The object of its fervour.

The realisation that Godwin's theories rested on faulty foundations came to him after he met Coleridge. He describes in Book X of *The Prelude* (1805) how he had turned to mathematics, a rational activity to which he had resorted in a desperate attempt to get relief from his morbid feelings, and how Coleridge had come as counsellor and friend.

I . . . for my future studies, as the sole
Employment of the enquiring faculty,
Turned towards Mathematics, and their clear
And solid evidence – Ah! then it was
That thou, most precious Friend! about this time
First known to me, didst lend a helping help
To regulate my soul. (902-16)

When he and Southey were launching Pantisocracy Coleridge had been favourably disposed to Godwin. He had read *Political Justice* and met Godwin in London, but even then had been less taken with his theories than Southey. 'I think not so highly of him as you do', he wrote to Southey on 21 October 1794. By 1796 he was a fierce opponent.

Writing to Benjamin Flower in December, he tells him that he plans a refutation of *Political Justice* (though the plan was never fulfilled):

> My answer to Godwin will be a six shilling Octavo; and is designed to shew not only the absurdities and wickedness of his System, but to detect what appears to me the defects of all the systems of morality before & since Christ, & to shew that wherein they have been right, they have exactly coincided with the Gospel, and that each has erred exactly where & in proportion as, he has deviated from that perfect canon.[6]

Coleridge's opposition was based on Godwin's atheism and his optimistic view of human nature. Although he had supported radical dissent, Coleridge had never been an atheist. Writing to his atheist friend Thelwall on 13 November 1796, he declared, 'I am daily more and more a religionist'. The lectures on religion and politics he had delivered the previous year in Bristol give a clear picture of his beliefs at the time. There is a marked similarity with today's 'liberation theology' in his injunction to 'Go, preach the GOSPEL to the poor' and in his claim, made to Thelwall, that Christianity is 'a religion for Democrats'. But Coleridge had a keen realization of sin, almost, indeed, a pathological sense of guilt which prevented him from any easy-going assessment of human nature. Although he believed in the eventual triumph of truth and in non-violence, he was convinced that Godwin's emphasis on reason ran counter to human nature. Coleridge's Christianity led him to believe that we are all members one of another, that society is, or should be, like a family. Perhaps when he prepared the third of his *Lectures on Revealed Religion* he had been reading Burke, for Burke believed in what Hazlitt called a 'natural prejudice' in favour of one's own family, as the best foundation for society; or it may simply have been his own Christian conviction which inspired the declaration in this lecture that the 'Love of our Friends, parents, and neighbours leads us to the love of our Country to the love of all Mankind'.

Coleridge had always tried to bring his reason and his feelings together. Writing to his brother George on 30 March 1794, he had already indicated the effect of this on his religious development. 'In short', he writes,

> my religious Creed bore and perhaps bears a correspondence with my mind and heart – I had too much Vanity to be altogether a Christian – too much tenderness of Nature to be utterly an Infidel. Fond of the dazzle of Wit, fond of subtlety of Argument, I could not read without some degree of pleasure the levities of Voltaire, or the reasonings of Helvetius – but tremblingly alive to the feelings

of humanity, and su[s]ceptible of the charms of Truth my Heart forced me to admire the beauty of Holiness in the Gospel, forced me to love the Jesus, whom my Reason (or perhaps my reasonings) would not permit me to worship – My Faith therefore was made up of the Evangelists and the Deistic Philosophy.[7]

Coleridge thought Hartley could satisfy his craving for unity and so, as he wrote to Benjamin Flower on 2 November 1796, he named his first-born 'in honor of the great Master of Christian Philosophy'.

Coleridge found it easy to detach Wordsworth from his allegiance to Godwin, for Wordsworth's personal experience was leading him to cast doubt on the principles of Social Justice.

Wordsworth and his sister Dorothy had come together after a long separation. Their relationship was founded on a deep and even passionate affection for each other and now they were able at last to set up home together; an arrangement that envisaged Annette living with them as well. To suggest, as Godwin had done, that family ties were of little consequence, cut across one of Wordsworth's most cherished beliefs. Again, Coleridge's support and the self-confidence he had given Wordsworth as a poet, made nonsense of the detached view Godwin had of friendship. His growing conviction that reason alone was an unreliable guide in human affairs was confirmed for him by Coleridge, whose endeavour, as he put it later in *Biographia Literaria*, 'to keep alive the heart in the head', was a powerful influence on him.

Like Wordsworth, Coleridge still counted himself a republican, but as he wrote to his brother George in March 1798,

I therefore consent to be deemed a Democrat & a Seditionist. A man's character follows him long after he has ceased to deserve it – but I have snapped my squeaking baby-trumpet of Sedition and the fragments lie scattered in the lumber-room of Penitence.

This letter shows how close Wordsworth and Coleridge had come together and how both were taking stock and examining their beliefs, or as Coleridge put it in the same letter, 'I have for some time past withdrawn myself almost totally from the consideration of immediate causes, which are infinitely complex and uncertain, to muse on fundamental and general causes.' It also shows the kind of help Coleridge gave Wordsworth, for the letter continues:

I devote myself to such works as encroach not on the anti-social passions – in poetry, to elevate the imagination and set the affections in right tune by the beauty of the inanimate impregnated, as with a living soul, by the presence of Life – in prose, to the seeking with patience and a slow, very slow mind . . . what our faculties are and what they are capable of becoming. – I love fields and woods and mounta[ins] with almost a visionary fondness – and because I have found benevolence and quietness growing within me as that fondness [has] increased, therefore I should wish to be the means of implanting it in others– and to destroy the bad passions not by combating them, but by keeping them in inaction.[8]

We see here how Coleridge helped Wordsworth realise that emotions such as fear, guilt, and sorrow are best dealt with not by repression or rational control, but by acceptance. The calmness of mind necessary for this acceptance can be cultivated by a contemplation of the natural world and the beauty of the landscape; and not only the beauty but also the feelings of sublimity that certain landscapes can inspire. In 'The Borderers', the tragedy in blank-verse Wordsworth was writing at this time, Marmaduke is given a speech which could be about Wordsworth himself as he recalled his experiences on Salisbury Plain:

Deep, deep and vast, vast beyond human thought,
Yet calm—I could believe that there was here
The only quiet heart on earth. In terror,
Remembered terror, there is peace and rest.[9]

Writing in Book I of *The Prelude* Wordsworth recognises how nature had influenced the growth of his mind in this way,

Fair seed-time had my soul, and I grew up
Fostered alike by beauty and by fear (305-6)

Not only was Wordsworth ready to abandon Godwin's teaching when he realised how it failed to match his own experience, but he found in Hartley a far more acceptable account of what he now felt to be the truth. Hartley's philosophy rested on the belief that all our knowledge comes through the senses and the sense-impressions stored away in our memories; our values and even our moral judgments derive from this body of knowledge, so that ultimately who we are depends upon the environment in which we have been brought up. Pushed to an extreme the theory leads to determinism and for a time Coleridge was ready to accept this. Even when he ceased to be a necessitarian, he was convinced that to have been brought up in the countryside gave one an enormous advantage and he felt a certain envy at Wordsworth's good fortune in growing up in the Lake District, while he had been taken from the West Country as a child of nine to be a scholar at Christ's Hospital in London. For Wordsworth, too, such ideas made explicit what he had always felt; the familiar landscape of his childhood, its lakes and mountains, had always been an influence upon him and had strengthened and consoled him with their memories through many years of absence.

The growing sensibility to landscape in the eighteenth century is a familiar story. Works such as Addison's *Spectator* essays 'On the Pleasures of the Imagination', Shaftesbury's *Characteristics*, Burke's *Enquiry into the Origin of our Ideas of the Sublime and Beautiful,* guide-books such as William Gilpin's *Tour of the Wye* and *Guide to the Lakes*, and the new taste in painting and landscape gardening, all mark this growth. The concept of sublimity, developed especially by Shaftesbury and Burke, with the notion that nature can inspire one with feelings of awe and terror, is an important part of this story.

Wordsworth and Coleridge both shared this new sensibility and knew these writers, but they gave an added depth to their appreciation of nature. With Wordsworth this came, as most of his convictions did, from personal experience, from his life as a boy in the Lake District and the knowledge that his surroundings had been a formative influence on his life and character. But Wordsworth was able to articulate this largely because Coleridge gave him the language in which to do so.

Coleridge's reading of Berkeley raised doubts in his mind about Hartley's philosophy which brought together mind and matter in a unitary system. He found this attractive, but it was a system heavily indebted to Locke and when he came to Berkeley, Coleridge found that there were serious objections which could be levelled at Locke and his followers. If we know objects outside ourselves only through sense impressions how do we know that such objects exist at all? All we can be certain of are the sense impressions themselves. Again, there was an obvious difficulty in the notion that a material object could act upon an immaterial one such as the mind, and Hartley's theory of vibrations faced serious objections on this score. If the dualism between mind and matter were to be resolved it was perhaps easier to do it by arguing, as Berkeley did, that what we assume to be external objects are not made known to us by sense impressions or ideas, they *are* the sense impressions or ideas. Berkeley went even further and maintained that God is the omnipresent perceiver in whose mind objects exist even when there is no-one else to perceive them. Instead of a material unity, as Hartley had proposed, it was possible to argue for a spiritual one in which God plays an essential part.

That the Unitarian Coleridge and, through him the 'semi-atheist' Wordsworth, should find the philosophy of an Anglican bishop congenial to their own thinking is less surprising than at first appears. *The Prelude* recounts several occasions when as a boy Wordsworth experienced 'visitations', when he felt nature as a spiritual presence and was at one with the universe in a mystical unity. Very often these experiences included not only pleasure, but also admonishment and a sense of moral guidance. His later description of these childhood experiences sounds remarkably like a psychological version of Berkeley's account of perception: 'I was often unable', he said, 'to think of external things as having any external existence, and I communed with all I saw as something not apart from but inherent in my own immaterial nature. Many times while going to school have I grasped at a wall or tree to recall myself from this abyss of idealism to the reality'.[10] Berkeley may have had little direct influence on Wordsworth, but he found in the new direction Coleridge's thought was taking a welcome reinforcement for what he had always felt instinctively.

It was a joke in the Coleridge circle that having named his first two children, Hartley and Berkeley, he should have been absorbed in Spinoza when the third child was expected. In the event the new baby was given the name Derwent, but Coleridge's admiration for Spinoza remained even when he abandoned his allegiance to a philosophy he felt inevitably led to pantheism. In *Biographia Literaria* Coleridge recounted how a Government agent was sent down to the Quantocks to watch the two poets and reported how he had heard them talking about a certain 'Spy Nozy'. That such an agent was sent on this mission has since been authenticated and even if Coleridge embroidered the story, there is little doubt that he and Wordsworth discussed Spinoza at this time. Certainly on 30 September 1799, in a letter to Southey, Coleridge says that he is 'sunk in Spinoza' and in spite of domestic troubles remains 'as undisturbed as a Toad in a Rock'. Spinoza was execrated by some as an atheist but Schleiermacher spoke for many when he called him a 'pious, virtuous, God-intoxicated' man. The starting point for Spinoza's philosophy was to substitute for Descartes' dualism of mind and matter a monism founded on Substance, 'that which is in itself and is conceived through itself'. Spinoza calls this Substance God, but it is not what is generally understand by the term, for Spinoza's God is not personal. Instead of separating thought and extension as Descartes had done, Spinoza regards them as attributes of the one Substance. All things then can be seen as 'in' God and for this reason he was accused of pantheism. Certainly Coleridge came to think this was so, but even more damaging for him was the realisation that Spinoza's God was an 'It' who could not pity or forgive frail humanity. This was why Coleridge wrote in *Biographia Literaria*:

> For a very long time indeed I could not reconcile personality with infinity; and my head was with Spinoza, though my whole heart

remained with Paul and John.[11]

J. D. Campbell in his *Life of Coleridge* quotes Southey as saying of Coleridge's intellectual progress, 'Hartley was ousted by Berkeley, Berkeley by Spinoza, and Spinoza by Plato'. Milton was a Christian Platonist and Coleridge's study of Milton and the debates of the seventeenth century was now leading him to a reassessment not only of Hartley and Locke's 'new way of ideas', but the whole of eighteenth-century thought. Milton's hopes of establishing a Christian Commonwealth in England had been dashed by the restoration of the monarchy and he withdrew from active life to seek 'a Paradise within', a happier state, as the angel told Adam and Eve after the Fall, than the one they were leaving. In his retirement Milton turned to his great epic, *Paradise Lost*, which recounts the Biblical story of man's creation, fall, and redemption. It was conceived not simply as a narrative poem, but as a defence of the Christian faith against those who preached a doctrine of materialism and state autocracy. Chief among these was Hobbes, whose Leviathan was described by their contemporary, Bishop Burnet, as 'a very wicked work'. Hobbes, Burnet tells us,

> seemed to think that the universe was God, and that souls were
> material, Thought being only subtil and unperceptible motion.[12]

Burnet goes on to describe the group known as the Cambridge Platonists who opposed Hobbes, a leading figure among them being Ralph Cudworth, the Master of Christ's, Milton's own college. In his *True Intellectual System* (1678) Cudworth argued that Hobbes's materialism meant banishing 'all mental and consequently divine causality, quite out of the world; and to make the whole world to be nothing else but a mere heap of dust, fortuitously agitated.'[13]

Coleridge borrowed Cudworth's *True Intellectual System* from the Bristol Library in 1795 and again in 1796 and it led him to realise that the doctrines of Godwin and Hartley had been anticipated by Hobbes and had been challenged with great effect by these seventeenth-century Platonists. This liberated him from the narrow confines of empiricism at the time when he was collaborating with Wordsworth in producing *Lyrical Ballads*, and together with his other reading, it convinced him that the materialist and devitalised account of the world given by eighteenth-century thought was no longer satisfactory. It was about this time that he read Wilberforce's *Practical View* with its insistence that the heart is at the centre of religion:

> It may therefore be laid down as an axiom, that infidelity is in
> general a disease of the heart more than of the understanding. If
> Revelation were assailed only by reason and argument, it would

have little to fear. (Ch. VII, Section 3)

Wilberforce's work ends with a section addressed to Unitarians which would have had a special interest for Coleridge. This maintains that the weakness of Unitarianism is its lack of passion, its coldness of heart. 'The Unitarian and Socinian', he writes,

> who deny, or explain away, the peculiar doctrines of the Gospel, may be allowed to feel these grand truths, and to talk of them with little emotion. But in those who profess a sincere belief in them, this coldness is insupportable. The greatest possible services of man to man must appear contemptible, when compared with 'the unspeakable mercies of Christ.

This probably struck a chord in Coleridge's mind for in May 1798, a month after Wilberforce's *Practical View* appeared, he wrote to his friend John Estlin, the Unitarian minister in Bristol:

> I have been too neglectful of practical religion – I mean, actual & stated prayer, & a regular perusal of scripture as a morning & evening duty! May God grant me grace to amend this error; for it is a grievous one! – Conscious of frailty I almost wish (I say it confidentially to you) that I had become a stated Minister. . . . But tho' all my doubts are done away, tho' Christianity is my Passion, it is too much my intellectual Passion: and therefore will do me but little good in the hour of temptation & calamity.[14]

The reference here to entering the Unitarian ministry looks back to January of that year when Coleridge had been invited to Shrewsbury to preach a trial sermon before the Unitarian congregation there. Hazlitt, who was then nineteen and whose father was the Unitarian minister at nearby Wem, recalled many years later in his essay 'My First Acquaintance with Poets', the effect this sermon had on him. Coleridge, he wrote, seemed 'like an eagle dallying with the wind'. 'Poetry and Philosophy had met together. Truth and Genius had embraced, under the eye and with the sanction of Religion'. He walked back to Wem with the feeling that 'there was a spirit of hope and youth in all nature, that turned everything into good'.

The sermon was a great success and, had Coleridge wished, he could have embarked on a career in the ministry, but while at Shrewsbury he received the offer of an annuity of £150 from Tom Wedgwood, on condition that he abandon this plan and devote himself to poetry and philosophy. While he expresses a lingering regret in his letter to Estlin, there can be little doubt that the Wedgwood offer was accepted with relief. It may be that Wilberforce's *Practical View* had sown the seeds of doubt in his mind about Unitarianism, for in 1799, he wrote in his Notebook, (an entry repeated in 1802):

> Socinianism Moonlight – Methodism etc. A Stove! O

for some Sun that shall unite Light and Warmth.[15]

Many years later when he was listing in *Biographia Literaria* the characteristics of Wordsworth's poetry, Coleridge wrote that he recognised in Wordsworth's work that 'union of deep feeling with profound thought' which he himself could attain only when he had found a philosophy of religion that satisfied him. For his part Wordsworth had little enthusiasm for philosophy or theology and as Coleridge observed, 'the weight and sanity of the thoughts and sentiments' in Wordsworth's poetry were 'won, not from books, but – from the poet's own meditative observation' (*Biog. Lit.* Ch XXII). But this should not obscure Coleridge's contribution to the peace of mind and sense of purpose Wordsworth found when they were neighbours in the Quantocks. Quite apart from his personal friendship and encouragement, Coleridge's philosophical speculation confirmed for Wordsworth the truth that came from his own experience. It delivered him from fallacious doctrines and gave him a renewed faith in the healing power of nature, in the importance of memory, and in the visionary sense of life as a spiritual unity, which led as Coleridge put it, to 'a sympathy with man as man'. It was this sympathy he shared with Coleridge, which brought both men close to Wilberforce in the endeavour to deliver their contemporaries from the etiolated and deistic theology of the times. They, no less than Wilberforce, wished to free their fellows from the lethargy of stale practices and beliefs and had written *Lyrical Ballads* with this in mind. When the poems had been published Coleridge wanted Wordsworth to embark on a great philosophical poem, which would set out at much greater length the foundations of their beliefs; this turned instead into *The Prelude* in which Wordsworth recounted what he knew best, the story of the growth of his own mind.

Wordsworth

In his *Natural Supernaturalism*, M. H. Abrams, writing about the 1805 version of Wordsworth's *The Prelude*, asks the rhetorical question, 'What role does God play within the poem itself?' 'To answer this question', he continues, 'it is not enough to list the passages in which reference is made to God; for the essential matter is, 'What does God do in the poem?' ' And to this the answer is patently, 'Nothing of consequence'. Abrams draws a distinction between Wordsworth's religious beliefs and the poem itself; he is not concerned, he tells us, with the 'autobiographical question' of whether Wordsworth was a 'pantheist, panentheist, Christian' or with what he would have 'been prepared to assert outside the poem'. His concern is only with the poem and here, he maintains, 'God is at intervals ceremoniously alluded to, but remains an adventitious and non-operative factor'. If all allusions to deity, he argues, 'were struck out of *The Prelude*, there would be no substantive change in its subject matter or development'.

The distinction he makes is an odd one for *The Prelude* is nothing if not autobiographical and its purpose is to give the reader an account of the growth of the poet's mind. Abrams contends that 'Wordsworth did not greatly trouble himself about the question of orthodoxy until incited to do so by Coleridge's alarm and the remonstrances of friends and reviewers' and that in *The Prelude* he describes his spiritual development 'within a system of reference which has only two generative and operative terms: mind and nature'. According to this account, God is either absent or irrelevant for Wordsworth.

We are faced here with two Wordsworths: one the poet who expressed his deepest thoughts and feelings in *The Prelude* (and to regard the poem in any other way seems perverse); the other, an individual separate from his poetry, who is either confused or hypocritical. This dichotomy seems very improbable and Abrams seeks to avoid it by suggesting that in *The Prelude* Wordsworth is the mouthpiece of what Hazlitt called 'the Spirit of the Age'. This is then extended to include the suggestion that Wordsworth speaks in terms which anticipate German and especially Hegelian Idealism, which reduces reality to subject and object. This anticipation of German philosophy, Abrams maintains, was the product of a process of conceptualisation and secularisation of Christian doctrine. But what kind of process is Abrams suggesting here? In *The Prelude* Wordsworth was articulating what was his own personal experience, but the poem hardly seems the product of a mind that was theologically illiterate. Indeed, Abrams's suggestion entails a certain theological sophistication on Wordsworth's part, for it implies that he made a decisive break with the tradition of the Church of England in which he had been brought up. If Abrams is suggesting that Wordsworth absorbed the most radical theological ideas of his day by some kind of mental osmosis without being fully aware of doing so, this seems highly unlikely. Coleridge would undoubtedly have been the main source of such ideas, but Abrams believes that Coleridge was alarmed by these developments in Wordsworth's opinions.

There seems a certain inconsistency here, for Abrams extends the argument beyond *The Prelude* to *Lyrical Ballads*, or at any rate to 'Tintern Abbey', one of the most important poems in that collection, and brings in Coleridge as someone whose views are now identical with Wordsworth's. 'Now notice', he writes,

> how this metaphysics of subject-object interaction parallels the exemplary lyric from which Wordsworth, following the instance of Coleridge's 'Frost at Midnight', established in 'Tintern Abbey'; an individual confronts a natural scene and makes it abide his question, and the interchange between his mind and nature constitutes the entire poem, which usually poses and resolves a spiritual crisis.

No doubt Abrams is correct in seeing in 'Tintern Abbey' an anticipation in miniature of *The Prelude* and to connect it with Coleridge's 'Frost at Midnight'. But again these two poems are nothing if not autobiographical and to understand them fully one must set them in the time and place to which they refer.

In 'Frost at Midnight' Coleridge reflects upon his own schooldays at Christ's Hospital in the middle of London, 'In the great city pent and cloisters dim'. Here he was cut off from his own family and the countryside of his native Devon and saw 'naught lovely but the sky and stars'. From these memories he turns his attention to his baby Hartley, asleep in his cradle at his side. The time is midnight and as one day ends and another begins he turns from the past to the future and vows that Hartley will be brought up to be influenced by nature and will

see and hear

The lovely shapes and sounds intelligible
Of that eternal language, which thy God
Utters, who from eternity doth teach
Himself in all, and all things in himself.

The importance given to nature here is clear, but the reference to God is more than perfunctory; indeed it is central to the whole poem. The echoes of Berkeley's Christian Platonism are unmistakeable, both in the notion that natural objects are the language in which God speaks to men and in the belief that God dwells in all things and that they have their being in him. This is very different from the reduction of reality to subject and object, which Abrams sees as the theme of *The Prelude*.

'Tintern Abbey' is also directly autobiographical and at an even profounder level than 'Frost at Midnight', for it deals with a crisis in Wordsworth's life. The poem starts with a precise chronological reference. Like 'Frost at Midnight' it was first published in 1798 and was completed by Wordworth as he and his sister walked down the hill from Clifton into Bristol on the conclusion of their visit to the

Wye. Wordsworth composed the poem in his head during their tour of the Wye valley and wrote it down only when they reached Bristol and handed it to Joseph Cottle, who was about to publish *Lyrical Ballads*. But the opening line of the poem sets the scene five years earlier when Wordsworth paid his first visit to the Wye. This time he was on his own and had made the nightmare journey across Salisbury Plain after parting from his friend Calvert.

In *The Prelude* he was to write of the period between the two visits to the Wye as one in which he had been haunted by terrifying dreams of the Terror, guilt concerning Annette, and fears for his own sanity; in many ways 'Tintern Abbey' is closer to 'The Ancient Mariner' than to 'Frost at Midnight'. But now in 1798 he has found peace of mind and self-confidence. 'Tintern Abbey' gives no details of this ordeal through which he has passed nor does it describe fully his state of mind on his first visit. Instead it contrasts two attitudes to nature. On his earlier visit the appearances of nature

> were then to me
> An appetite: a feeling and a love,
> That had no need of a remoter charm,
> By thought supplied.

This has been replaced with a more mature response in which he has learned

> To look on nature, not as in the hour
> Of thoughtless youth.

Nature now is more than a source of sensory pleasure; its healing influence has led him to see it as the agency of a spiritual power which animates all things and unites the mind of man with the universe. This reciprocity is more than one between subject and object, for as in Berkeley's philosophy, subject and object are brought together in the mind of a supreme Being who speaks to man in the language of nature:

> Therefore am I still
> A lover of the meadows and the woods,
> And mountains; and of all that we behold
> From this green earth; of all the mighty world
> Of eye and ear, both what they half-create,
> And what perceive; well pleased to recognize
> In nature and the language of the sense,
> The anchor of my purest thoughts, the nurse,
> The guide, the guardian of my heart, and soul
> Of all my moral being.

It is easy to trace in the poem the influence of Berkeley and Hartley, but it was Wordsworth's own experience which led him to this new awareness. In the peaceful surroundings of the Quantock hills he had found mental stability and spiritual refreshment, had discovered in himself a creative power and developed a new poetic style, which he employed in 'Tintern Abbey' itself and which was to lead him forward to his best work. This transformation had been brought about not only by the ministrations of nature, but through the encouragement of Coleridge and above all, the companionship of Dorothy. So the poem ends with an affectionate tribute to 'my dear, dear Sister', his love for whom is more profound than even his love for nature:

> We stood together; and that I, so long
> A worshipper of Nature, hither came,
> Unwearied in that service: rather say
> With warmer love, oh! with far deeper zeal
> Of holier love. Nor wilt thou then forget,
> That after many wanderings, many years
> Of absence, these steep woods and lofty cliffs,
> And this green pastoral landscape, were to me
> More dear, both for themselves, and for thy sake.

These are the sentiments expressed in the last book of *The Prelude* (references are to the 1805 edition which does not differ materially from the 1850 one at this point) where Wordsworth recalls his friendship with Coleridge, for whom the poem was written, and his reunion with Dorothy,

> At a time
> When Nature, destined to remain so long
> Foremost in my affection, had fallen back
> Into a second place, well pleased to be
> A handmaid to a nobler than herself. (XIII, 236-40)

The importance of personal affection which Dorothy brought with her was increased by the friendship of Coleridge,

> O most loving Soul!
> Placed on this earth to love and understand.

Coleridge gave Wordsworth not only affection but the intellectual foundations for his new-found conviction:

> Thy gentle spirit to my heart of hearts
> Did also find its way; and thus the life
> Of all things and the mighty unity
> In all which we behold, and feel, and are,
> Admitted more habitually a mild
> Interposition, closelier gathering thoughts
> Of man and his concerns, such as become
> A human creature. (XIII, 252-59)

The thoughtless reverence for nature has given way under the influence of Coleridge to a more considered frame of mind; his earlier rapture is now

> balanced by a reason which indeed
> Is reason, duty and pathetic truth;
> And God and Man divided, as they ought,
> Between them the great system of the world
> Where Man is sphered, and which God animates. (XIII, 264-68)

Wordsworth writes very precisely. God, man, and nature are all intimately related, but all are separate. There is no hint of pantheism or Spinozism, nor a reduction of reality to a man-nature relationship independent of God and no possibility of regarding the reference to God as merely a pious flourish. These passages show us how difficult it is to keep Wordsworth out of his own poetry and to separate the man from his work and they challenge the assumption that God was a meaningless concept in his thought and an absentee in his life.

This said, we still have to clarify his religious beliefs. A good starting-point for this is the biographical evidence.

A straightforward account of this can be found in Hoxie Fairchild's *Religious Trends in English Poetry* and in Mary Moorman's *Life*. At Hawkshead grammar school, a Church of England foundation whose headmaster was a clergyman, Wordsworth would have received the Anglican teaching of the day, which was Protestant with a tendency perhaps to Erastianism. There are no references to this in *The Prelude*, but in middle age when he was composing his *Ecclesiastical Sketches* he tells us that he was brought up in the High Church tradition. He belonged to this when he made the remark, but this does not mean that either in childhood or in later life he owed anything to the emerging Anglo-Catholic or Tractarian movement, only that he was politically and ecclesiastically conservative.

The changes in Wordsworth's beliefs between his childhood and his later orthodoxy are not easy to chart. There is no evidence that the Unitarianism and left-wing politics which attracted Coleridge at Cambridge meant much to Wordsworth while he was at the university, but the French Revolution certainly turned him into a republican in politics and probably a deist in religion. It had been understood by his family that he would become a parson but, as Jane Austen's novels demonstrate, many who entered the ministry at the time did so with little sense of vocation and only a vague belief in Christian doctrine. That Wordsworth refused to take this step when he left France and returned to England, suggests that any remaining commitment to Christian belief was at the most merely nominal, and as we have seen, in 1796 Coleridge considered him' a semi-atheist'.

On the death of their mother, Dorothy Wordsworth lived with relatives at Halifax and then at Forncett near Norwich. In both these places she knew several prominent Unitarians whom William met while visiting her; this acquaintance with Unitarians was extended when he met Coleridge. But when he was living in the Quantocks, Wordsworth never showed any inclination to become a Unitarian or share even occasionally in their worship, and there is no evidence that he went to hear Coleridge preach at the Unitarian chapels around Bridgwater. It is unlikely, in fact, that he and his sister attended any place of worship when they lived in Somerset and this probably compounded the suspicion and dislike they encountered in the neighbourhood and led to the termination of their tenancy at Alfoxden.

All this confirms the description of Wordsworth as an atheist or semi-atheist in 1796, however, the term 'semi' may suggest some change in his opinions, and Helen Darbishire goes so far as to maintain that 'at no time of his life, except perhaps at the brief period of disillusionment after his return from France in 1793, was Wordsworth a disbeliever in Christianity'.[16] Certainly 'Tintern Abbey' is capable of a theistic interpretation, although Coleridge thought the God 'Whose dwelling is the light of setting suns' was not the Christian one. The poem is not of course a philosophical or theological argument, but a celebration of the joy which comes to Wordsworth as he leaves behind his past frustrations and guilt, sustained now by nature and the love of his sister and friend. Even though it may not be Christian it shows a belief in a beneficent and transcendent power. In January 1801, less than three years later, Wordsworth was writing to Wilberforce acknowledging an identity of purpose in their published work.

The following year saw Wordsworth and his sister in Calais, where they had gone to meet Annette Vallon and Wordsworth's daughter Caroline, and to let Annette know that he proposed marrying Mary Hutchinson. It must have been a highly emotional visit, and one of the sonnets Wordsworth wrote about it shows in its Biblical imagery a deeply religious awareness of what the relationship with his daughter meant to him. For Wordsworth his small daughter is the innocent intermediary who takes the place of the priest and asks God to forgive the harm he has caused her and her mother. There can be no doubt that the God she approaches on his behalf is more than a perfunctory or vacuous figure:

Dear Child! dear Girl! who walkest with me here,
If thou appear untouched by solemn thought
Thy nature is not therefore less divine:

Thou liest in Abraham's bosom all the year;
And worshipp'st at the Temple's inner shrine,
God being with thee when we know it not!

By the time of this visit both volumes of *Lyrical Ballads* had appeared. In the first volume 'We are Seven' shows the simple belief of the child in an after-life, and in the second 'The Brothers' provides the affectionate portrait of a parish priest who gives faithful service to his people. But apart from 'Tintern Abbey', and even this remains questionable, Wordsworth's contributions to the collection are hardly what most people would regard as religious poetry. What then did he mean when he told Wilberforce he thought they shared a common purpose? The best answer to this is to be found in Coleridge's *Biographia Literaria*, written many years later but, nonetheless, providing an account of what the two poets had in mind when they collaborated in their joint venture. 'During the first year that Mr. Wordsworth and I were neighbours', writes Coleridge in Chapter XIV of *Biographia Literaria*, 'the thought suggested itself . . . that a series of poems might be composed of two sorts.' They agreed to divide the poems between them and that Coleridge's 'should be directed to persons and characters supernatural, or at least romantic; yet so as to transfer from our inward nature a human interest and a semblance of truth sufficient to procure for these shadows of imagination that willing suspension of disbelief for the moment which constitutes poetic faith.'

Coleridge proceeds to distinguish his own contribution from Wordsworth's which, he makes clear, is opposite and yet complementary to his own. Wordsworth's object, he tells us, is

> to give the charm of novelty to things of everyday, and to excite a feeling analogous to the supernatural, by awakening the mind's attention from the lethargy of custom, and directing it to the loveliness and wonders of the world before us; an inexhaustible treasure, but for which in consequence of the film of familiarity and selfish solicitude we have eyes, yet see not, ears that hear not, and hearts that neither feel nor understand.

The term 'natural supernaturalism' was used by Carlyle to characterise the secularised version of Christianity he preached in *Sartor Resartus*, but this is very different. It is impossible to mistake the genuinely religious tone of this passage with its Biblical references to Isaiah and Jeremiah and one cannot dismiss these as simply a stylistic device. That the Bible and religion were present to Wordsworth's mind in some of the poems in *Lyrical Ballads* can be seen in the comment he made in a letter about 'The Idiot Boy', in which he writes of the religious veneration given to idiots in some communities. 'I have often applied to idiots, in my own mind', he writes, 'that sublime expression of Scripture, that their life is hidden with God.'[17] These poems are not religious in a conventional sense perhaps, but they are meant to make the reader more spiritually aware. Coleridge commented that those who admired them were to be found

> chiefly among young men of strong sensibility and meditative minds; and their admiration . . . was distinguished by its intensity,
> I might almost say, by its religious fervour.

Most of the poems in *Lyrical Ballads* are narrative or dramatic and do not follow the pattern of 'Tintern Abbey' which combines meditation and landscape. Their subject is men and women, often at a moment of crisis in their lives; in some poems influenced for the better by nature, in others injured by a repressive or vicious set of circumstances. They are simple country people because in them human nature is free from the conventions and stock-responses of those brought up in the artificial surroundings of urban society. As with Blake's *Songs of Innocence* Wordsworth's poems celebrate the innocence of the child, not only in the infant but in the adult, and in both poets this vision of innocence had a political significance, for both nursed millennarian hopes of a new society. Wordsworth had based these hopes on the French Revolution and its failure was a devastating blow to him, but his recovery from the disillusionment that followed his return to England brought with it the conviction that he could best serve the cause of political justice through his poetry.

This passion for justice is found in many of his poems in the first edition of *Lyrical Ballads*. It is seen in its most radical and political form in the earliest written poem in the collection, 'The Female Vagrant'. The last of the poems, 'Tintern Abbey', only mentions in passing the vagrants who frequented the abbey ruins, the 'vagrant dwellers in the houseless woods', and this has caused adverse criticism in some quarters. But such criticism misunderstands the poem, for it is about his own personal crisis and its resolution.[18] In turning away from revolutionary politics in 1796, Coleridge had declared in 'On Having Left a Place of Retirement',

> I therefore go, and join head, heart and hand,
> Active and firm, to fight the bloodless fight
> Of Science, Freedom, and the Truth in Christ.

Now Wordsworth, too, as he faces the failure of the French Revolution, turns to his poetry to carry on the struggle for a new world of freedom and justice. We do not know whether at this date he would have included Coleridge's 'Truth in Christ' as part of his manifesto, but

'Tintern Abbey' echoes some of the themes to be found in Coleridge's poems, including the belief that peace of mind is an essential preliminary and that this comes, as he wrote in 'This Lime Tree Bower My Prison', from a knowledge 'That Nature ne'er deserts the wise and pure'. During the years of collaboration over *Lyrical Ballads* Coleridge ceaselessly urged Wordsworth to embark upon a great philosophical poem. In a letter to his friend James Losh on 11 March 1798, Wordsworth announced that he had started on this and that its title would be *The Recluse: or Views of Nature, Man, and Society.* When the second volume of *Lyrical Ballads* had been completed in 1800, Wordsworth wrote 'Home at Grasmere', which formed the first and only book of *The Recluse* proper. But while he and his sister were in Germany in 1799, cut off in the Hartz mountains by 'the worst winter of the century' and feeling homesick for England, he began to draft poetic passages of childhood autobiography and it was this material which came increasingly to occupy his attention and which became the long autobiographical poem which he finished in 1805. He went on revising this poem until 1839 but it was not published until shortly after his death in 1850. It was his widow who entitled it *The Prelude*, a title chosen because the poem was seen as the introduction to a much longer work consisting of the unfinished *Recluse* and *The Excursion.* Until its publication it was known in the family circle as 'the poem to Coleridge' or as a poem 'on my early life or the growth of my own mind'. The qualification 'early' is important, for the poem carries the story of Wordsworth's life only down to the publication of *Lyrical Ballads*.

M. H. Abrams perceives *The Prelude* as a secularised version of Christianity, a replacement for Wordsworth's faith in the French Revolution, the god who had failed, and it is true that both Wordsworth and Coleridge aspired to write a poem which would articulate their mature beliefs after the failure of their earlier hopes. The poem they had in mind would attempt to match *Paradise Lost* and revive for their generation the heroic virtues of Milton's epic. Coleridge relinquished this ambition in favour of Wordsworth, whom he regarded as the greatest poet since Milton and a worthy successor to him, and it was with Coleridge's repeated exhortations and encouragement that Wordsworth took up the task. Milton's epic had retold the Biblical story of man's creation, fall, and redemption, but Coleridge urged upon Wordsworth a great philosophical poem. This was something Wordsworth found difficult to accomplish and, as we have seen, he postponed it in favour of a poetic autobiography. But in writing this, Milton was still very much in his mind and throughout

The Prelude there are references to and near-quotations from *Paradise Lost* and behind these again the unmistakeable echoes of the Biblical narrative.

Not only had Wordsworth been brought up in a Church of England school, but like most of his contemporaries he had attended his parish church, where the weekly lectionary covered the entire Biblical story in the course of the church's year. His poetry shows, then, a more than conventional knowledge of the King James's Bible and a regard for its language. Moreover, most Englishmen at this time had been brought up to see the life of the individual as a replication of the Biblical story of man's fall and redemption, and some at least of the events of their lives mirrored in incidents from the Bible, such as the wandering in the wilderness, Jacob wrestling with his unknown God, and St John's vision of the new Jerusalem. It was a tradition which went back to St Augustine's *Confessions*, but it had been recovered and featured prominently in the Protestantism of the seventeenth and eighteenth centuries.

How extensive this influence was can be seen in the way it permeated the hymnody of the period, especially the hymns of Isaac Watts and the Wesleys. Their hymns trace the Biblical story of man's pilgrimage from the loss of Eden to his redemption by Christ, but unfold it as a drama of the individual's inward spiritual experience. The hymns of the Wesleys go with the traveller on his life's journey and provide an accompaniment for every stage of it, whether it be joy or sorrow, victory or defeat. We encounter the same pattern again in Bunyan's *Pilgrim's Progress* and even in works of popular fiction such as *Robinson Crusoe*, whose hero disobeys his father by running away to sea and after suffering many privations returns home again with the realisation that his life has mirrored not only the parable of the Prodigal Son, but the entire Old Testament story.

We should not be surprised, therefore, to find that Wordsworth viewed his life within a similar framework and that his poem should tell the story of his loss of innocence and his eventual recovery of an earthly Paradise at Grasmere. We should remember, too, that his 'fall' was not only his loss of hope at the failure of the French Revolution, but a more personal guilt at having deserted Annette and their child; something he could hardly mention directly in *The Prelude*. But we do not need to conclude from this internalisation of the Biblical narrative that he secularised the Christian faith, if by this is meant a rejection of the objective truth of the gospel. Certainly those who sang the Wesleys' hymns or who found inspiration in *Pilgrim's Progress*, had no difficulty in bringing objective and psychological truth together in a unity of belief. Indeed, the whole history of Christianity has been a process of secularisation in the sense that the Christian faith has had to relate to cultural changes and use contemporary language to express itself. Chapter XIV of *Biographia Literaria* suggests that Wordsworth's share of *Lyrical Ballads* was to show how ordinary secular life has a spiritual significance, and by this was meant a Christian significance. This becomes clearer if we consider Coleridge's part in the joint volume and especially if we look at 'The Ancient Mariner', which marked the beginning of their collaboration.

Although there are formal differences between them there is the same pattern of belief in 'The Ancient Mariner' and 'Tintern Abbey' and this is true (although on a much larger scale) of *The Prelude*. The Ancient Mariner, like Robinson Crusoe, sets out on a sea-voyage with an unreflective innocence that is shattered by the events that follow his sinful act of shooting the albatross. He returns home to do penance for his sin, hoping to recover a new and more mature innocence. Like Adam, the type of all such figures, his story is that of the whole human race as narrated in the Bible. The poem is not explicitly Christian; an equivalent, perhaps, today would be C. S. Lewis's Narnia stories which also require 'a willing suspension of disbelief for the moment' in making the supernatural natural. The counterpart in Wordsworth's poems in *Lyrical Ballads* is their perception of a spiritual reality in what Coleridge, in Chapter XIV of *Biographia Literaria*, described as 'ordinary life, the characters and incidents . . . as will be found in every village and its vicinity'. With Wordsworth the Christian dimension is not so evident and this may be because his commitment to Christianity was less certain than Coleridge's or, more likely, as we shall see later, because he did not wish to make his poetry a vehicle of religious affirmation, only a means of creating in his readers a new spiritual awareness.

In reading *The Prelude* one realises that it becomes more explicitly religious as it reaches its end and this is even truer of the revised version published after Wordsworth's death. At first he had intended not to publish it until *The Recluse* had been finished, but when this remained uncompleted he realised that *The Prelude* must stand on its own and began to make changes in his original text. He carried out these changes from 1805-06, the date of the original manuscript, until a radically revised version was made for the final edition, published in 1850. But before this, in the 1814 Preface to *The Excursion* (which was meant to form part of a larger whole including *The Prelude* and *The Recluse*) Wordsworth had written that his then unnamed autobiographical poem and *The Recluse* 'have the same relation to each other, if I may so express myself, as the ante-chapel has to the body of a gothic church'.

Whatever one thinks of *The Excursion* (and the poem has received a bad press ever since Jeffrey's savage verdict in *The Edinburgh Review* – 'This will never do!') it takes the religious commitment of the early version of *The Prelude* a stage further and this is probably what Wordsworth had in mind by his metaphor. If *The Prelude* is not explicitly Christian, *The Excursion* was criticised by some as no more than Anglican propaganda. Noted Evangelicals such as Hannah More welcomed it, and the hymn writer, James Montgomery, though he criticised it for not mentioning justification by faith or the Atonement, praised it warmly in *The Eclectic Review*.

The Excursion is a dialogue in the Platonic manner and Wordsworth knew modern examples of this form in Shaftesbury's *The Moralists* and Berkeley's *Alciphron*.[19] Shaftesbury's work is a prose argument in favour of theism, inspired by the feelings of sublimity and awe aroused in us by those aspects of nature which 'spell out that mysterious Being, which to our weak Eyes appears at best under a Veil of Cloud'. In Book IX of *The Excursion* the Wanderer communes with nature in a similar manner and celebrates in rhapsodical terms what he calls 'an active principle [that] pervades the Universe':

from link to link
It circulates, the Soul of all the worlds. (IX, 3-15)

It is not surprising then that in the 'Essay, Supplementary to the Preface' Wordsworth praises Shaftesbury as 'an author at present unjustly depreciated'. Berkeley's *Alciphron* moves the argument forward from theism to an outright defence of Christianity, but he and Shaftesbury both advanced a Platonic philosophy inimical to the rationalistic thought of the Enlightenment. Both gave a spiritual account of life which accords with what Wordsworth had in mind in the prose Argument that prefaces Book IV of the poem, where he compares 'the dignities of the Imagination with the presumptuous littleness of certain modern Philosophers'. Both rejected the clock-maker picture of God advanced by the deists and believed that 'in him we live and move and have our being'.

This was Wilberforce's faith which Wordsworth approved of and adopted in *The Excursion*, and in his 'Essay, Supplementary to the Preface', he once more makes the comparison between poetry and religion he had made in writing to Wilberforce years before. There is 'an affinity', he writes, 'between religion and poetry', and continues,

'Religion makes up the deficiencies of reason by faith; . . . and poetry
– ethereal and transcendent, yet [is] incapable to sustain her existence
without sensuous incarnation. ' He insists that his poetry is not religious
argument dressed in verse and many years later, in February 1840, in a
letter to the Rev. Henry Alford, who had contributed an article, mainly
on *The Excursion*, to Dearden's *Miscellany*, he elaborates on this. 'I
was particularly pleased', he writes,

> with your distinction between religion in Poetry and versified
> Religion. For my own part, I am averse to frequent mention of the
> mysteries of Christian faith; not from a due sense of their
> momentous nature, but the contrary. I felt it far too deeply to venture
> on handling the subject as many scruple not to do.

This may explain why Christian doctrine does not figure more
prominently in his poetry and why in *The Prelude* he restricts himself
to recounting his own spiritual experience.

It is impossible to know how *The Recluse* would have developed
if Wordsworth had persevered with it. Although it was meant to be
a great philosophical poem, 'Home at Grasmere', which he
described as Book I of *The Recluse*, is not philosophical in any
way, even if Coleridge in *Table Talk* in 1832 spoke of its purpose
as

> illustrative of, a redemptive process in operation, showing how
> this idea reconciled all the anomalies, and promised future glory
> and restoration. Something of this sort was, I think, agreed on. It
> is, in substance, what I have been all my life doing in my system
> of philosophy.

But Wordsworth was no Dante, and Coleridge no Thomas Aquinas;
in *The Prelude* Wordsworth had already achieved what his genius was
best suited to.

The philosophy of religion for which he had little aptitude seemed
ruled out, then, as a subject for his great poem and, as we have seen,
he had reservations about using the Biblical story as Milton had done;
perhaps history and especially ecclesiastical history might have taken
their place. Certainly when he turned aside from *The Recluse* once
again it was to write his *Ecclesiastical Sketches*, a long series of
sonnets started in 1821 and published in 1822, but with additions
made as late as the 1840s.

These sonnets trace the history of the English church from Saxon
times up to the Glorious Revolution of 1688. They are not doctrinal
or devotional, but purely historical and leave no doubt that while he
had a sympathy for the medieval church and even for monasticism,
Wordsworth was a firm believer in the Reformation. They were inspired

by a visit to Cambridge, where he was moved by the beauty of King's College chapel to write three sonnets, including the well-known 'Tax not the royal Saint with vain expense'. The sonnets concerned with the seventeenth century, while still admiring Milton, praise Charles I and Laud as defenders of the established church. By now Wordsworth was a High Church Tory for whom the Church of England stood as the guarantee of civil order and individual liberty; like many of his contemporaries, however, he combined without any sense of irony, a love of freedom with apprehension about Catholic Emancipation and a dislike of Nonconformity.

Although he welcomed the Oxford Movement he was reluctant to support it publicly and was never a Catholic in doctrine.

Indeed, he took a rather detached view of doctrine, disliking the Evangelicals not on doctrinal grounds, but for the emotional and personal nature of their religion. In many respects he was a liberal in theology and a Tory in politics, both secular and ecclesiastical. The failure of the French Revolution and the guilt he felt for the part it had played in his life had led Wordsworth to retreat to the peace of Grasmere and his own family circle. The title of *The Recluse* indicates his retirement from active politics throughout the years he was engaged with the poem, but the struggle of Britain against Napoleon induced in him a feeling of patriotism, expressed so eloquently in his Poems dedicated to National Independence and Liberty; a patriotic strain which when joined with his religious beliefs led him to view church and state as almost identical.

Admiration for the *Ecclesiastical Sketches* and, indeed, for Wordsworth himself was not widespread at the time of their publication and Byron, who had unfurled the flag of freedom for a new generation, was the popular hero throughout Europe. In his later years, however, Wordsworth had a growing band of devotees and by the time *The Prelude* appeared he had become the poet of the age. *The Prelude* was published in 1850, the year that also saw the publication of Tennyson's *In Memoriam*. The public that admired *In Memoriam*, a poem George Henry Lewes called 'the solace and delight of every house where poetry was loved', welcomed it, not because it proclaimed a dogmatic faith, but because they found in it consolation for their sorrows and reassurance in its confession that 'there lives more faith in honest doubt, / believe me, than in half the creeds'. The same public also welcomed Wordsworth's poem for its inner conviction and healing power; Byron was now seen as the poet of the *mal du siecle* whereas Wordsworth gave his readers health and moral strength.

The jibe that for the Victorians reading Wordsworth (like gin) was one of the quickest ways out of Manchester, fails to understand his poetry, for while it gave refreshment to those who lived in the squalor and poverty of the new industrialised cities, it was not escapist. In Book VIII of *The Excursion* he writes with discernment of the effects of industrialisation. He is no luddite and appreciates the advantages of manufacturing, but he is also aware of the ugliness of the rapidly expanding towns and the exploitation of labour and especially of child labour. J. T. Coleridge, a nephew of the poet, and a friend and contemporary of John Keble at Oxford, gives an account in his Memoir of the Rev John Keble of the occasion in 1839 when Keble presented Wordsworth for an honorary doctorate at Oxford. At the end of his presentation address Keble described Wordsworth as a poet who 'above all has exhibited the manners, the pursuits, and the feelings, religious and traditional of the poor', and he advises his hearers to read Wordsworth's poetry if

> they sincerely desire to understand and feel that secret harmonious
> intimacy which exists between honourable Poverty, and the severer
> Muses, sublime Philosophy, yea, even our most holy Religion.

This recognises both the political radicalism and the religious sincerity of Wordsworth's poetry, a combination which inspired Broad Churchmen such as F. D. Maurice and Charles Kingsley, the founders of the Christian Socialist movement. There were others, like Newman, who felt that Wordsworth had delivered them from the cold and deistic religion of the eighteenth century; for them this was the greatest gift of the Romantic movement. But Romanticism needed more than emotional warmth, more even than the 'Joy in widest commonalty spread' that came from Wordsworth's personal vision of a spiritual reality in and behind all things. The solemnity of the occasion led Keble to claim too much when he spoke of Wordsworth's 'sublime Philosophy'. In the prose Argument of Book IV of *The Excursion*, Wordsworth had spoken of the need for a 'union of the imagination, affections, understanding, and reason', but it was Coleridge who attempted to construct a philosophy that would accomplish this. Thinking Christians in the Victorian period who admired Wordsworth, welcomed the writings of Coleridge, for they opened a door to a greater understanding of Wordsworth's poetry. To approach Wordsworth through the pages of Coleridge is still a rewarding introduction, for there is more than a grain of truth in the remark that Wordsworth was Coleridge's best work, even if, like all his other works, he left it unfinished.

Coleridge

A once popular view of Coleridge was that his interest in philosophy was a dangerous preoccupation for a poet and that if he had not been led away into metaphysical speculation he might have fulfilled his early promise and become the greatest poet of his age. This view was thought to have been supported by his own poem 'Dejection', in which he spoke of 'abstruse research' stealing from his 'own nature all the natural man', and by Wordsworth, who declared that 'Coleridge had been spoilt for a poet by going to Germany'. 'If it had not been so', Wordsworth maintained, 'he would have been the greatest, the most abiding poet of his age'.[21] But such a view hardly fits the facts of Coleridge's own life or what he himself said. He was immersed in the study of philosophy before he went to Germany and this at a time when he was writing his greatest poetry. There is no reason to believe that this study brought about any decline in his poetic powers and when those powers did decline, philosophy gave him consolation and strength. Moreover, Coleridge believed that poetry and philosophy, far from being inimical, were intimately related, and in Chapter XV of *Biographia Literaria*[22] he went so far as to claim that 'No man was ever yet a great poet, without being at the same time a profound philosopher'. This leads one to ask what light his poetry and his philosophy throw on each other. We have seen that in 1794, Coleridge counted himself a materialist, but in 1797 he incorporated in 'The Destiny of Nations' the Christian and Platonic notion found in the writings of Berkeley, that the world of nature is the language of God. In 'Frost at Midnight' which emphasises the importance of natural surroundings in the formation of character, he vows that the baby Hartley will be brought up away from the din and squalor which surrounded his father's childhood in London. (There is a sad irony here, for Hartley grew up to be a gifted but wayward character who lost his fellowship at Oriel and took to drink.) Coupled with this empiricism in the poem there is again the Berkeleyan doctrine of nature as a divine alphabet.

Coleridge's early poetry shows his changing philosophical ideas, but to suggest that it is simply a versified version of philosophy would do less than justice to both. Philosophy is a conceptual discipline which says what can be said clearly and unambiguously, whereas poetry is what T. S. Eliot called 'a raid on the inarticulate', an attempt to explore those states of mind where thought and feeling meet. What impressed Coleridge in Wordsworth's poetry was 'the union of deep feeling with profound thought'[23], a union he sought in his own life and attempted to capture in his poetry.

We see this when we read his major poems and nowhere more clearly than in 'The Ancient Mariner'. Some readers of the poem have regarded it as written in the Gothic style of the German poet Bürger, the English translations of whose *Lenore* were in great vogue at the time. Even Southey, who should have known better, assumed this in a review of *Lyrical Ballads* he wrote in *The Critical Review* in October 1798. 'We do not', he wrote, 'sufficiently understand the story to analyse it. It is a Dutch attempt at German sublimity. Genius has here been employed in producing a poem of little merit. ' Coleridge knew Bürger's poetry and may even have been influenced by it, but his poor opinion of the Gothic in literature can be gauged from a letter he wrote in March 1797, only a few months before he began writing his poem. In this letter to the poet William Lisle Bowles, he declares that he is 'weary of the Terrible' since for the 'last six or eight months' he has been reviewing in *The Critical Review* the novels of Ann Radcliffe, Mary Robinson, and M. G. ('Monk') Lewis,

> in all of which dungeons, and old castles, & solitary Houses by the Sea Side, & Caverns, & Woods, & extraordinary characters, all the tribe of Horror & Mystery, have crowded on me – even to surfeiting.[24]

The epithet 'Dutch' which Southey borrows from painting implies a rather dull and painstaking version of the German Sturm und Drang school of literature, but few today would agree with this charge of pedestrianism. Southey's confession that he does not understand the poem explains a good deal, but the charge of unintelligibility anticipated many later judgements, for even when they admire it, some critics find it a magical poem that has no meaning and requires no explanation. For them it is the story of an amazing sea-voyage told in ballad style and nothing more; a poem which has no reference beyond itself and, when read, leaves only the memory of our own enchantment. But this view can hardly be sustained in the face of the text, for at the end of the poem there is a very simple moral:

> He prayeth best, who loveth best
> All things both great and small;
> For the dear God who loveth us,
> He made and loveth all.

Coleridge later came to regret the inclusion of this and in his *Table Talk* answered the criticism of Mrs Barbauld, herself a poet, who had said that 'she admired the Ancient Mariner, but there were two faults in it, – it was improbable, and had no moral'. Coleridge candidly admitted the charge of improbability, but as for the lack of a moral, he now felt that the real fault was 'the obtrusion of the moral sentiment so openly on the reader'.[25]

Mrs Barbauld may have been rather obtuse, but there are still readers who make the same or similar mistakes. Because they read it as a literal narrative they fail to recognise in the poem the quality Coleridge attributed to Wordsworth, 'the original gift of spreading the tone, the atmosphere, and with it the depth and height of the ideal world around forms, incidents and situations' which belong to real life.[26] This is what distinguishes Coleridge's poem from the romanticism of poets such as Bürger and Sir Walter Scott. The voyage the Mariner makes, in spite of its improbability, is a real one, but the changing sea-scape and the adventures that befall him are symbolic of a spiritual and moral world. This is true even of the framework within which the narrative is set, for the poem starts with a wedding, regarded by many as a sacrament, and for all a symbol of new life; seen in the New Testament as an image of the union between God and his people. It is significant that on the Mariner's return from his voyage he is not invited to the wedding-feast. The woman Life-in-Death, who gambles with Death for the soul of the Mariner, is a dreadful reversed image of the bride, and the two represent the opposed forces of good and evil between which the action of the poem takes place:

Her lips were red, her looks were free,
Her locks were yellow as gold:
Her skin was as white as leprosy,
The Nightmare LIFE-IN-DEATH was she,
Who thicks man's blood with cold.

The poem is not an allegory in which every feature has its spiritual counterpart and in Lecture VIII of his 1818 Lectures Coleridge makes a distinction between allegory and symbol which applies to 'The Ancient Mariner':

The Symbolical cannot, perhaps, be better defined in distinction
from the Allegorical, than that it is always a part of that, of the
whole of which it is the representative.[27]

The voyage is one of spiritual testing in which the mist and snow which obscure the vision and chill the resolution of the sailors have their spiritual counterparts. The Mariner when his shipmates have all perished is both physically and spiritually lonely. The shooting of the albatross at first glance may seem insignificant, but is an act of gratuitous wickedness, for it has no motive; only afterwards do the crew blame the bird for the bad weather. In this it is like the Fall, symbolised in Genesis by the trivial eating of an apple, which is, nevertheless, an act of disobedience against God. The killing of the albatross is a violation of what Coleridge in 'The Aeolian Harp' called 'the one Life within us and abroad', and it, too, is an act of disobedience running counter to God's natural order. When the drought comes, the albatross is hung around the Mariner's neck in place of the Cross as an emblem of his sin and when he finds he can pray, it falls away and sinks into the sea. This moment comes when, moved by the beauty of the water-snakes, he 'blessed them unaware'. His blessing is followed by sleep and then rain, both instruments of God's grace. There is a roaring wind, which calls to mind the wind that heralded the coming of the Holy Ghost at Pentecost, and the ship moves on, not by the wind but by a supernatural agency:

> The loud wind never reached the ship,
> Yet now the ship moved on!

The Mariner's voyage sees him leaving his home port and returning there, but changed from the unreflecting man who set out on this strange journey. The poem shows the same pattern as the Biblical story of man's Fall and redemption. That Coleridge was preoccupied with the doctrine of the Fall can be seen also in 'Kubla Khan', which was probably written in 1798, just after he had finished 'The Ancient Mariner'. 'Kubla Khan' was not published until 1816, but its reception was not unlike that given to 'The Ancient Mariner', and even today it is often regarded as an unfinished psychological curiosity rather than a work of superb artistry. This is largely the result of Coleridge's account of how he wrote the poem, of how he fell into a dream-like state after taking 'two grains of Opium . . . to check a dysentry' while resting at a farmhouse between Porlock and Linton.

The term 'a psychological curiosity' was Coleridge's own in a note he added to the poem when it was first published, and this also included the story of how after waking, he began to write the 'two to three hundred' lines he had composed in his sleep, but was interrupted by 'a person on business from Porlock'. Even if the poem we have is only a quarter of what Coleridge composed while asleep, we should not assume it lacks meaning and is merely a series of images which emerged from his unconscious mind. In a further note, which Coleridge added to a manuscript version of the poem now in the British Library, he describes his sleep as 'a sort of reverie' and this suggests that he had a much more conscious control of his material than has been assumed. Certainly we should dismiss the idea that the poem is no more than part of a dream induced by opium. No doubt the two grains of opium influenced the poem, but the artistry it displays cannot be accounted for in this way. The taking of drugs does not turn a man into a poet, otherwise all addicts would be poets. Even allowing that opium played a necessary part in the genesis of the poem it is not sufficient to explain its greatness. Coleridge took opium, but he was also a poet of genius and if he had not given us his account of the poem we should regard it as meaningful and perhaps complete.

Ever since J. L. Lowes's *Road to Xanadu* critics have sought for the origins of 'Kubla Khan' in Coleridge's extensive reading, especially Bartram's *Travels to Discover the Sources of the Nile*, Maurice's *History of Hindostan*, and *Paradise Lost*. Lowes also demonstrated that some of its imagery owed something to Coleridge's walking-tour in North Wales in 1794, but it was Geoffrey Grigson in an article in the Cornhill magazine for 1947 who pointed out the similarity between the landscapes of 'Kubla Khan' and Hafod in Cardiganshire. As well as being what he termed 'a library cormorant', Coleridge was also a keen observer of nature and his poetry contains many images taken from natural scenery, and this is especially true of 'Kubla Khan'. Not far from the farmhouse where Coleridge fell asleep the river Lyn rushes down to the sea through a steep and rocky gorge. He would also have seen Wookey Hole in the Mendips, since it lay on the route between Nether Stowey and Cheddar, which we know he visited. Here the river Axe descends from the Ebbor Gorge to run underground into a great limestone cavern in which the stalagmites and stalactites give the appearance of a palace made of ice. All these come together in the poem, but it is Hafod especially which contributes to its meaning as well as its visual imagery.

Hafod was an estate at Devil's Bridge, near Aberystwyth, which Coleridge visited during his tour of Wales. It was laid out by its owner, Thomas Johnes, in the 1780s to recreate the Happy Valley described by Johnson in *The History of Rasselas Prince of Abyssinia*. Johnes employed two of the most distinguished landscape artists of the day, Richard Payne Knight and Uvedale Price, to lay out his grounds, which were enfolded in the steep hills that descend to the river Ystwyth, but the idea of creating a paradise was his own. He also designed the little Garden of Eden which lay within it hidden by the woods and approached by a stone gateway bearing the figures of Adam and Eve. The house, which was later destroyed by fire, was finished in 1788, only a few years before Coleridge's visit, and was designed in the picturesque Gothic style made fashionable by Horace Walpole at Strawberry Hill. It stood at the head of the valley and in front, on the far side of the lawn, ran the river. On its completion Johnes added a large octagonal library to the roof and on top of this a beautiful dome in the style of a Mogul palace. This elaborate representation of an earthly paradise, which he encountered only four years before he wrote 'Kubla Khan', was probably still fresh in Coleridge's mind, but the memory of it would have been revived by *An Attempt to Describe Hafod*, which appeared in 1796 and which was written by George Cumberland, a friend of Joseph Cottle, who was about to publish *Lyrical Ballads*.

The literary and topograhical memories come together in 'Kubla Khan'. The river Alph, whose name is close to the first letter of the Greek alphabet and hence to the Biblical story of Creation, brings to mind the river Alphaeus, an underground river which in ancient legend was thought to emerge as the Nile, and also the river Axe which runs below the Mendip Hills. The names *Ebbor, Aberystwyth*, and *Abyssinia*, run together in Coleridge's invention of Abora, which is close to Milton's Amara. In Book IV of *Paradise Lost* Milton describes the true Paradise where Adam and Eve live in innocence before the Fall and contrasts it with false paradises such as Amara,

where *Abassin* Kings their issue Guard,
Mount *Amara*, though this by some suppos'd
True Paradise, under the *Ethiop* line
By *Nilus* head, enclos'd with shining Rock. (280-83)

The first two sections of 'Kubla Khan' describe the creation of an earthly paradise, which has been built like the Garden of Eden by the side of a river, but unlike Eden it has been built by an earthly potentate. Like the Happy Valley in *Rasselas*, or Johnes's estate at Hafod, or Milton's Amara, it is one of those follies that try to make a new heaven on earth. It may not be false in any wicked sense, but it remains imperfect; it is subject to change and decay, its impermanence foreshadowed by the 'Ancestral voices prophesying war. ' Since the Fall any such earthly paradise can only be an imperfect copy of the original Garden of Eden or an incomplete approximation to the Paradise laid up in heaven; ours is a fallen world and only a shadow of the reality now lost to us.

This Christian and Platonic notion, reinforced no doubt by his reading of Plato and the English Platonists while he was writing the poem, leads in the next section to Plato's doctrine of Ideas. An entry in one of his Notebooks at the end of 1796, copies a sentence from Book VII of Plato's *Republic*.[28] This comes from the allegory of the Cave which was also in Coleridge's mind when he wrote 'The Destiny of Nations'. In elaborating this allegory Socrates tells Glaucon that men cannot perceive the Absolute directly; only after a gradual progression from the darkness of the cave into the light of day can they 'look at the sun and observe its real nature, not its appearance reflected in water'. In the cave men are imprisoned and their only knowledge comes from the shadows cast on the wall in front of which they are chained; they are unaware of any other world and mistake appearances for reality. If one of them were to ascend into the sunshine it would take him time to adjust to the light, and if he then returned to the cave he would be blinded by the darkness and incur the disbelief and derision of his fellow prisoners. The difference between appearance and reality, permanence and impermanence, is duplicated in Coleridge's use of another Platonic image, the fountain whose waters are always changing but whose form remains the same. (An image Wordsworth also used in his account of Crossing the Alps in Book VI of *The Prelude*, where he describes the mountain cataracts as 'Characters of the great Apocalypse, /The types and symbols of Eternity'.) In these lines in 'Kubla Khan' we no longer perceive the dome itself; all we see is its reflection on the surface of the water:

The shadow of the dome of pleasure

Floated midway on the waves.

The sun, which Coleridge employs throughout his poetry as a symbol of God, or the Absolute, casts its light upon the dome but it is a reflected light and the icy interior of this shadowy palace is as cold as the water it floats on and the vision of perfection it offers an illusion.

In Book VII of *The Republic* Socrates had spoken of a music that transcends earthly sound of which our own human music is only a faint echo, and as we contemplate the dome we hear this Platonic harmony, 'the mingled measure /From the fountain and the caves'. The theme of music leads on to the final section of the poem where the Abyssinian maid sings of the paradise hidden in her native mountains. She leads the poet to believe that if he could capture her magic in his poetry he, too, could build 'That sunny dome! those caves of ice!' This recalls the legend of Orpheus whose sacred lyre possessed supernatural powers, but the description of the poet with 'flashing eyes' and 'floating hair' comes from Plato's *Ion*. In *The Republic* Socrates dismisses poets as deceivers, concerned only with appearances and not reality. In *Ion* they are described in terms perhaps more favourable, but still ambiguous, for Plato may be writing satirically. Socrates speaks of them here as not in their right minds, but 'like Bacchic maidens who draw milk and honey from the rivers when under the influence of Dionysus'. This suggests that poetry is a kind of divine madness, a gift that confers on the poet a supernatural and Orphic power. The end of 'Kubla Khan' leaves one with a similar ambiguity. Does the poet deal only with appearances? Does he create illusions or give us a vision of reality itself? If Coleridge had completed his poem he might have answered these questions. Perhaps leaving them unanswered was deliberate and similar to Keats's 'Ode to a

Nightingale', which ends with a question,

Was it a vision, or a waking dream?

Fled is that music: – do I wake or sleep?

It was left to *Biographia Literaria*, where Coleridge analyses the workings of the poetic imagination, to attempt an answer to these questions.

The other poem of the supernatural started at this time was 'Christabel'. The first part of the poem was written in Somerset in 1797-1798, the second at Keswick in 1800, after a long interval during which Coleridge made his visit to Germany. When it was published in 1816, along with 'Kubla Khan', it was unfinished. The reason Coleridge gave for publishing it was that he felt others were plagiarizing his work and borrowing the metre he had used for his poem, and that if it were not published then, he himself would risk the charge of plagiarism. Like 'The Ancient Mariner', 'Christabel' takes the kind of story popularised by the English translations of Bürger's poems and gives it 'the depth and height of the ideal world', but although the poem starts with this quality it fails to sustain it.

Like 'The Ancient Mariner', 'Christabel' is concerned with the theme of evil and guilt. Christabel, an innocent girl whose mother died in giving her birth, goes at night into the woods surrounding her father's castle to pray for her lover who is far away. There she meets Geraldine and takes her home to rescue her from some supposed threat. As the poem progresses we become aware that Geraldine is a Lamian figure, a snake-like sorceress, and Christabel like a dove caught in the toils of a serpent. The poem suggests that Christabel will pass from unreflecting innocence to a knowledge of good and evil, but through divine grace in acquiring the wisdom of the serpent will retain the innocence of the dove. There were four contemporary accounts of how Coleridge planned to complete the poem: two by James Gillman, the physician with whom he lived from 1816 until his death, the other two by his son Derwent Coleridge. The most succinct of these is Derwent Coleridge's who thought the poem was 'founded on the Roman Catholic notion of expiation for others' sins; that Geraldine is a divinely appointed penance imposed upon Christabel for the redemption of her lover who had committed some crime'.[29]

The first part of 'Christabel' is successful in creating an atmosphere of unexplained dread, but this falls off in the second part and it was probably Coleridge's awareness that the poem was losing its hold that led him to abandon it. Certainly it fails to give any sense of genuine religious feeling and provides only a vague evocation of the supernatural; it has the trappings of medieval belief but they are no more than literary devices.

Coleridge's poems of the supernatural played a smaller part in modifying the religious sensibility of their time than Wordsworth's. Nevertheless, one should not underestimate their importance in bringing about a deliverance from the cold rationalism of eighteenth-century deism and the superficiality of so much Augustan poetry which saw nature as no more than picturesque. Newman was not alone in regarding Coleridge as one who had aroused the church from spiritual torpor and he was not thinking only of Coleridge's theological writings. Even so, Coleridge moved away from this kind of poetry; a change brought about partly by his admiration for the style developed by Wordsworth, partly by the lukewarm reception given to 'The Ancient Mariner' by Southey and Wordsworth, but most of all by changes in his own personal fortunes.

On coming back from Germany, Coleridge had moved his household from Nether Stowey to Keswick to be near to Wordsworth, 'his god' as Lamb described him. Coleridge's wife disliked the move since all her family and friends lived in the West Country and she became increasingly resentful of the time her husband spent with the Wordsworths; a resentment fanned into jealousy when she realised that Coleridge was in love with Sara Hutchinson, whose sister Mary was soon to become Wordsworth's wife. Coleridge himself was suffering from the damp climate of the Lakes and now began to take opium to relieve the pains of rheumatism, and the depression, anxiety, and guilt that afflicted him.

In April 1802, less than two years after moving to Keswick, he wrote the verse-letter to Sara Hutchinson, which in a revised version, with the personal references removed, was published in the *Morning Post* in October as 'Dejection: An Ode'. There is a sad irony in the date, for it appeared on Wordsworth's wedding-day. At one time Coleridge would have felt that nature's healing power could remove the depression that had settled on his mind and destroyed his creative powers, but now as he looks from his windows and views the mountains and lake he has to confess:

I see them all, so excellently fair!
I see, not feel, how beautiful they are.

The contrast with Wordsworth becomes clearer in the version published in the *Morning Post*, for there the name Edmund, who is Wordsworth, is substituted for Sara. As Wordsworth finds contentment on his wedding-day, Coleridge faces the death of his hopes, his poetic ambitions, and his personal happiness. The healing power of nature can only operate where there is an inner and joyful reciprocity and this is denied him:

> Joy, Sara! is the Spirit and the Power,
> That wedding Nature to us gives in Dower
> A new Earth and new Heaven,
> Undreamt of by the Sensual and the Proud!

The contrast between his own and Wordsworth's fortunes became more pronounced with the passage of time and this is seen in his lines 'To William Wordsworth', written in January 1807, a few months after his return from Malta, when he listened with mixed emotions to Wordsworth's reading of the poem known in their circle as 'The Poem to Coleridge'. Coleridge had left for Malta in 1804, in search of health, freedom from marital discord, and a kinder climate. When he returned to England he was still in the grip of opium and had started to drink brandy to counteract the depression it produced. In a letter to her friend Catherine Clarkson on 6 November 1806, Dorothy Wordsworth wrote:

> Never, never did I feel such a shock at first sight of him. . . . He is
> utterly changed, and yet sometimes, when he was animated in
> conversation . . . I saw something of his former self. . . . That he is ill
> I am well assured, and must sink if he does not grow more happy.

It was about this time that Coleridge decided to separate from his wife and listening to Wordsworth reading the poem that was to become *The Prelude*, he must have felt acutely the contrast between his own misery and the domestic happiness that surrounded Wordsworth. But more than this, he realised that *The Prelude* was a great achievement comparable to *Paradise Lost*. Coleridge's own poem 'To William Wordsworth' composed, as one manuscript version relates, 'for the greater part of the Night, on which he [Wordsworth] finished the recitation of his poem (in thirteen Books) concerning the growth and history of his own Mind', is full of Miltonic echoes. Coleridge sees Wordsworth as Milton's heir, but writes of himself in imagery that recalls not *Paradise Lost* but 'Lycidas'. He looks back over the years since he had known Wordsworth and feels his own waste of talents when compared with his friend's success:

> Sense of past youth, and Manhood come in Vain;
> And Genius given, and Knowledge won in vain;
> And all which I had culled in wood-walks wild,
> And all which patient toil had reared, and all,
> Commune with thee had opened out – but flowers
> Strewed on my corse, and borne upon my bier,
> In the same coffin, for the self-same grave!

Coleridge does not lose himself in self-pity, but is generous enough to salute his friend's achievement and to look forward with hope, 'even as Life returns upon the drowned'. *The Prelude* gave him, as it gave so many after him, strength and guidance; hearing it read for the first time was almost a religious experience and his own poem ends:

I sate, my being ended in one thought
(Thought was it? or aspiration? or resolve?)
Absorbed, yet hanging still upon the sound –
And when I rose, I found myself in prayer.

Coleridge was soon to find himself in desperate circumstances. Without a permanent home he stayed with the Wordsworths for a time, but this ended with the famous quarrel that brought their friendship to an end for many years. He moved to London, then Bristol, then with friends at Calne, and finally for the last eighteen years of his life with Dr and Mrs Gillman at Highgate, making a living from journalism, lecturing, and writing. When he was in Germany he had acquired a greater knowledge of philosophy, theology, and Biblical studies, and was attracted especially by Kant who, as he declared in *Biographia Literaria*, took hold of his mind 'as with a giant's hand'. He had brought back from Germany a box of books he hoped would lay the foundations of a philosophy which would answer his deepest needs and it was to this that he now turned in earnest. Although he never satisfactorily completed a system of thought, this is true of some of the greatest philosophers and may even be an advantage. Certainly what he accomplished played a decisive part in meeting the challenges to religious belief in the century which followed.

Biographia Literaria, which tells the story of the growth of his own mind can be seen as a prose equivalent of *The Prelude*. One is struck in reading it with its religious images and overtones. It tells the story of how Hartley and the empiricists had led him into a wilderness of doubt and a darkness of mind and how he had been delivered from these to reach the promised land of renewed faith. He had been led from darkness into light with the help of the Neoplatonists, Plotinus, Proclus, and Gemistus Pletho, and the seventeenth-century mystics George Fox, Jacob Boehme, and Boehme's English disciple, William Law. 'They contributed' he wrote, in Chapter IX of *Biographia Literaria*,

to keep alive the heart in the head ... if they were too often a moving cloud of smoke to me by day, yet they were always a pillar of fire throughout the night, during my wanderings through the wilderness of doubt, and enabled me to skirt, without crossing, the sandy deserts of utter unbelief.

Alongside these stood his friend Wordsworth, whose poetry showed that 'union of deep feeling with profound thought' which meant so much to Coleridge. It was repeated reflection on this poetry, he tells us, that led him to assign a central place to the imagination when he came to construct his philosophy. Compared with the greater part of eighteenth-century poetry, Wordsworth's work had a quality which suggested that there were two powers of the mind; one an associative power which produced works of fancy, the other a creative one which produced works of the imagination. As early as 1801, Coleridge had become convinced that the mind is active in perception and not merely a receptacle for sense impressions. Writing to Thomas Poole, he had declared:

> If the mind be not *passive*, if it be indeed made in God's Image, and that, too, in the sublimest sense – the Image of the *Creator* – there is ground for suspicion that any system built on the passiveness of the mind must be false as a system.

The mind for Coleridge is a counterpart of nature, which is not matter governed by mechanical laws, but a living body animated by the divine spirit, – not *natura naturata* but *natura naturans*. The human mind creates the world it perceives in a manner analogous to God's creation of the world out of chaos; it imposes order on the manifold of sense experience. It does this by what Coleridge called the primary imagination, which he describes as 'a repetition in the finite mind of the eternal act of creation in the infinite I AM'.

This process operates in art as well as perception. Some poetry can be explained in terms of images taken from the memory and brought together by association; this is how most seventeenth and eighteenth-century theorists had accounted for poetic composition. Coleridge accepted that some poetry could, indeed, be explained in this way, but considered this the work of the fancy and the poet who wrote it the poet of talent. The poet of genius, however, possesses a creative power that forms from the materials of perception a new world; one like the everyday world, but reorganised and transcending ordinary perception. This secondary or poetic imagination creates a world of 'seeming objects', a world like that of our ordinary experience, but carrying also a weight of meaning and significance. The world of the poet, as Aristotle had argued, is more universal than that of the historian. So Hamlet or King Lear and even the characters and events in Shakespeare's history plays, when compared with Holinshed's *Chronicles*, 'may be termed ideal realities':

> They are not the things themselves, so much as the abstracts of the things, which a great mind takes into itself, and then naturalises them to its own conception.[30]

Coleridge in the prospectus to his last lectures on literature, delivered in 1818-1819, described Shakespeare as 'the great Philosophic Poet' and Wordsworth, too, although he failed to complete any great philosophical poem, remained for him one whose work was a supreme example of the imagination at work.

The importance given to the imagination by Coleridge can be seen in Chapter IX of *Biographia Literaria* where he claims that the poetic imagination creates symbols and that 'An IDEA in the highest sense of that word cannot be conveyed but by a symbol'. This follows from the distinction he makes between the understanding and the reason. The understanding frames concepts and is concerned with discursive knowledge derived from sensory perception; the reason goes beyond this and is the 'source and substance of truths above sense' that have their own evidence. The reason is concerned with principles that are not empirically verifiable, but have to be accepted if experience itself is to make sense. Coleridge called the secondary imagination 'the agent of the reason'; it creates a world that lies beyond conceptual knowledge, one that can be represented only in symbols. But there is a reciprocity between symbol and concept, for conceptual knowledge stimulates and feeds the poetic imagination, and criticism attempts to interpret works of art in conceptual terms, even if without total success.

The distinction between reason and understanding goes back to Plato and was upheld by the English Platonists of the seventeenth century, including Milton, who believed that reason belonged to the angelic part of human nature and that poetry had a special role in revealing divine truth. But it was Kant who deepened and refined Coleridge's theory of the imagination. The understanding, for Kant, views nature as governed by mechanical laws; the reason, on the other hand, views it as a work of art, the parts of which contribute to a unity which transcends the parts. According to Kant this idea of wholeness can only be a product of reason; it cannot be constructed from the senses and although it cannot be proved empirically our aesthetic experience demands that we accept it as true. Coleridge welcomed this as a confirmation of what he himself had always believed. As early as 1797 he had written to his friend Thomas Poole about the importance of imaginative literature in education:

> I know of no other way of giving the mind a love of the Great and the Whole. Those who have been led to the same truths step by step through the constant testimony of their senses, seem to me to want a sense which I possess. They contemplate nothing but *parts*, and all *parts* are necessarily little. And the universe to them is but a mass of *little things*.[31]

Nevertheless, there were important points on which Coleridge parted company with Kant. Kant set severe limits to what the human mind could know and considered it limited to 'phenomenal' knowledge and unable to apprehend 'things in themselves'. Coleridge found it difficult to accept this and even refused to believe that this was in fact Kant's teaching. At one time he had been attracted by the Neoplatonic claim that art could penetrate the world of perception to apprehend the supersensuous, but Plato himself had denied this, and we saw in 'Kubla Khan' that Coleridge left the question unanswered. For Kant art represents an idea in the artist's mind, for the Neoplatonists it provides an access to ultimate reality. Although he flirted with Schelling, who tried to reconcile these two positions with a philosophical monism that identified nature and the mind, Coleridge rejected this because it left no place for a transcendent deity and led to pantheism.

A more serious disagreement with Kant was over moral theory, for Coleridge could not accept Kant's notion that the only virtuous action is one done from a sense of duty. Actions prompted by affection, family ties, or a regard for consequences, are all for Kant expedient and not moral. This was a more sophisticated version of what Coleridge had criticised in Godwin and in a letter to J. H. Green on 13 December 1817, he wrote, 'I reject Kant's *stoic* principle, as false, unnatural and even immoral . . . he treats the affections as indifferent'.[32] Coleridge always felt that the love found in one's family circle (or sadly lacking in his own) was the foundation of social ethics. Coleridge also disagreed with Kant's famous dictum 'I ought, therefore I can', since for him any philosophy worth its salt had to speak to the human condition. His constant endeavour was to find or construct a philosophy that matched his own experience and needs, and at this time his greatest need was a longing for forgiveness and a freedom from guilt at missed opportunities. To be told that 'I ought, therefore I can', as he reflected on the waste of his own great gifts, his broken marriage, and his opium addiction, must have seemed like telling a drowning man he could swim if he set his mind to it. His feelings were expressed in the cry of despair recorded in a Notebook entry: 'But O! not what I understand, but what I *am*, must save or crush me!'[33]

This explains why he turned to a philosophy concerned with religion and, in doing so, brought help to those in his own and succeeding generations who sought a faith that could stand up to the intellectual challenges of the times. When he wrote *Aids to Reflection*, published in 1825, natural theology was at a low ebb. The traditional arguments for the existence of God had been seriously weakened; only the argument from design carried any conviction and Paley's comparison of the world with a watch was still very popular. Coleridge found this comparison odious; for him the best evidence was the human heart and Paley's argument little different from the deism which had been bled white from the wounds inflicted by Hume.

Revealed religion was in little better shape. Its twin foundations of the church and the Bible were both under attack. Gibbon had criticised the history of the church with a savage and effective irony, and the authority of the Bible had been called into question by the Higher Criticism of German scholars. Coleridge's theology is rooted in personal experience and especially moral experience. In Chapter X of *Biographia Literaria* he emphasises his moral concern: 'I became convinced', he writes, 'that religion, as both the corner-stone and the key-stone of morality, must have a *moral* origin; so far at least, that the evidence of its doctrines could not, like the truths of abstract science, be wholly independent of the will'. It is not that we act virtuously to achieve a heavenly reward, or that one cannot be virtuous without belief, but the realisation that there is an ideal always beyond our moral capabilities. We are faced with the demands of a moral imperative that cannot be met from our own resources and this is recognised and met in Christianity with the promise of forgiveness and grace. Although a theological truth, this is a matter not of speculative but practical knowledge. Coleridge's theology is existential in the same way that the Bible's is; this is made clear in the final chapter of *Biographia Literaria* where he writes: 'We can only *know* by the act of *becoming. Do the will of my Father, and ye shall KNOW I am of God.*'

One of Coleridge's reasons for going to Germany was to collect material for a *Life of Lessing*, the author of the famous *Laocöon*; like so many of his projects this was never completed (or even started), but Lessing remained a considerable influence. This influence started, as Lessing's own interests did, with literary theory, but Lessing turned in later life to theology and Biblical studies, where his pioneering views scandalised the German Lutherans. Coleridge began by sharing many of Lessing's doubts about the authority of the Bible and these were increased by the lectures given by Eichhorn (one of the leading, and in Coleridge's description, most 'daring' of the Biblical scholars) when Coleridge was at Gottingen. The New Testament writers who claimed that Jesus was the Son of God and who declared that Jesus himself said so, were reporting something they felt was true, but the fact is only that they made such a claim; the claim itself has still to be proved. After all, there were contemporaries of Jesus who never accepted such a claim. Reason cannot validate such claims: 'That is the ugly wide ditch' wrote Lessing, 'which I cannot get over, though I have often and earnestly attempted to leap it'.[34] The only way across is by faith, a leap in the dark as Kierkegaard described it, that will land you in the arms of God; and so it was to faith and its relation to the Bible that Coleridge increasingly turned his attention.

In *Confessions of an Inquiring Spirit*, published posthumously in 1840, Coleridge faced a two-fold challenge to the Scriptures. On the one hand he had to counter the view current in England in his day that the Bible was literally true throughout; 'dictated' in fact by God. On the other he had to answer the attacks of those radical German critics who regarded the Bible as no different from the collections of myth found in pagan religions. The one he called 'Bibliolatry', a view of the Bible that the rationalists with some reason dismissed with contempt. The other, he believed, failed to see that the Bible, although subject to the same scholarly criticism as any other book, was different from any other book. Coleridge maintained that the Bible carried the evidence of its own truth. 'The Bible and Christianity', he declared, 'are their own sufficient evidence'. As Lessing had argued, Christianity is not true because the apostles and evangelists taught it; they taught it because they believed it to be true. Not everything the Biblical authors wrote is revealed truth, for they were men of their own times with patterns of thought and even prejudices that coloured their narrative: something to be seen in the evolving religious awareness that shows itself between Genesis and Revelation. Nevertheless, argued Coleridge, although not every part of Scripture is revealed truth, all of it is inspired.

It is here that Coleridge's prolonged thinking about literature informs his view of the Bible. His life-long study of Shakespeare led him to see that a great deal of the Bible expresses thought and records experience through the medium of literature and he recognised similarities between Shakespeare's plays and large parts of the Bible. This does not mean that the Bible is fiction, but that the inspiration of the Biblical writers worked through the imagination. Just as Shakespeare took the chronicles of English and Roman history and turned them into plays with a universal significance, so the Biblical writers were concerned not simply with the facts, but with interpreting them in the light of their faith. The difference for the believer, of course, is that the Biblical writers – and this is especially true of the New Testament – were telling a story with a unique significance and importance. Coleridge expressed this well in 1816 in *The Statesman's Manual*, entitled *A Lay Sermon*, where he contrasts the imaginative writing of the Old Testament and the pallid abstractions of modern histories:

The histories . . . of the present and preceding century partake in . . . its mechanistic philosophy, and are the *product* of an unenlivened generalizing Understanding. In the Scriptures they are the living *educts* of the Imagination; of that reconciling and mediatory power, which incorporating the Reason in Images of the Sense . . . gives birth to a system of symbols . . . consubstantial with the truths, of which they are the *conductors*.

The characters of the Old Testament are individuals and not allegorical figures and yet in them we perceive universal truths; they provide, writes Coleridge, both 'Portraits and Ideals': 'The truths and the symbols that represent them move in conjunction and form the living chariot that bears up (for us) the throne of the Divine Humanity.'

Coleridge's teaching on the Bible was generations ahead of general opinion in England and even runs contrary to what many simple people hold dear today. But this was not his only contribution to religious thought. He was also a distinguished philosopher of religion, something fairly rare in England, and his influence has been the greater because he was not a systematic thinker. His great achievement was not the construction of a system, but the opening out of lines of enquiry, and above all in challenging the empiricist philosophy that had become the British orthodoxy. The effect of this philosophy on religion had reduced Christianity either to a variant of deism, a cold, intellectual assent to what could be empirically verified, or to a fundamentalist belief in the verbally inerrant text of the Bible. Methodism reacted to this with an appeal to the heart, which was echoed by Evangelicals like Wilberforce, and which was welcomed by Coleridge. His endeavour was to give this tribunal of inner experience a philosophical defence which could withstand the assaults of scepticism.

In a well-known essay in *The Westminster Review* J. S. Mill described Coleridge (along with Bentham) as one of the two great seminal minds of the century. The term 'seminal' is apt, for his writings provided a seed-bed of ideas which were brought to fruition by his successors. These included men of letters, literary critics, and political theorists, and in religion men as diverse as Arnold, Newman, F. D. Maurice, and Kingsley. Julius Hare in his *Mission of the Comforter*, 1846, called him 'the great religious philosopher to whom the mind of our generation in England owes more than to any other man' and John Tulloch in *Movements of Religious Thought in Britain during the Nineteenth Century* (1853), said of him that 'the later streams of religious thought in England are all more or less coloured by his influence'.

II

Carlyle and Arnold

Virtually no-one today reads Carlyle. The publication of his and his wife's letters in the splendid now complete edition undertaken by Edinburgh and Duke universities has done something to revive an interest in and even a degree of sympathy for him, but the florid style of his published writings, their hectoring tone and frequent bad temper, together with opinions that many modern readers find repellent, have left him on the side-lines of history. And yet to his contemporaries he was a prophetic figure. George Eliot said that 'there is hardly a superior or active mind of this generation that has not been modified by Carlyle's writings'. Nor was George Eliot alone. James Hutchison Stirling, the first serious expositor of Hegel's philosophy in Britain, looking back on his youth some forty years later, could declare, 'He [Carlyle] was every literary young man's idol, almost the God he prayed to. Even a morsel of white paper with the name of Carlyle upon it would have been picked up from the street as a veritable amulet.'[1]

What gave Carlyle this reputation was that he led the way in helping his contemporaries adjust to the massive dislocations brought about by the French Revolution, the Romantic movement, and the growth of a new industrialised society. The appeal he made was hardly perhaps consciously articulated, but nevertheless brought coherence and stability at a time of profound intellectual and political change. Central in the transition from one age to another was the transformation of religious thought and belief. Orthodox religion had been under attack since the end of the eighteenth century and the efforts of a thinker such as Coleridge to defend Christianity on philosophical grounds had scarcely entered the minds of ordinary people. It was here that Carlyle made his most striking contribution to the troubled sensibility of his age. He was not a systematic or original thinker but rather a social critic and historian. Nevertheless, he brought answers to the anxieties and problems that beset men's minds by bringing into England and popularising many of the ideas of German philosophy. Above all, it was Carlyle who held out the promise of a vitalistic philosophy which could replace the materialist and mechanistic thought of the preceding century.

Wordsworth and Coleridge both played an important part in this transition and their influence extended far beyond poetry. T. S. Eliot was quick to realise this for in *The Use of Poetry and the Use of Criticism* he writes, 'there is, in his [Wordsworth's] poetry and in his Preface [to *Lyrical Ballads*] a profound spiritual revival, an inspiration communicated rather to Pusey and Newman, to Ruskin, and to the great humanitarians, than to the accredited poets of the next age'.[2] The same could be said of Coleridge and here the list would have to be extended to include at least F. D. Maurice and Matthew Arnold, though it was Coleridge's religious and philosophical writings rather than his poetry that counted with them. Where Carlyle modified and indeed challenged the influence of Wordsworth and Coleridge was in his attempt to bring about a religion free from dogma. Speaking through the mouth of his hero in *Sartor Resartus* he declared that the present age needed to replace 'The Mythus of the Christian Religion', with 'the divine spirit of that Religion in a new Mythus'. Already in his early writings Carlyle realised that he was witnessing the birth of a new age and that the underlying principles of the old society were being challenged more radically than ever before. The title of his popular tract for the times, *Past and Present*, is an indication of this, but already in 1831, in 'Characteristics', he had written, 'The Old has passed away, but, alas the New appears not in its stead; the Time is still in pangs of travail with the New.'[3] At the centre of this change for Carlyle was the search for a religion that would meet the needs of modern man, for he believed that 'a man's religion is the chief fact with regard to him'.[4]

Carlyle was brought up in the strict tradition of Scottish presbyterianism, which was steeped in Calvinism and puritanism. His family belonged to a simple rural community set in a harsh physical and economic environment in which his father's occupation as a stone-mason gave Carlyle a life-long respect for hard work well done. But it was his mother who was the more dominant influence on his character and her strict moral teaching remained deeply embedded in his personality. Throughout her long life he kept up a regular correspondence with her and she remained a formidable figure to her daughter-in-law, Jane Welsh Carlyle. When the old lady's portrait arrived at their house in Cheyne Row,

Chelsea, Carlyle wished it to be hung over the sitting-room fireplace, but Jane insisted that it be kept in her husband's study. 'I could never feel alone with that picture over me!', she wrote, 'I almost *screamed* at the notion.'[5] Shortly before her death in 1853 Carlyle wrote to his mother, 'If there has been any good in the things I have uttered in this world's hearing, it was *your* voice essentially that was speaking thro' me: essentially, what you and my brave father meant and taught me to mean'.[6]

His parents intended Carlyle for the ministry, but at Edinburgh university, where his increasing scepticism was brought to a head by reading Gibbon, he decided not only that he could no longer follow this path but that Christianity was no longer true. His parents reluctantly accepted the first part of this and he was careful, especially with his mother, to conceal or at least soften the full force of the second. It is significant that it was Gibbon rather than his fellow Scot, David Hume, who led him to abandon his Christian faith. Carlyle, unlike Coleridge, was never steeped in eighteenth-century empiricism. His mind had a historical rather than a philosophical bent and it was what he felt to be Gibbon's demolition of Christianity as a historical institution rather than Hume's undermining of Christian doctrine that proved the deciding factor in his loss of faith.

Carlyle's upbringing left him with a legacy of Biblical Christianity which psychologically he could never shake off. His imagination was steeped in the Bible which he would probably have heard read daily at home and certainly every Sunday at the kirk. Even when he abandoned his faith the Bible left him with the deep-seated conviction that human existence was a great historical drama whose end still awaited consummation. Coupled with this was the sense that behind this historical process there was a transcendent world of spiritual powers and values in which the individual life participates; that this present world is one of appearances only, a mere approximation to a reality which has still to be fully manifested. By the time Carlyle began to write, the study of history was developing into a serious academic discipline, but whereas Gibbon, Hume, and Robertson adopted a positivist and scientific approach to their subject, Carlyle saw history not as the product of impersonal forces, but as

> at bottom the History of the Great Men who have worked here
> ... all things that we see standing accomplished in the world
> are properly the outer material result, the practical realisation
> and embodiment, of thoughts that dwelt in the Great Men sent

into the world.[7]

This was close to the Biblical view of history and especially to the Old Testament, with its story of kings, prophets and heroes.

Carlyle's abandonment of his Christian faith left him at first in a state of severe depression and with the feeling that life was meaningless. This ended only when he underwent what can best be described as a conversion experience, and Carlyle used this word in recounting what happened to him. The most graphic account of this is provided in his quasi-autobiographical work *Sartor Resartus*, where it is attributed to his hero, Herr Teufelsdrockh, whose story Carlyle tells. What happened to Teufelsdrockh in the Rue Saint-Thomas de l'Enfer in Paris did in fact happen to Carlyle himself in Leith Walk, Edinburgh. Even if we did not know from other sources that the experience was Carlyle's own, the narrative at this point is clearly about Carlyle himself and the incident he recounts remained for him something that marked a crisis in his life.

In the chapter of *Sartor Resartus* entitled 'The Everlasting No' Carlyle speaks for the whole generation of young men with whom he had grown up. This was a generation which still felt the effects of the French Revolution and its aftermath, but it was not only social and political unrest which brought perplexity and confusion. The defeat of Napoleon heralded a new age and a shaking of the foundations of belief. What Carlyle called 'the withered, unbelieving, secondhand Eighteenth Century' had been found wanting, but what was there to put in its place? The Church and the Bible which had provided the bearings for an earlier generation, were now felt to be inadequate. The old formularies were still there but they lacked vital meaning; they were empty husks whose kernel had vanished. Carlyle found himself in a slough of despond in which he wrote, 'To me the Universe was void of all Life, of Purpose, of Volition, even of Hostility: it was one, huge, dead, immeasurable Steam-engine rolling on, in its dead indifference'.

At first Carlyle could see no way through what he called the 'howling desert of infidelity' which surrounded him, but he now experienced a spiritual rebirth. 'I asked myself ', he wrote, 'What *art* thou afraid of ? Wherefore, like a coward, dost thou forever pip and whimper? . . . what is the sum-total of the worst that lies before thee? Death?' When he faced this ultimate question he found that all his doubts and fears had dropped away:

> then it was that my whole ME stood up, in native God-created
> majesty, and with emphasis recorded its Protest. Such a Protest,

the most important transaction in Life, may that same Indignation and Defiance, in a psychological point of view, be fitly called. The Everlasting No had said: 'Behold, thou art fatherless, outcast, and the Universe is mine (the Devil's)'; to which my whole ME made answer: 'I am not thine, but Free, and forever hate thee! 'It is from this hour that I incline to date my Spiritual New-birth, or Baphometic Fire-baptism; perhaps I directly thereupon began to be a Man.[10]

Some may see this as an account of a psychological crisis of the kind any young man may undergo in achieving maturity and independence, and such a view is supported by Carlyle's consideration of suicide as an answer to his problems. But this reductionist interpretation does not fit in with Carlyle's own view. Although the psychological element was certainly present, for him it was predominantly a religious experience which led to a spiritual rebirth. The echoes of Biblical language and imagery, the use of the old-style 'thee' and 'thou', and the dialogue with the Devil, all demonstrate that for him it had a religious dimension. But the religion he preaches in *Sartor Resartus* is free of any dogma and independent of any church. On the negative side it was a revolt against the empiricist philosophy of his day, against the view of society as a machine, against the calculating prudential morality of the times, against the search for happiness rather than virtue, against the greed and materialism that animated many of his contemporaries. On the positive side it proclaimed man as a free being subject only to the moral law, as a being who lived in a spiritual as well as a material dimension, or as he put it in the chapter entitled 'The Everlasting Yea',

thou art not engulfed, but borne aloft into the azure of Eternity. Love not pleasure; love God. This is the THE EVERLASTING YEA, wherein all contradiction is solved: wherein whoso walks and works it is well with him'.

Although Carlyle considered the rituals and formularies of traditional Christianity to have lost their meaning, he did not seek to abolish them, for man cannot walk into the world naked; he needs clothes to protect him and to give him respectability. Religious symbols, like those of the Law and Parliament, are a necessary part of a civilised society and represent in outward form what has real significance. Indeed, for Carlyle all life is sacramental and natural phenomena and laws can be seen as miraculous. But a failure of confidence has come about, Carlyle maintains, because men invest the outward forms with a significance that belongs only to the inner reality. It is this confusion of appearance and reality, according to Carlyle, which has brought with it a contempt for the spiritual and a cynicism which has undermined the whole of society. What is needed then is a transvaluation of the old dogmas and ceremonies, a regeneration of the spirit, and a reverence before the mystery of existence.

There were two important components of this new vision of reality. One of these was a renewed moral awareness, a reverence for the moral law and the importance of the individual conscience. The 'recognition of Man, and his Moral Duty', he observes, 'comes to be the chief element only in purer forms of religion'.[11] The other was the belief in history as a dynamic process; a conviction that society is neither fixed and immutable nor, on the other hand, a meaningless flux, but moving forward to a future consummation if only men are ready to meet the challenge of events with a sense of purpose. For Carlyle the 'Great Men', whether kings, statesmen, priests, or men of letters, are those who evince this purpose. 'Great Men', he declares, 'are the inspired . . . Texts of that divine Book of REVELATIONS, whereof a Chapter is completed from epoch to epoch, and by some named HISTORY'.[12] History is for him a continuous revelation. Is not 'Man's History, and Men's History a perpetual Evangel?', he asks, and answers, 'Listen, and for organic music thou wilt ever, as of old, hear the Morning Stars sing together.'[13] The purpose revealed in history, he believed, was a moral one. All the great events of history such as the Civil War and the French Revolution, which to their contemporaries seemed catastrophic, were turning points which directed men forward to a final goal in which evil will be subsumed in the good. So, in the last of his Lectures on Heroes, he asserts that 'What Napoleon *did* will in the long-run amount to what he did *justly*; what Nature with her laws will sanction.'

All this is, of course, a variant of the Christian teaching which left its mark on Carlyle's mind even after he had abandoned it. Indeed, the 'clothes philosophy' he advances in *Sartor Resartus* was probably derived from the verses in Psalm CII, 'And thou Lord in the beginning hast laid the foundations of the earth, and the heavens are the work of thy hands. They shall perish, but thou shalt endure: they shall all wax old as a garment; And as a vesture shalt thou change them, and they shall be changed: but thou art the same, and thy years shall not fail.' Carlyle's millennarian view of history is derived from the Bible and his emphasis upon the moral imperative comes from his Puritan upbringing. But this secularised version of Christianity which he designated in *Sartor Resartus,* Natural Supernaturalism, had a parallel in the idealist philosophy which had developed in Germany from the time of Kant.[14] Certainly Kant's teaching that the only moral action is one done from a sense of duty alone chimed in with Carlyle's austere temperament and upbringing. More than this, the development of German idealism by Kant's successors provided a way of thinking which helped to shape his own version of religion. In his early essay, The 'State of German Literature' which he contributed to the *Edinburgh Review* in 1827, he writes approvingly of Fichte who had taught the notion of 'a 'Divine Idea' pervading the visible Universe; which visible Universe is indeed but its symbol and sensible manifestation, having in itself no meaning, or eventual existence independent of it'. Carlyle follows Fichte in believing that 'To the mass of men this Divine Idea of the world lies hidden: yet to discern it, to seize it, and live wholly in it, is the condition of all genuine virtue, knowledge, freedom'. Schelling, who at one time had attracted Coleridge, also provided something Carlyle was looking for: a self-authenticating intuitive knowledge which could unite the self and the objective world. Kant had argued persuasively that such knowledge was not available to the pure reason; only the practical reason whose concern was morality could prescribe laws which were self-authenticating. Coleridge accepted the truth of this and came to see that Schelling's philosophy led to pantheism, but Carlyle seemed unaware that his belief that all natural laws are miraculous and all natural phenomena sacramental leaves one with no miracles and no sacraments.

Only dogmatic religion could give Carlyle what he wanted and it was perhaps a dawning realisation of this that led him to put more weight on action rather than belief. In fact he was temperamentally impatient with speculative thought and his knowledge of German philosophy was not very precise; it was German literature which helped him to articulate his thought and above all Goethe who inspired him. In his Lecture on 'The Hero as a Man of Letters', he wrote of Goethe, 'I consider that, for the last hundred years, by far the notablest of all Literary Men is Fichte's countryman, Goethe'. He advised his own countrymen to 'close your Byron, and open your Goethe'.

What attracted Carlyle to Goethe is made clear in the essay he devoted to him in the *Foreign Review* in 1828. In Goethe he found someone who had experienced the same doubt and perplexity he himself had suffered and who had risen above them to a new spiritual awareness. 'For Goethe has not only suffered and mourned in bitter agony under the spiritual perplexities of his time; but has also mastered them, he is above them, and has shown others how to rise above them.' Carlyle found in Goethe not only a romantic version of post-Kantian philosophy expressed with poetic sensibility, but the story of a spiritual pilgrimage that ran parallel to his own. He had already translated into English the semi-autobiographical account of Goethe's spiritual education recounted in *Wilhelm Meister's Apprenticeship,* and now went on to further Goethe's reputation in England with translations and encomiastic essays. For many people Carlyle was now regarded as the main channel through whom German literature and thought came into England.

This was a role hitherto given to Coleridge and there is plenty of evidence to suggest that Carlyle was jealous of Coleridge's reputation in this matter and always ready to diminish it. In his essay *On The State of German Literature* he gives a disquisition on Kant which fails to mention Coleridge and by implication rules him out with the statement that no British writer has shown any real knowledge of Kant. The faint praise he gives Coleridge in his essay on Novalis published in the *Foreign Review* in 1829 at least shows that he had read *Biographia Literaria* and the *Friend* and one can hardly doubt that Carlyle profited from his study of Coleridge.[15]

Temperamentally, however, the two men were poles apart and a good deal of what came to be Carlyle's active dislike of Coleridge had its origin in what amounts to a contempt for Coleridge as a man, although there remained differences of opinion between them which were rooted in Carlyle's suspicion of speculative thought. One of Carlyle's central beliefs was the need for action and the importance he gave to this goes back to his childhood. In his *Reminiscences* he wrote that his father believed 'man was created to work, not to speculate, or feel, or dream'.[16] This remained Carlyle's own opinion and when he came to launch his attack on Coleridge in his *Life of Sterling* he contrasted his father's character with that of Coleridge.

The entire chapter he devotes to Coleridge is an extended *argumentum ad hominem,* brilliantly written with a satirical edge, and is one of the most sustained pieces of demolition-work in our literature. Carlyle begins with a picture of Coleridge as remote and with little relevance to the issues of the day; one of yesterday's men:

> Coleridge sat on the brow of Highgate Hill, in those years
> looking down on London and its smoke-tumult, like a sage
> escaped from the inanity of life's battle; attracting towards him
> the thoughts of innumerable brave souls still engaged there.

He then goes on to sow the seeds of a legend that has survived into
our own day, that Coleridge was not only irrelevant but indolent:
'His express contributions to poetry, philosophy, or any specific
province of human literature or enlightenment, had been small
and sadly intermittent.' Modern editions of Coleridge's writings,
including *The Collected Works* (not yet completed), which will
run to twenty-two volumes, contradict this charge of laziness; and
by an ironical reversal Coleridge's reputation as a thinker, quite
apart from his reputation as a poet, has grown as fast as Carlyle's
has diminished.

The sarcasm mounts as Carlyle tells us that Coleridge was
'thought to hold, he alone in England, the key of German and
other Transcendentalism; knew the sublime secret of believing by
the reason' what 'the understanding' had been obliged to fling out
as incredible.' Men of common sense and practical men 'reckoned
him a metaphysical dreamer: but to the rising spirits of the young
generation he . . . sat there as a kind of *Magus*.' He then passes on
to a physical description of Coleridge:

> Brow and head were round . . . but the face was flabby and
> irresolute. . . . The whole figure and air, good and amiable
> otherwise, might be called flabby and irresolute; expressive of
> weakness under possibility of strength . . . in walking, he rather
> shuffled than decisively stept; and a lady once remarked he never
> could fix which side of the garden walk would suit him best,
> but continually shifted, in corkscrew fashion, and kept trying
> both.

Carlyle employs here a device Dickens was to use so brilliantly, of
using physical characteristics to mirror qualities of mind and
personality, for his attack on what he regards as the irresolution
and evasiveness of Coleridge's thinking:

> His talk, alas, was distinguished, like himself, by irresolution:
> it . . . loved to wander at its own sweet will, and make, its auditor
> and his claims . . . a mere passive bucket for itself. . . . He had
> knowledge about many things and topics, much curious reading
> but generally all topics led him . . . into the high seas of
> philosophic theosophy, – the hazy infinitude of Kantean
> transcendentalism, with its 'sum-m-mjects' and 'om-m-mjects'.

Page after page of persistent and bitter criticism seem to be modified
in places when Carlyle writes more in sorrow than in anger: 'To the

man himself Nature had given, in high measure, the seeds of a noble endowment; and to unfold it had been forbidden him'. But this is the patronising attitude which infuriated Lamb when people spoke of his friend as 'poor Coleridge' and was another manoeuvre on Carlyle's part to make Coleridge look ineffective.

One can easily challenge the justice of these charges against Coleridge and Carlyle's qualifications as a critic are not enhanced by the naivety of remarks such as 'the hazy infinitude' of Kant's philosophy, but one has to realise that the whole of this chapter of his *Life of John Sterling* is a sustained piece of special pleading. One needs to appreciate the place Sterling occupied in the religious debates of the time to understand Carlyle's diatribe and to grasp his purpose in writing his biography of Sterling.

John Sterling was one of the most gifted men of his generation, whose ill-health and early death in 1844, at the age of thirty-eight, denied him any great achievement. His contemporaries all regarded him as a man of enormous promise and intellectual distinction; a judgement almost unanimous across a wide spectrum of opinion. The Sterling Club, a dining and debating club established in 1838 and named after him, included in its membership most of the talented men of the day and his friends included such diverse figures as Coleridge, J. S. Mill, F. D. Maurice, Carlyle, and J. C. Hare. Hare, who had been his tutor at Cambridge had a decisive influence upon him; he owned the most extensive library of German writings in Britain and introduced Sterling to German literature and philosophy and it was through Hare that Sterling became acquainted with Coleridge. While at Cambridge Sterling was invited to become a member of the 'Apostles', recently founded by Maurice, another pupil of Hare's and said by his tutor to possess 'metaphysical powers among the greatest he had ever come in contact with'.[17] Sterling and Maurice were very different personalities. Hare said that Maurice was 'so shy that it was almost impossible to know him', while of Sterling he wrote, 'his conversational powers were certainly among the most brilliant I have witnessed. In carrying on an argument I have known no one comparable to him'. In spite of these differences Sterling and Maurice became close friends. They jointly edited the *Athenaeum* and went on to marry sisters. (Later Hare also married Maurice's sister.)

When Sterling was at Cambridge some of the more influential members of the university had come under the spell of Wordsworth and even more of Coleridge and were conscious of a new current of thought sweeping through the university. 'At that time', wrote Hare, looking back to 1829 in his *Memoir of Sterling*, 'it was coming to be acknowledged that Coleridge is the true sovereign of modern English thought'. By then Sterling was in London contributing poems and articles to the *Athenaeum* in whose columns he paid handsome tribute to Coleridge, and already in 1827 while still at the university he had visited Coleridge at Highgate. Still later he became a constant visitor and a valued friend, especially during Coleridge's last years, and he was among the few at Coleridge's graveside. What Sterling owed to Coleridge, and it was a debt he always acknowledged, even later when he became more critical of his teacher, was a renewal of his religious faith brought about by Coleridge's vitalistic philosophy, his new approach to the Bible, and a theology inspired by Platonism and reinforced by German idealism. Sterling summed it up when he told Hare in 1836:

> To Coleridge I owe *education*. He taught me to believe that an empirical philosophy is none, that Faith is the Highest Reason, that all criticism, whether of literature, laws or manners, is blind, without the power of discerning the organic unity of the object.

It was the prospect Coleridge offered of a religion of greater tolerance, open to criticism, and concerned above all for the truth, which encouraged Sterling to be ordained into the ministry of the Church of England. Maurice himself was ordained in the same year and Hare who was now rector of Hurstmonceaux invited Sterling to become his curate. His ministry lasted for only eight months and ended in the year that saw the publication of Strauss's *Leben Jesu*, the translations of which heralded a period of bitter religious debates in England. It was perhaps disgust with the rancour between his fellow Anglicans which led finally to what Carlyle considered a repudiation of his faith, but Carlyle was wrong in asserting that a loss of faith brought about Sterling's departure from Hurstmonceaux. The evidence from letters, his own testimony and that of friends make it clear that the immediate cause of giving up his ministry was the threat of tuberculosis and his doctor's advice to withdraw. It is true that Sterling seemed to recover quickly, but the recovery was brief and his health remained precarious. Even the short time he spent in London on leaving Hurstmonceaux was devoted to philosophical and theological studies. By these he hoped to continue his ministry and help reform a church which he felt needed new bearings if it were not to be shipwrecked on the rocks of archaic dogmatism.

It was now that Sterling met Carlyle and came increasingly under his influence; a development regretted by Hare and Maurice, both of whom distrusted what they considered Carlyle's sophistry. Maurice was at this time chaplain of Guy's Hospital and could witness the growing intimacy between Carlyle and Sterling; indeed there was something of a rivalry between the two men for rescuing Sterling from what each thought was the other's pernicious influence. In a letter to Sterling on 11 September 1836, Carlyle treats Maurice with heavy sarcasm, 'I ought to esteem his way of thought at its full worth', he writes, 'and let it *live* in me if I could. Hitherto, I regret to confess, it is mainly moonshine and *Spitzfindigkeit*, and will not live. But the man is good and does live in me.'[18] The terms Carlyle uses are similar to those he was to use against Coleridge, but he is careful not to offend Sterling by attacking his friend too vehemently and so draws a distinction between Maurice's character and his beliefs. However, in writing to his brother John, on 1 February 1838, he does not bother to conceal his real feelings and dismisses Maurice: as 'One of the most entirely uninteresting men of genius that I can meet with in society is poor Maurice to me. All twisted, screwed, wire-drawn; . . . I do not remember that a word ever came from him betokening clear recognition of healthy free sympathy with anything'.[19]

This is manifestly unfair. There is a painting, to which the artist Ford Madox Brown gave the title *Work*, which depicts Carlyle and Maurice looking at a group of navvies working in Heath Street, Hampstead. Maurice as much as Carlyle had a sympathy for the poor and a concern for the effect of industrialization upon their lives; a concern with a more practical outcome than anything achieved by Carlyle, for it led Maurice to found the Working Men's College. In fact the two men had much in common and Maurice told Edward Strachey that 'he has been more edified by Carlyle's Lectures [On Hero Worship] than by anything he had heard for a long while, and that he has the greatest reverence for Carlyle, but that it is not reciprocal, for he is sure Carlyle thinks him a 'sham'[20] Maurice recognised in Carlyle's pronouncements some of the features of Coleridge's teaching. Inspired by Kant, Coleridge had taught that we should regard people as ends in themselves and not as means only, that religion had its origins in the moral consciousness, that a sense of duty should lead to action, and that society was not a machine but an organic whole. Some of this also informed Carlyle's pronouncements and Maurice sympathised with his attempt to awaken in the nation a sense of spiritual renewal and purpose; what he objected to was Carlyle's vague pantheism, his belief in personal sincerity as the only criterion of faith, and his prejudice against the church, especially the established church.

Sterling had appointed Hare and Carlyle as his literary executors and on his death in 1844 it was agreed between them that the preparation of his unpublished work together with a Memoir should be undertaken by Hare. Hare thereupon arranged the publication in 1848 of the two volumes of Sterling's *Essays and Tales* with an introductory Memoir running to 230 pages. It was clear to Hare at the outset that his task was likely to lead to controversy, not only with the traditionalist right wing of the church who regarded Sterling with suspicion and questioned his orthodoxy, but also with Carlyle who might challenge any attempt to claim Sterling as a Christian at all. And so it proved. Sterling's religious opinions would hardly cause comment in Christian circles today but his friends had been upset by his refusal to dismiss Strauss's *Leben Jesu* out of hand and by his sympathetic article on Carlyle in the *Westminster Review*. Schleiermacher with his emphasis on religious experience had become a major influence on his thinking and along with this went a desire to see the Scriptures demythologised and treated as poetry rather than history, but both of these now fall within a liberal orthodoxy. We catch an authentic glimpse of Sterling shortly before his death in an entry made by Barclay Fox in his Journal on Sunday 9 July 1843. The Foxes were a wealthy and cultivated Quaker family who lived in Falmouth where Sterling and his wife and children had settled in search of a mild climate:

> Sterling came to breakfast & then accompanied us to Meeting. He confessed afterwards to me that no service had given him as much satisfaction. He felt, however, somewhat tempted to address a few words to the Meeting on the danger of supposing that you possess the principle of Truth on account of an overweening attachment to some of its outward & accidental appendages. [21]

Whatever the reasons, Sterling's own family were not satisfied with Hare's portrait and his father, Captain Edward Sterling (whose editorial pronouncements in *The Times* gained him the nick-name of 'The Thunderer'), suggested that another version of his son's Life should be written. There was talk of John Stuart Mill undertaking this, but when he refused, Carlyle gladly took up the task with the intention of correcting what he thought was Hare's false account.

It becomes clear in reading Carlyle's *Life of Sterling* that its author saw his subject as a symbolic figure in the history of his times. In writing his Life he was doing more than giving his readers the portrait of an attractive and gifted person who had been robbed by an untimely death of the great achievements his talents promised. He saw Sterling as a representative figure. Though written in a more urbane and less ranting style than the *Latter Day Pamphlets* his *Life* remains, nevertheless, a piece of polemical writing, and more powerful for its avoidance of the mannerisms which often detract from any appeal Carlyle may have for the modern reader. Carlyle was fully aware of what he was doing, for his fundamental belief was that the lives of men reveal the hidden meaning of history. At the end of his book he sums up what he sees as the importance of Sterling,

> whose Life-pilgrimage accordingly is an emblem, unusually significant, of the world's own during those years of his. A man of infinite susceptivity; . . . whose history therefore is, beyond others, emblematic of that of his Time.

Carlyle's ostensible purpose in writing his *Life* may have been to rescue Sterling from the theologians and to show him as a poet and man of letters, but behind this was the wish to demolish Coleridge, the Coleridgeans such as Hare and Maurice, and their defence of the Church of England, and to present Sterling as one who had emancipated himself from this futile enterprise. Carlyle's contemptuous remarks on the Church of England in his *Life of Sterling* border on the hysterical. His attitude had always been derisory, but in this work his dislike breaks out in fierce sarcasm at Hare's description of Sterling's discharge of his clerical duties, and even more when he writes of Coleridge's attempt to revive 'this dead English church'. He speaks disparagingly of the 'Shovel-hatted Coleridgean *Schwamerei*' in which Coleridge was lost and of the delusion that he could 'by logical alchymy, distil astral spirits' from 'the burnt ruins' of the defunct churches. Carlyle's contempt for speculative thought led him to regard Coleridge's endeavour to construct a philosophy of religion as no more than 'logical swim-bladders, transcendental life-preservers' to stop him sinking into a sea of doubt.

Carlyle presses home the question of doubt and charges Coleridge with cowardice, with a failure to admit his own lack of conviction. Carlyle met Coleridge only once and this accusation must depend upon the testimony of others. It is true that Sterling is recorded by Caroline Fox, as saying on 28 January 1842, that 'Coleridge professed doctrines which he had ceased to believe in, in order to avoid the trouble of controversy', but this may have been because Coleridge hesitated to become a stumbling block to other people's beliefs rather than cowardice. That Coleridge never doubted the essential truth of Christianity can be confirmed by the Note he wrote on a blank sheet of the first volume of Southey's *Life of Wesley*, including a request that the book be returned to its author on Coleridge's death. His letters and notebooks in places criticise Wesley for his egoism and Methodism for the hysteria of its followers, but here he writes that Southey's biography has been 'more often in my hands than any other' and how it has succoured him in times of 'sickness and langour'. This private Note could hardly have been written by an unbeliever.

Nevertheless, Carlyle makes full use of this criticism of Coleridge and incidentally in doing so he shows his close reading of *Biographia Literaria*. In Chapter IX of *Biographia Literaria* Coleridge writes with gratitude of the mystical writers, especially Jacob Boehme and William Law, who at a time when he had been likely to fall into infidelity, 'contributed to keep alive the heart in the head'; 'they were', he writes, 'always a pillar of fire throughout the night, during my wanderings through the wilderness of doubt.' It was these mystics who enabled him 'to skirt without crossing, the sandy deserts of unbelief '.

Carlyle seizes upon this image of the desert to substantiate his accusation of spiritual cowardice. Coleridge, he writes, had admitted skirting 'the howling deserts of Infidelity' and continues, 'this was evident enough: but he had not had the courage, in defiance of pain and terror, to press resolutely across the said deserts to the new firm lands of Faith beyond; he preferred to create logical fatamorganas for himself on this hither side'. The 'fatamorganas' Coleridge solaced himself with were all the Church of England could provide: the 'strange Centaurs, spectral Puseyisms, monstrous illusory Hybrids, and ecclesiastical Chimeras'.

There is an implicit comparison here with Carlyle himself. He *had* crossed the desert of infidelity and found a new faith. But he is far from precise about this Everlasting Yea. Certainly his contemporaries found his new gospel compelling and his *Life of Sterling* made an impact that Hare's *Memoir* never approached. But for the details of his gospel we have to look at his other writings. Nearly all its main features derive from a secularised version of the Biblical story seen through his Puritan upbringing. He views history as a dynamic process, a great drama moving ever forward in hopeful expectation, with its great men standing like Old

Testament prophets pointing the way to the establishment of the kingdom of righteousness. In his more optimistic moods he expresses a belief that the kingdom is at hand. If our era is the 'Era of Unbelief', he asks in *Sartor Resartus* (Bk. II, ch. 3) 'why murmur under it; is there not a better coming?' Such optimistic versions of history became fashionable in the nineteenth century and were nourished by its ideas of evolution, progress, and improvement. They received their most developed form in Hegel's philosophy of history and in Marx's material version of this, both secularised variants of the Biblical story, and we know that Marx and Engels read Carlyle with approval.

Carlyle's message, like the Bible, was not concerned with metaphysics but with conduct and this, too, offered a welcome solution to many Victorians puzzled and weary with the problems of faith that pressed in on them. It was a relief to turn from speculation to action and to be exhorted in ringing tones, 'Up, up! Whatsoever thy hand find to do, do it with all thy might. Work while it is called Today; for the Night cometh wherein no man can work.'[22] This was a note sounded throughout the Victorian period. Even Newman, who might have been thought to have little in common with Carlyle, agreed that action was the test of true religion, since 'man is not a reasoning animal; he is a seeing, feeling, contemplating, acting animal'. 'Life', he assures us, 'is for action. If we insist on proof for everything, we shall never come to action; to act you must assume, and that assumption is faith.'[23] Newman was always mindful of the limits of speculation.

Conduct and sincerity of belief rather than subscription to dogma or doctrine were what counted for Carlyle. But he was more than an Old Testament prophet in secular guise, castigating a perverse and wayward generation; he provided his own version of New Testament salvation. For him contemporary society was sick; the fever of Romanticism had left it weak and needing healing. Sterling, was for him, a tragic example of the sickness that threatened society; he had succumbed to the debilitating influence of the times. The tuberculosis that killed him was only the immediate cause of his death. 'In this', he writes, 'as in other cases known to me, ill-health was not the primary cause but rather the ultimate one, the summing-up of innumerable far deeper conscious and unconscious causes.'[24] This sickness in society was why Carlyle enjoined his contemporaries to close their Byron and to open their Goethe, for Goethe was a physician of the soul who could bring spiritual health and well-being. Salvation for Carlyle, as one can see in *Sartor Resartus*, was a therapeutic experience.

All this proved an attractive message for Carlyle's contemporaries. It offered the challenges as well as the consolations of religion without any need for credal assent. Many who looked at the church of the day, beset by quarrels and rivalries, with rituals and liturgies that had lost their appeal, found reading Carlyle a liberating experience. His influence was pervasive in Victorian life and few leaders of thought remained unaffected by it. The churches themselves were aroused from their dogmatic sleep by his call to spiritual renewal. They were stung by remarks such as those when, at Sterling's request, he attended a church in Cheapside and wrote, 'bright lamps, gilt prayer-books, baize-lined pews, Wren-built architecture; and how, in almost all directions, you might have fired a musket through the church and hit no Christian life'.[25]

It would be wrong to exaggerate Carlyle's influence on the life of the church, for the church was not as moribund as he supposed. Moreover, his denunciation of *laissez-faire* doctrines and his support of radicalism were often a matter of rhetoric rather than the action he proclaimed. The practical measures of education for working men, the crusade for higher education for women and women's suffrage, and discussions with the Chartists were initiated by the Christian socialists whose leaders were Maurice, Kingsley, John Ludlow, and Thomas Hughes. Even so, one cannot doubt that Carlyle's influence in moulding the spirit of the age was immense. Nearly all the foremost thinkers and writers of the time counted themselves his friends. There were positivists such as J. S. Mill and George Eliot, Unitarians like Harriet Martineau, and Christians of all persuasions including Tennyson, Browning, Dickens; and even Thackeray, whose worldly cynicism met with Carlyle's disapproval, was a visitor at the Carlyles' house in Cheyne Row.

Although Arnold belonged to a slightly younger generation and differed from Carlyle in many things, describing him as 'part man of genius, part fanatic – and part tom-fool', he agreed with Carlyle in believing that they lived in a sick society. This sickness, they believed, came from an industrialised and *laissez-faire* economy which treated men as parts of a machine and not as ends in themselves. In 'The Scholar-Gipsy', probably written in 1852-3, Arnold contrasts the doubts and distractions of his own day with the freshness and innocence of earlier times,

Before this strange disease of modern life,
With its sick hurry, its divided aims,

Its heads o'ertaxed, its palsied hearts, was rife.

At about the time, in 1851, when most of his fellow countrymen were celebrating Britain's industrial and commercial achievements at the Great Exhibition in Hyde Park, Arnold was lamenting in 'Dover Beach' the impoverishment of life brought about by the loss of faith:

> The Sea of Faith
> Was once, too, at the full, and round earth's shore,
> Lay like the folds of a bright girdle furled.
> But now I only hear
> Its melancholoy, long withdrawing roar,
> Retreating, to the breath
> Of the night-wind, down the vast edges drear
> And naked shingles of the world.

While Arnold's diagnosis did not differ a great deal from Carlyle's, there were significant differences in the remedies they prescribed. One can see this already in the 'Memorial Verses' Arnold wrote on Wordsworth's death in 1850. As a young man Arnold was indebted to Carlyle for many of his beliefs; with Carlyle he looked to the great men of the past for inspiration and saw them as sources of spiritual strength in an age when religious belief had decayed. One of these for both of them had been Byron, and as an undergraduate at Oxford Arnold, along with many other young men, looked to Byron as a hero who had won for himself a European reputation for romantic passion and courage. 'Memorial Verses' looks back on those years when a whole generation had felt Byron's influence,

> like the thunder's roll.
> With shivering heart the strife we saw
> Of Passion with Eternal Law;
> And yet with reverential awe
> We watch'd the fount of fiery life
> Which serv'd for that Titanic strife.

Even now, while he confesses that Byron 'taught us little', he looks back and finds inspiration in a life which remains an example of fortitude. In 'Courage' composed in the same or the previous year, he writes:

> And, Byron! let us dare admire,
> If not thy fierce and turbid song,
> Yet that, in anguish, doubt, desire,
> Thy fiery courage still was strong.

Always Arnold looks for strength and security in a world adrift and without bearings:

> Our bane, disguise it as we may,
> Is weakness, is a faltering course.
> Oh that past times could give our day,
> Joined to its clearness, of their force!

Nevertheless, Arnold was not slow in taking Carlyle's advice to close his Byron and open his Goethe. In 'Stanzas from the Grande Chartreuse', probably composed in 1852 or 1853, he writes disparagingly of Byron's parading through Europe 'The pageant of his bleeding heart', and in a letter to his friend Clough, written as early as 29 September 1848, on a journey which takes him across the Alps, he describes the locality round Lake Geneva as 'spoiled by the omnipresence there of that furiously flaring bethiefed rushlight, the vulgar Byron'.[26] Towards the end of his life when he published a selection of Byron's poems, he made clear what he thought had been the fatal defect in Byron and quotes Goethe to support his criticism. Goethe, like Arnold, had been a warm admirer of Byron's poetry and indeed regarded him as the greatest English poet of his day, but Goethe, Arnold writes 'lays his finger on [Byron's] . . . real source of weakness both as a man and as a poet. "The moment he reflects, he is a child" '.[27]

Arnold tells us that he came to Goethe, 'the greatest voice of the century', through Carlyle, 'the voice of Goethe'[28], but his knowledge of the German writer became more extensive than Carlyle's and Goethe remained with him, even as a diminishing influence, throughout his life. In the Preface to the 1853 edition of his own Poems he refers to him as 'the greatest poet of modern times, the greatest critic of all times'. He sums up the effect Goethe had on him in 'Memorial Verses' where he writes of Goethe as the physician who diagnoses the ills of modern society:

> He took the suffering human race,
> He read each wound, each weakness clear –
> And struck his finger on the place
> And said – *Thou ailest here, and here.* –
> He look'd on Europe's dying hour
> Of fitful dream and feverish power;
> His eye plung'd down the weltering strife,
> The turmoil of expiring life;
> He said—The *end is everywhere;*
> *Art still has truth, take refuge there.*

Even if modern civilisation is in terminal decline, however, the individual can still save himself, for Goethe had found peace in what Arnold calls this 'Iron Age':

> And he was happy, if to know

Causes of things, and far below
His feet to see the lurid flow
Of terror, and insane distress,
And headlong fate, be happiness.

For Arnold as a young man this note of Stoic resignation came as a welcome relief from the self-indulgent poetry popularised by Byron. It appealed to his temperament and to a mind educated in the classical tradition of Rugby and Balliol, and pointed the way in which he might develop his own poetic style. Coupled with the suggestion that art allows an escape from subjection to the passions in aesthetic contemplation, it proved irresistible.

Goethe derived his view of art from Kant and passed it on to his friend Schopenhauer, who developed it into a philosophy which has attracted writers as diverse as Tolstoy, Conrad, and Proust. But it was Schelling, whose philosophy had been brought into England by Coleridge, who took this view of art to an extreme by maintaining that the highest kind of thinking expresses itself in this form. It is significant that in the list of books Arnold had read we find not only Carlyle and Goethe, but Kant and Schelling.[29] These for him were the thinkers whose work had been 'really subversive of the foundations on which the old European order rested' and, he continues in his essay on Heinrich Heine, none are 'so thoroughly modern, as those who have felt Goethe's influence most deeply'.[30]

This explains why Arnold, with regret for the past and still venerating the writers of classical antiquity, was eager to see society move forward into a modern age. How he thought this could come about and its implications for religion can best be approached through his writings about Wordsworth. *Memorial Verses* moves from Goethe to praise of Wordsworth, but his admiration for the one does not imply a rejection of the other. Wordsworth himself disliked what he knew of Goethe and although this may not have been a great deal, there was in fact an important difference between the impact each of them made on Arnold. In 'Courage', the opening stanza, written under the influence of Goethe, tells us that we 'Must learn to wait, renounce, withdraw'. When he wrote this Arnold was already beginning to realise that he had repressed a good deal of his own nature in a spirit of Stoic renunciation. Writing to Clough on 12 February 1853, he laments the lack of feeling that has become habitual with him and declares, 'I am past thirty and three parts iced over'.[31]

Where Goethe encouraged self-control, Wordsworth promised

liberation. Wordsworth himself had come close to a breakdown by repressing his feelings while under the influence of Godwin and had been delivered by Coleridge, his sister Dorothy, and the healing power of nature. Now he was to provide the same service for Arnold. Nor was Arnold alone in paying tribute to Wordsworth for this kind of liberation. John Stuart Mill's *Autobiography* was to recount a similar experience. Mill, too, was to turn at first to Byron, the poet of the passions *par excellence*, but found no relief from his depression in 'the vehement sensual passion of his Giaours, or the sullenness of his Laras'. It was Wordsworth's poetry, writes Mill, which brought him 'the very culture of the feelings, which I was in quest of'.

Where Byron offered passionate excitement and Goethe renunciation, Wordsworth provided for Arnold a healthy outlet for feelings that needed expression and cultivation. He writes of how Wordsworth released pent-up emotion and provided a rebirth of the personality by taking it back to childhood. The language he uses echoes the Scriptural injunction that we must become as little children and this is part of the authentic Wordsworthian experience of spiritual renewal and growth:

> He found us when the age had bound
> Our souls in its benumbing round;
> He spoke, and loos'd our heart in tears.
> He laid us as we lay at birth
> On the cool flowery lap of earth;
> Smiles broke from us and we had ease.
> The hills were round us, and the breeze
> Went o'er the sun-lit fields again.
> Our foreheads felt the wind and rain.
> Our youth return'd: for there was shed
> On spirits that had long been dead,
> Spirits dried up and closely-furl'd,
> The freshness of the early world.

The Arnold family spent a good deal of each year at their holiday home, Fox How, where they were friends and neighbours of the Wordsworths at nearby Grasmere, and through this friendship Wordsworth took a personal interest in the young Arnold and his poetry. This led to a sense of indebtedness and an admiration for Wordsworth which remained throughout Arnold's life. His mature opinion of Wordsworth's work is best seen in the Preface he wrote for his selection of Wordsworth's poems published in 1879, nearly thirty years after *Memorial Verses*. This is where Arnold warns us that 'we must be on our guard against the Wordsworthians' who 'lay far too much stress upon what they call his philosophy'. One Wordsworthian he had in mind was Leslie Stephen, who claimed for Wordsworth 'an ethical system . . . as distinctive and capable of exposition as Bishop Butler's'. Arnold dismisses this and argues that 'His [Wordsworth's] poetry is the reality, his philosophy, – so far, at least, as it may put on the form and habit of 'a scientific system of thought', and the more that it puts them on, – is illusion'. Arnold admits that there are passages in Wordsworth's poetry which read like philosophy and cites *The Excursion*, a poem which pleases those admirers of Wordsworth who find in it 'doctrine such as we hear in church, religious and philosophic doctrine'. But this he thinks is to admire Wordsworth for the wrong reason. 'Perhaps', he argues, 'we shall one day learn to make this proposition general and to say: Poetry is the reality, philosophy the illusion. But in Wordsworth's case, at any rate, we cannot do him justice until we dismiss his formal philosophy.'[32]

These remarks have led to endless confusion. The logical positivists of the first half of this century, who divided all language into referential or emotive language, welcomed Arnold as a critic because, they believed, he regarded poetry, along with religion and ethics, as no more than the expression of emotion. I. A. Richards, although he later modified his views, was one of these at a time when his influence was greatest. In *Science and Poetry* Richards made the familiar distinction between 'scientific statement, where truth is ultimately a matter of verification . . . and emotive utterance' and argued that 'it is not the poet's business to make true statements'. Poetry, he maintained in his *Principles of Literary Criticism* is, strictly speaking, meaningless, but nevertheless by harmonising our passions it can produce mental calmness and health. Richards thought modern society on the brink of disintegration because of the collapse of traditional beliefs and values. 'If this should happen', he wrote, 'a mental chaos such as man has never experienced may be expected. We shall then be thrown back as Matthew Arnold foresaw, upon poetry. It is capable of saving us; it is a perfectly possible means of overcoming chaos.'[33] This interpretation of Arnold's critical ideas, especially when associated with his religious views, has had an enormous influence, but it is doubtful whether it does justice to either.

Given his strictures on Byron's inability to think, one can hardly suppose Arnold considered Wordsworth deficient as a thinker. His criticism of *The Excursion* is a criticism of explicitly didactic poetry and is in tune with his dislike of the eighteenth century as 'an age of prose' and his dismissal of its poets, with the exception of Gray, as too preoccupied with argument. But this does not mean that Arnold took what one can call the 'low' view of poetry advanced by Richards, that is, one which gives it a merely therapeutic role with no concern for the truth. In a phrase reminiscent of Coleridge, Arnold looked back on the Athens of the fifth century BC as one characterised by the 'imaginative reason'. It was a period, he writes, 'in which poetry made, it seems to me, the noblest, most successful effort she has ever made as the priestess of the imaginative reason, of the element by which the modern spirit, if it would live right, has chiefly to live'.[34] Indeed, one can argue that Arnold took a 'high' view of poetry that led naturally to an association with religion as it had done in ancient Greece.

An understanding of what he had in mind can be found in another controversial statement of Arnold's which has led to endless argument. This is the claim he makes in *The Study of Poetry* that poetry is 'a criticism of life'. By criticism in this context Arnold means holding up an ideal by which we can judge life as we know it. This goes back to the Renaissance and Sidney's *Apologie for Poetrie* where a contrast is drawn between the world of nature, that is, the world we know, and the world created by poetry which contains 'forms such as never were in nature'. The world of 'nature is brazen', Sidney tells us, 'the poets only deliver a golden'. This golden world of poetry provides a vision of life as it might be and in doing so acts as a guide for our conduct. It is this high view of poetry which leads Arnold to declare that 'The best poetry is what we want; the best poetry will be found to have a power of forming, sustaining, and delighting us, as nothing else can. '[35]

For Arnold the truth of poetry is not the truth of propositions. The poet is a maker; he tells a story, creates a dramatic representation of life, or composes a lyric. In all he does, however, he makes something and although not propositional this does not lack meaning. Indeed, it has a richness of meaning denied to other forms of discourse. Arnold had learnt from the German idealist philosophers and especially, perhaps, Kant's *Critique of Judgment*, that the meaning of a work of art is not exhausted by conceptual analysis.

For Arnold the analogy with religion was manifest. Indeed, poetry and religion were so close that they might almost, but not quite, be seen as the same. At the beginning of 'The Study of Poetry' there is a long passage which needs to be quoted in full. 'The future of poetry', writes Arnold,

> is immense, because in poetry, where it is worthy of its high destinies, our race, as time goes on, will find an ever surer and surer stay. There is not a creed which is not shaken, not an accredited dogma which is not shown to be questionable, not a received tradition which does not threaten to dissolve. Our religion has materialised itself in the fact, in the supposed fact; it has attached its emotion to the fact, and now the fact is failing it. But for poetry the idea is everything; the rest is a world of illusion. Poetry attaches its emotion to the idea; the idea is the fact. The strongest part of our religion to-day is its unconscious poetry.

Arnold is not saying that all poetry is religion but that religious affirmations are best expressed in poetry, that is, in imaginative writing rather than logic. One of the pillars of Christian belief had been the Bible but Arnold lived at a time when the new German criticism had questioned the historicity of the Scriptural story and a good deal of what had been accepted as fact had not survived the scrutiny of modern scholarship. 'The Study of Poetry' was written at the end of his life when Darwin had put a final nail in the coffin of the literal interpretation of the Genesis story. As for the New Testament writers, they were all relating events separated from modern man by Lessing's 'wide and ugly ditch'; a point emphasised by the *Lives of Jesus* by Renan and Strauss.

For Arnold religious dogmas were all attempts to express religious convictions based upon experience and this was best expressed in literary forms. Already in *Culture and Anarchy*, but even more in *St Paul and Protestantism*, he inveighs against those, especially the Calvinists, who had turned the imagery of St Paul into technical and legalistic formulae and by doing so had betrayed Paul's central message that we should live by the spirit and not the letter of the law. Such misunderstanding, says Arnold, could have come 'from no-one but the born Anglo-Saxon man of business'.[36]

In the Preface to the 1884 edition of *God and the Bible* Arnold offended both extremes in the religious debates of the time, the atheists who wished to see an end of Christianity, and the orthodox churchmen, when he wrote:

> At the present moment two things about the Christian religion must surely be clear to anybody with eyes in his head. One is, that men cannot do without it; the other, that they cannot do with it as it is.[37]

Arnold regarded himself as a defender of the faith who wanted to find a sure foundation on which Christian belief could rest and resist the attacks being made upon it. But where could this be found? His liberal approach to the Bible was matched by an equally liberal opinion of church authority. In this he followed his father, Dr Thomas Arnold, the famous headmaster of Rugby, who once said that he rejoiced on coming down to breakfast every morning to find that every question was an open question. This open-mindedness was responsible, perhaps, for Newman's question about Dr Arnold, 'but is *he* a Christian?'.

But it was more than this that separated Newman and Dr Arnold. The Oxford Movement started from a fear of Erastianism and was inaugurated by Keble's famous Assize Sermon of 1833 with its warning of 'National Apostasy'. Keble and Dr Arnold had been friends and undergraduates together at Oxford, but later each saw the other, as reported in Dean Stanley's *Life of Arnold*, as 'in error pernicious to the faith and dangerous to himself'. G. M. Young in his *Victorian England: Portrait of an Age* observes that Dr Arnold saw in religion a training ground for rulers, 'and the rulers needed a new faith which was to be found . . . in the Bible . . . interpreted not by tradition, but by science, scholarship, and, above all, political insight.' Dr Arnold made no sharp distinction between the spiritual and the secular, and envisaged a national church consisting not only of Anglicans but all Protestant Christians. With these views one can understand the mutual antipathy between Dr Arnold and Newman. Arnold had no patience with the claim to apostolic succession and the importance given to the clergy by the Tractarians. They for their part saw Arnold as a secularist and an Erastian, with little appreciation of the supernatural in religion.

Matthew Arnold had a great respect for his father and shared and developed many of his religious opinions, especially those concerning the church, but he differed from him in his respect for Newman. As an undergraduate at Balliol he had attended St Mary's to hear Newman deliver his Sunday afternoon sermons and in a famous passage written many years later, he described the effect this had on him. 'Who could resist the charm', he writes, 'of that spiritual apparition, gliding in the dim afternoon light through the aisles of St. Mary's, rising into the pulpit, and then, in the most entrancing of voices, breaking the silence with words and thoughts which were a religious music, – subtle, sweet, mournful. I seem to hear him still.'[38]

Many have treated this as recounting simply an aesthetic experience, but it was clearly more than that, and one critic was nearer the truth when he wrote of Arnold's appreciation of 'the beauty of holiness' in Newman's appearance and personality. The experience must have had a profound effect for him to recall it so vividly many years later and there is reason to believe that Arnold was attracted to Newman for more than the music of his voice or the sanctity of his life, great as this last was. There is evidence that Arnold went to hear Newman give a series of sermons in London in 1848, and again, many years later he wrote to Newman, 'I cannot forbear adding, what I have often wished to tell you, that no words can be too strong to express the interest with which I used to hear you at Oxford, and the pleasure with which I continue to read your writings now.' Then rather surprisingly, he adds, 'There are four people, in especial, from whom I am conscious of having learnt – a very different thing from merely receiving a strong impression – learnt habits, methods, ruling ideas, which are constantly with me; and the four are – Goethe, Wordsworth, Sainte-Beuve, and yourself.'[39]

What did Arnold learn from Newman and what especially were these 'ruling ideas'? They did not include Newman's theology and in particular did not embrace his doctrine of the church, for in his lecture on Emerson he writes, 'Cardinal Newman . . . has adopted, for the doubts which beset men's minds today, a solution which, to speak frankly is impossible'. The *Stanzas from the Grande Chartreuse*, written between 1851 and 1855, show Arnold's rejection of the contemplative life of the religious orders and by implication the Roman Catholic church, although his *Pagan and Mediaeval Religious Sentiment* displays a warm admiration for St. Francis of Assisi. It is doubtful, however, whether Newman was among those he addressed at the Grande Chartreuse:

> For rigorous teachers seized my youth,
> And purged its faith, and trimmed its fire,
> Showed me the high, white star of Truth,
> There bade me gaze, and there aspire.
> Even now their whispers pierce the gloom
> *What dost thou in this living tomb?*

He describes himself in the poem as

> Wandering between two worlds, one dead,
> The other powerless to be born.

Newman's church belonged to the first of these; nevertheless Arnold came to realise that there was common ground between them and that from Newman he had discovered the way to a new faith.

One common ground was the primacy of moral experience and the final authority of the conscience. Newman was adamant that even the church could not ask a man to act against his conscience, 'that solemn Monitor, personal, peremptory, unargumentative, irreparable, minatory, definitive', which acts independently of dogma or the Scriptures. This moral consciousness, common to all men, makes itself known as a command, an imperative which cannot be disobeyed without a sense of ignoring an obligation or breaking a law. This is all a matter of natural religion, but for both men Christian faith was built on this foundation. Faith, for both, was not only a matter of the intellect, for it makes claims on the whole person, on the reason, the emotions, and the will. Newman might have been speaking for both of them when he wrote that in 'this special feeling, which follows on the commission of what we call right and wrong, lie the materials for the real apprehension of a Divine Sovereign and Judge'.[40]

When he came to read Coleridge, Newman was surprised at the extent to which Coleridge had anticipated him in developing the relation between faith and reason.[41] Faith, for Coleridge, starts not with the intellect, but with a recognition of our own need for forgiveness in failing to meet the demands of a moral imperative. This need is met in the Bible with the promise of forgiveness and grace. Newman, too, argued that the moral law gives us a sense of responsibility for our actions and this is because it comes from a personal God. 'If', he writes in *The Grammar of Assent*, 'we feel responsibility, are ashamed, are frightened, at transgressing the voice of conscience, this implies that there is One to whom we are responsible, before whom we are ashamed, whose claim upon us we fear.'[42] This faith is a living one which is vindicated as it is lived out. Coleridge developed this approach to religion in his later works, but he had summed it up already in the final chapter of *Biographia Literaria* where he writes, 'we can only *know by the act of becoming. Do the will of my Father, and ye shall KNOW I am God!*' In making this the foundation of belief he was stating something with which Newman would have been in full agreement.

Arnold, too, would have approved since for him religion starts in morality or, as he preferred to call it, righteousness. *In Literature and Dogma* he differentiates between certainty and conjecture: 'And a certainty', he declares, 'is the sense of *life*, of being truly *alive*, which accompanies righteousness.' A living faith is an 'experimental process' which leads one to a greater understanding of the religious life and if this 'does not rise to be stronger in us, does not rise to the sense of being inextinguishable, that is probably because our experience of righteousness is really so very small; and here we may well permit ourselves to trust Jesus, whose practice and intuition both of them went, in these matters, so far deeper than ours.'[43]

On the foundation of the moral law Newman argued for the existence of a divine law-giver who manifested himself in Jesus and in an infallible church. Instead of building such a superstructure, Arnold engaged in a process of stripping down religion to what he considered its essentials, a process many thought he carried too far. He saw righteousness manifested in Jesus, but in *Literature and Dogma*, his critics alleged, what he calls 'the *epieikeia*, the sweet reasonableness of Jesus', turns the Jesus of the Gospels into an English gentleman, educated at Rugby and Balliol. But for Arnold this quality is at the heart of Christianity, and the Bible is important since 'only through the Bible-records of Jesus can we get at his *epieikeia*'. Arnold recognises the limitations of this: 'Even in these records, it is and can be presented but imperfectly; but only by reading and re-reading the Bible can we get at it at all.' This reading for Arnold involves a radical demythologising of the New Testament and an emphasis on its literary aspects together with a neglect of the historical and theological ones, since, he writes, 'Terms which with St. Paul are *literary* terms, theologians have employed as if they were scientific terms.' His interpretation of the Gospel text offended many believers when they read passages such as the following:

> Jesus had said: 'If a man keep my word, he shall never see death'; and by a kind of short cut to the conclusion thus laid down, Christians constructed their fairy-tale of the second advent, the resurrection of the body, the New Jerusalem.[44]

He answers these objectors by maintaining that 'the fantasy hides the grandeur of the reality' and this reality is the *epieikeia* of Jesus which we can achieve for ourselves by adopting it as a way of life.

This 'sweet reasonableness' which leads to 'the necessity of righteousness', is for Arnold the kernel of the Christian religion. The miracles in the Bible, even if authentic, are neither sufficient nor necessary for faith. In *God and the Bible* Arnold explains for those who were upset by this treatment of the miraculous, that 'It was not to discredit miracles that *Literature and Dogma* was written, but because miracles are so widely and deeply discredited already.'[45] This dismissal of the miraculous left his critics feeling that he had reduced religion to morality alone. Arnold, indeed, claimed that conduct was three parts of life, but he never reduced religion to morality since religion, he declared, was morality 'touched by emotion'. This phrase and his other notorious remark that God is 'a tendency not ourselves that makes for righteousness', received rough treatment from the philosopher F. H. Bradley. In his *Ethical Studies* Bradley countered the first by observing that all morality is touched by emotion of one kind or another, and he dismissed the second with the crushing remark that one might equally well say that 'washing is a tendency not ourselves that makes for cleanliness'. T. S. Eliot also had a poor opinion of Arnold's capacity for logical thought and in *The Use of Poetry and the Use of Criticism* declared that in philosophy and theology Arnold was an undergraduate and that 'The effect of Arnold's religious campaign is to divorce religion from thought'.

There is some truth in these charges, of course, but they miss the point Arnold is making, which is that religion carries with it a feeling of awe associated with the moral law and, more than this, it also supports the individual and leads him forward in the ways of righteousness. The church plays a part in this and in his *Last Essays on Church and Religion* he presents a conception of the church as 'a great national society for the promotion of goodness', an instrument for uniting all classes in a fellowship dedicated to righteousness. This would not have satisfied Newman and fell short of what many others thought the real nature of the church, which for them was a supernatural agency. Many have seen Arnold as simply a member of the Broad Church movement but his radicalism in religion goes far beyond this and places him in this century. His demythologising of the Bible, his emphasis on morality as the ground of belief, and his non-sacerdotal view of the church are all common elements in the religious thinking of today. Although he made less of an impact than Carlyle on his own contemporaries his influence has been longer-lasting and more pervasive. Most influential has been what many people see as his identification of religion with poetry; an identification Arnold never made although he believed that religious language is closer to poetry than to scientific, theological, or logical language. Religious experience for him was primary and the attempt to express this in any but imaginative language a mistake and one the Scriptures did not commit, even if modern readers of the Bible failed to recognise this; a point well put by one of our own contemporaries, the distinguished theologian, Hans Kung, when he writes,

'Proclamation, preaching, catechesis are somewhat different from science, whether of theology or history . . . their goal and therefore also their language are different'.[46] Arnold never wished to make poetry a surrogate religion, but like St Augustine and the Church Fathers, and Milton, he believed that the great myths of classical antiquity express truths common to all men and able to inspire the Christian as well as the pagan imagination. For this reason it may be wrong to describe him as a demythologiser. He saw great poetry as a glass in which men could discern an image of eternal truth, at once a source of wisdom and virtue. The Bible for him was the supreme example of this and because of Jesus also one that was unique.

III

George Eliot and Dickens

George Eliot's *Adam Bede* opens in 1799, a year after the publication of *Lyrical Ballads*, and in Chapter V Arthur Donnithorne tells the rector's wife that he has received a parcel of books, including a volume of recently published poems. 'I know you are fond of queer, wizard-like stories.', he says,

> It's a volume of poems, 'Lyrical Ballads': most of them seem to be twaddling stuff; but the first is in a different style – 'The Ancient Mariner' is the title. I can hardly make head or tail of it as a story, but it's a strange, striking thing.

Arthur Donnithorne's literary taste is certainly not George Eliot's, but several critics have seen in *Adam Bede* parallels with the 'Ancient Mariner'.[1] In Chapter XLV when Hetty is in prison she says her baby had been 'like a heavy weight hanging round her neck' and in Chapter XLII George Eliot herself writes, 'Deep, unspeakable suffering may well be called a baptism, a regeneration, the initiation into a new state'; a conviction central to the 'Ancient Mariner'. Certainly she was writing with her tongue in her cheek when Arthur Donnithorne describes Wordsworth's poems as 'twaddling stuff', for we know that her admiration for Wordsworth lasted throughout her life. *Adam Bede* itself in its story and its characters is a very Wordsworthian novel. Not only do incidents such as Hetty's burial of her dead baby recall 'The Thorn', but the emphasis upon the feelings rather than doctrine as the inspiration of true religion is in tune with Wordsworth's poems in *Lyrical Ballads*. Looking back in old age Adam Bede reflects on the difference between the old rector, Mr Irwine, and his more recent successor, who is a doctrinal zealot:

> I've seen pretty clear, ever since I was a young'un, as religion's something else besides notions. It isn't notions sets people doing the right thing – it's feelings. . . . I look at it as if the doctrines was like finding names for your feelings, so as you can talk of 'em when you've never known 'em, just as a man may talk of tools when he knows their names, though he's never so much as seen 'em, still less handled 'em. (Ch. XVII)

George Eliot herself drew the parallel with Wordsworth when writing not about *Adam Bede*, but *Silas Marner*. In a letter to her publisher, John Blackwood, on 24 February 1861, she remarks that she is surprised to find anyone interested in her story 'since William Wordsworth is now dead', and suggests that it 'would have lent itself best to metrical rather than prose fiction'.[2] Basil Willey is right when he observes in the chapter on George Eliot in his *Nineteenth Century Studies*, that 'she abundantly shows the power attributed to Wordsworth by Coleridge, that of spreading the depth, height and atmosphere of the ideal world around situations, forms and incidents "of which, for the common view, custom had bedimmed all the lustre, had dried up the sparkle and the dew-drops".' One can also see in some of her novels Coleridge's own interest in *Lyrical Ballads*, an endeavour 'directed to persons and characters supernatural', for as well as the plain style of her earlier novels she developed an increasing use of mythology to give her narratives added depth.

Leslie Stephen suggested, in an obituary notice he wrote for *The Cornhill Magazine* for February 1881, that a decline in George Eliot's reputation came about because the reflective element in her later work robbed it of the charm of her earlier novels. This may be true and, if so, it is because her early fiction portrays the world of her childhood and youth and not that of her mature years. 'Amos Barton' is a story taken from what her biographer, Gordon Haight, rightly describes as 'those earnest Evangelical years of her adolescence'. *Adam Bede* is set in 1799 and depicts a society already passing away when she was a child. *The Mill on the Floss* is rooted in the provincial life she knew well as a girl and *Silas Marner* she considered, as we have seen, a story that belonged to the time of Wordsworth. In all these earlier novels she was looking back at the lost innocence of her childhood before the great changes in her beliefs which were brought about by the intellectual and social forces sweeping across Europe.

Already, before she started her career as a novelist, she had ceased to be a Christian, a decision encouraged by the Brays, who lived near her home in Coventry and were her close friends for many years. Charles Bray had been an ardent Evangelical Christian but he abandoned his religious beliefs to become a rationalist and necessitarian. His brother-in-law, Charles Hennell, published in 1838 *An Inquiry into the Origins of Christianity*, which brought to the New Testament the kind of critical scrutiny which had generally been reserved for secular texts. He argued that parts of the Gospel story could not be accepted as historically true, not because the Evangelists attempted to deceive their readers, but simply that they wrote many years after the events they described and used the mythological and supernatural devices common in Eastern religions. In the Preface to his *Inquiry* Hennell wrote, 'Christianity, thus regarded as a system of elevated thought and feeling, will not be injured by being freed from those fables, and those views of local or temporary interest which hung about its origin.' His demythologising led him to conclude that while it was not a revealed religion and Jesus only a great teacher and religious leader, Christianity nevertheless remained the highest of all religions.

Charles Hennell's *Inquiry*, with its honest, searching, and yet reverent approach to Christianity, probably had a greater influence on her than Charles Bray's *The Philosophy of Necessity* which appeared in 1841. Charles Bray thought the new and fashionable study of phrenology would provide what Hartley had sought, a system which would solve the body-mind problem; this for him entailed a necessitarian account of human behaviour and he gave his book the sub-title *The Law of Consequences as Applicable to Mental, Moral and Social Science.* Although George Eliot may have owed more to Hennell than Bray she seems to have taken phrenology seriously. A year after Bray's book was published she had a cast of her head made by a phrenologist and in a letter to the Brays in May 1852 she describes Dickens's appearance as 'disappointing – no benevolence in the face and I think little in the head – the anterior lobe not by any means remarkable'.[3] She may not have adopted such a radical theory of necessity as Bray, but she was convinced that every individual acted out of an inner predisposition of character and she believed firmly in the inexorability of the moral law. In Chapter XVI of *Adam Bede*, Mr Irwine speaks to Arthur Donnithorne in terms the author would have endorsed when he says, 'Consequences are unpitying. Our deeds carry their terrible consequences, quite apart from any fluctuations [i.e. of motives and moral struggle] that went before – consequences that are hardly ever confined to ourselves.' This theme recurs throughout her novels and in the later ones is brought to bear on society as well as the individual.

The free-thinking circle of the Brays and their friends led her to turn her back on her old Evangelical mentors such as Wilberforce and Hannah More, but she abandoned her old beliefs with regret. Her scepticism was never destructive and when she ceased to be a Christian she still valued the personality and teaching of Jesus and some of his followers and respected other religions, especially Judaism. In his *Westminster Review* essay on Coleridge, J. S. Mill observed that of any statement Bentham would ask, 'Is it true?', whereas Coleridge would ask 'What is the meaning of it?'.[4] She was with Coleridge in this and her respect for Christianity had little to do with its claim to be historically true but rested on the inner meaning of the Gospel story, and the same could be said of her approach to Judaism and the myths of classical antiquity.

She brought this generous but sceptical spirit to her translation of Strauss's *Leben Jesu*, undertaken at the suggestion of Charles Hennell, but the scepticism certainly deepened as she worked at her task. Strauss wrote his book in the belief that he was defending the Gospel against those who would destroy it; on one side the rationalists who dismissed it as unacceptable to the reason, on the other, those who by rejecting any suggestion that modern scholarship could throw light on the New Testament put it beyond the consideration of intelligent readers. Strauss tried to steer a course between these extremes of rationalism and dogmatism, but as George Eliot came to realise, it was not easy to keep to this middle way. Her translation took her two years and she found the work demanding, both intellectually and spiritually. Nothing illustrates more graphically her state of mind than the well-known account of how she worked with a small cast of Thorwaldsen's *Risen Christ* in front of her and an engraving of Christ on the wall.

Her translation was published in three volumes in 1846 and marked a new development in English religious thought; for some its effect was as disturbing as the appearance of Darwin's *Origin of Species* in 1859. Strauss's book gave what he considered a strictly historical account of the life of Jesus without any dogmatic assumptions about the supernatural events of the Gospels. What gave it novelty was his refusal to dismiss this supernatural element as a deliberate imposture or as the crude and magical beliefs of a primitive people. His central conviction was that the Gospels were not a factual record, but 'ideas, often most poetical and beautiful ideas . . . such as were natural to the time and at the author's level of culture'. Strauss, as a disciple of Hegel, discounted the supernatural as beyond the scope of historical enquiry and treated the miraculous as myth, often embodying the highest thoughts and aspirations of mankind. He saw Jesus as a Jewish religious leader and thinker who for his followers embodied and expressed the myth of Messianism.

Strauss later discarded his Christian faith but when he wrote his *Leben Jesu* he thought he was presenting Jesus in the light of recent developments in German philosophy. Jesus could be seen as the representative human incarnation of what in Hegel's philosophy had been pure spirit. Jesus the son of Man was a new Adam, who like the first Adam, stood for the whole of humanity. 'Is not an incarnation of God from eternity', he asked, 'a truer one than incarnation limited to a particular point in time?' The whole of human history could now be regarded as a progressive revelation of God. But this attempt to accommodate the Incarnation to Hegel's philosophy left the unique status of Jesus in doubt; the emphasis upon the divine in the God-man formula now gave way to an insistence upon the humanity of Jesus.

The notion that a good deal of the Bible was mythical and no different in kind, even if generally superior in its moral awareness, from classical myth and other non-Biblical religions, was given support by Robert Mackay's *The Progress of the Intellect, as Exemplified in the Religious Development of the Greeks and Hebrews*, (1850). His publisher, John Chapman, brought Mackay to Rosehill, the Brays' home in Coventry, and it shows the reputation she now enjoyed that he asked George Eliot to review Mackay's book in the *Westminster Review*. Her long review reveals clearly her realisation that Mackay's work along with Strauss's had implications that went far beyond the recognition of the mythical element in the Biblical narrative. By this time George Eliot had already read Carlyle's *Sartor Resartus* with its emphasis upon history as the unfolding drama of mankind's religious progress and she realised that the same historical perspective informed Strauss's and Mackay's approach to Christianity. They agreed with Carlyle that the symbols appropriate to the expression of faith in earlier ages were no longer suitable for modern man since faith itself was always developing. The study of history, she wrote in her review, will enable us to grasp this:

> if by a survey of the past it can be shown how each age and each race has had a faith and a symbolism suited to its needs and its stage of development . . . to dream of retaining the spirit along with the forms of the past, is as futile as the embalming of the dead body in the hope that it may one day be resumed by the living soul.[5]

It followed from this that the central place in history traditionally assigned to the Incarnation was no longer secure and this began to press in on orthodox Christianity from several quarters. One of the most influential of these was Feuerbach whose *Das Wesen des Christenthums* was translated by George Eliot with the title *The Essence of Christianity*.

Feuerbach, like Strauss, was a disciple of Hegel, but like Marx he turned Hegel upside down and changed the dialectical movement of history which Hegel had seen as a mental or spiritual process into a material one. But whereas Marx saw religion as something which would disappear with the coming of the communist state, Feuerbach regarded it as a necessary feature of man's self-consciousness. For him religion was a fact of human nature, but he believed that the object of man's religious interest would move from a God who was only imaginary to man himself. God was a projection at best of man's own highest aspirations; at worst, a neurotic symptom (a point Freud was to develop later). 'The question as to the existence or non-existence of God', he wrote, adopting the tones of the Hegelian dialectic, 'the opposition between theism and atheism, belongs to the sixteenth and seventeenth centuries, but not to the nineteenth. I deny God. But that means for me that I deny the negation of man.' So, in turning Hegel upside down he also turned Christianity upside down. Christianity brought down God into man; he believed that man could be raised up to being God. 'Thus do things change. What yesterday was still religion, is no longer such today; and what today is atheism, tomorrow will be religion.' The supernatural element in Christianity was no longer a problem; it was merely a picture-book language in which man expresses his own dreams. This religion of humanity for Feuerbach promised a freedom from the guilt-ridden oppression of conventional religion, a spirit of liberation which would lead men to achieve their full potential.

One can hear in Feuerbach's work the romantic note sounded by English revolutionary writers such as Godwin and Shelley and nowhere is it clearer than in Feuerbach's reversal of the doctrine that God is love into the dogma that love is God. This not only opened up Utopian vistas of a new society, but promised a new freedom in personal relationships; not libertinism but a love which finds fulfilment in loving another. 'The monks', he writes, 'made a vow of chastity to God; they mortified the sexual passion in themselves, but therefore they had in Heaven, in the Virgin Mary, the image of woman – an image of love. They could the more easily dispense with real woman, in proportion as an ideal woman was an object of love to them.' But in Feuerbach's new religion love is expressed physically, 'a real love, a love which has flesh and blood'; sexuality is a celebration of man's divinity. The only true marriage is one based on the acceptance of this; 'a marriage the bond of which is merely an external restriction, not the voluntary, contented self-restriction of love . . . is not a true marriage'. Such a claim made an instant appeal to the passionate nature which combined in George Eliot with a deep moral conviction, and no doubt sanctified her union with George Henry Lewes.

Stauss and Feuerbach were both Hegelians and, although critical of his idealism, accepted Hegel's view of history as a self-contained and ever-developing process. But Strauss gave Hegel's account of religious development a human face by seeing in Jesus the embodiment of the historical process, whereas Feuerbach in an even more radical modification of Hegel gave his account of history a material basis. G. H. Lewes, who was familiar with Feuerbach's work before George Eliot started her work on the *Essence of Christianity* and had referred to him in his *History of Philosophy* (1846), was also critical of Hegel's idealism but, nevertheless, wrote approvingly of his *Philosophy of History*. One can discern in Lewes the makings of a Young Hegelian (the name given to the predecessors of Marx), but any tendency in this direction was modified by the influence of English empiricism and French positivism.

In 1853, the year before the *Essence of Christianity* appeared, Lewes had published Comte's *Philosophy of the Sciences*, the proofs of which George Eliot helped to correct. Comte's *Cours de philosophie positive* (1830-1840) traced the history of human thought and society through three stages: the primitive period dominated by religious explanations of reality; the metaphysical which conceptualised these; and finally the scientific which, by the observation and correlation of facts and a disregard of useless speculation about ultimate causes, gave man a positive understanding of his environment and society. Comte regarded himself as the founder of a new science of sociology which would explain social structures by the same methods as those of the natural sciences.

George Eliot shared some of Lewes's enthusiasm for Comte's positivism, but both had certain reservations. Comte offered more than an explanatory theory; he promised a new society and a new religion of humanity. The leaders of this society would be philosophers in the manner of Plato's Guardians, and their rule would confer among other benefits, freedom of expression, the equality of the sexes, full-employment, and the end of war; the last guaranteed by the formation of a great Western Republic comprising France, England, Germany, Italy, and Spain. Orthodox religion would be replaced by a secular priesthood, a liturgical calendar, and meetings for worship to commemorate the worthy departed and to encourage service to society. The focus of this secular religion would be collective humanity. The immortality it offered its followers could not be a personal one, but the good passed on by one generation to another; an article of the new faith George Eliot expressed in the opening lines of one of her poems:

O may I join the choir invisible
Of those immortal dead who live again
In minds made better by their presence

Not many English admirers of Comte accepted his proposals for a secular ritual modelled on that of the Roman Church and T. H. Huxley called it 'Catholicism minus Christianity'. George Eliot, too, although she upheld a religion of humanity, was dubious about this side of Comte's positivism and even more sceptical about the Utopian character of his Republic. She had few illusions about human nature and although optimistic about historical progress, remained a realist about people. She was a conservative by temperament and did not share Comte's disregard for the past; her inclination was always to assimilate what was valuable in the past into a new pattern. In her review of Mackay's *The Progress of the Intellect* in the *Westminster Review*, where she speaks in her own voice and not as a translator of Strauss and Feuerbach, she is critical of those positivists who, she writes,

Holding, with Auguste Comte, that theological and metaphysical speculation have reached their limit, and that the only hope . . . is to be found in positive science, . . . urge that the thinkers . . . in the van of human progress should devote their energies to the actual rather than the retrospective.

On the contrary, she argues,

it would be a very serious mistake to suppose that the study of the past and the labours of criticism have no important practical bearing on the present.[6]

Comte had dismissed the myths of ancient civilisations as irrelevant to the needs of modern man, but George Eliot felt that properly interpreted they contained valuable insights into human nature and she welcomed Mackay's recognition of this. 'The introduction of a truly philosophic spirit into the study of mythology – an introduction for which we are chiefly indebted to the Germans'[7], appealed to her artistic imagination and was to inform her novels.

History for George Eliot, whether of the individual or the community, was of the greatest importance.

One of the great differences between the eighteenth and the nineteenth centuries was that brought about by the new interest in history as a basis of explanation for the natural world as well as society. For the eighteenth century the physical world and society were both static, whereas for the nineteenth they were subject to change. The dominant science in the eighteenth century had been physics, but this was now being replaced by zoology. Nowhere is the point put more graphically than by two remarks made by Darwin. The first was in a letter to John Lubbock, who had written to thank him for an advance copy of the *Origin of Species*, published in 1859. In his letter he goes back to his time as an undergraduate at Cambridge when Paley's *Natural Theology* had been a standard text. 'I do not think', he wrote, 'I hardly ever admired a book more than Paley's *Natural Theology*. I could almost formerly have said it by heart.' But his admiration had disappeared long ago and in his later autobiography he rejects Paley's comparison of the physical universe with a watch. 'The careful study of [Paley's] works', he now writes, was the 'part of the academical course which ... was of the least use to me in the education of my mind.'[8] By Darwin's time the picture of the universe as a piece of clockwork and God as a divine watchmaker had largely disappeared.

Darwin was not the first to advance a theory of evolution. The idea that history as an explanatory concept could be extended to account for the development of the natural world, including the zoological species, was fairly common by the time he published the *Origin of Species*. The Biblical criticism introduced from Germany by George Eliot had been accompanied by a new interest in geology, marked by the publication of Lyell's *Principals of Geology* in 1830-3 and Chambers's *The Vestiges of Creation* in 1844, which made it difficult to accept literally the Biblical stories of the Creation and the Flood. Tennyson's *In Memoriam*, published in 1850, to which we shall turn in a later chapter, illustrates the challenge to Christian belief made by evolutionary theories even before Darwin's book appeared. The novelty of Darwin's work, apart from its wealth of scientific detail and observation, lay in its title, which in full is, *On the Origin of Species by Means of Natural Selection, or the Preservation of Favoured Races in the Struggle for Life*. The phrase 'by Means of Natural Selection' suggested that the evolutionary process worked by chance not design, and seemed to remove any purpose from history and any divine providence from the universe.

The effect on many in the Victorian period was devastating and led to the loss of their religious faith. The 1860s were years of often fierce and troubled debate which saw a great increase in the number of 'honest doubters'. Several who had intended to take holy orders gave up their vocation, among them John Morley, who when he became editor of the *Fortnightly Review* declared its policy to be 'the diffusion and encouragement of rationalistic standards in things spiritual and temporal alike'. The combination of Mill's positivism and Darwin's evolutionary theory proved too much for Morley, who, nevertheless, looked back as many others did with regret on 'those old ages of noble, brave belief'. George Meredith, who had less sympathy for the old days than Morley, declared with some truth, 'Cut him open and you will find a clergyman'.

The same was true of many others, including George Eliot, who carried over into their agnosticism a reverence derived from a religious upbringing. Others, like Leslie Stephen who had been a priest in the Church of England, looked back with no regret. In 'Are we Christians?', which first appeared in *Fraser's Magazine* and was later published in his *Essays on Freethinking and Plainspeaking* (1873) he wrote with the zeal of the convert to his new rationalist principles: 'Let us shake the dust off our feet, and taking reason for our guide, and Mr. Darwin for the best modern expounder of the Universe, go boldly forward to whatever may be in store for us.' He had little sympathy for liberals like Jowett or Matthew Arnold. In his essay, 'Religion as a Fine Art', he accused both of intellectual dishonesty, with trying to eat their Christianity and still have it:

> Whether you evade the conflict between science and theology by saying that the ancient dogmas are to be accepted without any reference to reason, or to be accepted because they may be twisted into any meaning whatever, or to be accepted simply because you can get up a sham belief in them if you try very hard, you are equally approximating to the same principle that they belong to the sphere of poetry instead of history.

Where did this leave George Eliot? She dismissed the historicity of the Gospel story, but valued it as literature and felt it still had meaning. This was because she set a high value on poetry and fiction. She could accept the removal of a divine providence from human affairs if this is what Darwinism entailed, since for many years she had been accustomed to doing without it. She and Lewes welcomed Darwin's *Origin of Species* with open arms. Lewes had been sent an advance copy for a review he had been asked to write in *Blackwood's Magazine* and he passed this on to George Eliot who greeted it with raptures. She recorded her approval in a Journal entry for 24 November 1859, 'A divine day. I walked out and Mrs Congreve [the wife of a well-known postivist] joined me. Then Music, Arabian Nights, and Darwin.'

But did she grasp the significance of the phrase '*by Means of Natural Selection*'? Certainly Darwin himself was unhappy with the implications of his theory. Writing to Asa Gray of Harvard, a year after his book appeared, he confessed, 'about Design. I am conscious that I am in an utterly hopeless muddle. I cannot think that the world, as we see it, is the result of chance; and yet I cannot look at each separate thing as the result of Design.'[9] George Eliot was left with a sense of awe rather than confusion. On 5 December 1859, a few days after reading the *Origin of Species*, she wrote to her friend Mrs Bodichon:

> it marks an epoch, as the expression of his thorough adhesion, after long years of study, to the Doctrine of Development . . . it will have a great effect in the scientific world, causing a thorough and open discussion of a question about which people have felt timid. So the world gets on step by step towards brave clearness and honesty! But to me the Development theory and all other explanation of processes by which things came to be, produce a feeble impression compared with the mystery that lies under the processes.[10]

The term Doctrine of Development reminds us that George Eliot was familiar with evolutionary theory long before she read Darwin. This was the usage adopted in the early 1850s when she was a close friend of Herbert Spencer with whom for a time her name was romantically connected. He was contributing articles on these and allied subjects to the *Westminster Review* of which she was sub-editor, and to *The Leader* of which their friend Lewes was joint editor. Spencer was beginning to make an enormous reputation for himself as the pioneer of the new discipline of sociology which he developed by endeavouring to apply scientific method to the study of society. He could not, of course, use the experimental method in which tests could be repeated, but in its place he substituted historical explanation, believing with Hegel that to understand anything one needs to know its history. He was also inspired, as Darwin was, by the theories of Adam Smith and Malthus. Malthus had argued that Adam Smith's competition in a free market must lead to a struggle for survival since the growth of population when unchecked outstrips the resources needed to sustain it. Darwin used this notion of a struggle for survival to explain the evolution of the species and Spencer extended it to cover the development of human society.

There were many points on which George Eliot and Spencer agreed. Spencer believed in a *laissez-faire* political system and in the need for gradual change, opinions which he derived from evolutionary theory. He believed that 'there is no way from the lower forms of social life to the higher, but one passing through small successive modifications'.[11] He shared her view that ancient myths have a value of their own. 'Instead of passing over as of no account', he writes 'or else regarding as purely mischievous, the superstitions of early man, we must inquire what part they play in social evolution.'[12] In *Social Statics*, published in 1851 when he and George Eliot were closely associated, he advanced a theory of evolution in which the changes in historical development are brought about by a power far above

> individual wills. Men who seem the prime movers, are merely the tools with which it works, and were they absent it would quickly find others.[13]

This, together with her belief in the universality of the law of causality, raised questions about the freedom of the will for George Eliot. She was never a strict determinist in the sense that denies one the freedom to make choices; the concept of duty and the importance of making moral choices are never far away in any of her novels. But there are several passages in her work which have given rise to the suggestion of determinism. One of these can be found in her review of Mackay's *The Progress of the Intellect*. 'Mr Mackay's faith', she writes, entails

> that divine revelation is not contained exclusively or pre-eminently in the facts and inspirations of any one age or nation, but is co-extensive with the history of human development, and is perpetually unfolding itself to our widened experience and investigation. . . . The master key to this revelation, is a recognition of the presence of undeviating law in the material and moral world – of that invariability of sequence which is acknowledged to be the basis of physical science, but which is still perversly ignored in our social organization, our ethics and our religion.[14]

This not only removes the Incarnation from its central place in history, but substitutes for the doctrine of grace what the ancient Greeks called the law of *dike*. Lord Acton put it well when he wrote, 'The doctrine that neither contrition nor sacrifice can appease Nemesis, or avert the consequences of our wrongdoing from ourselves and others, filled a very large space indeed in her scheme of life and literature.'[15]

But must this inexorable law of causality lead to the denial of free-will? Her answer to this was provided in large part by Spinoza, who remained a dominant influence in all her thinking. In May 1843 Lewes had written a long article on Spinoza in the *Westminster Review* which was reprinted in a pamphlet and later incorporated in his *Biographical History of Philosophy*. Before she met Lewes, however, George Eliot was engaged in translating Spinoza's *Tractatus Theologico-Politicus* at the request of Charles Bray, who then failed to find a publisher for it. After she met Lewes she worked hard at a translation of Spinoza's *Ethics* which Lewes had arranged to supply for Bohn, but again this remained unpublished. But though she was never rewarded financially, her work gave her a rich return, for that 'pious, virtuous, God-intoxicated man' became a source of spiritual illumination and a compensation for the loss of her early faith.

Spinoza's God is not a personal one, but he (or it) is the ground of the universe in whom we have our being. He is not separate from the universe for all things exist in him and everything that happens must happen as it does. 'Everything is determined by the necessity of the divine nature.' (*Ethics*, Pt. 1, Proposition 29) Spinoza repeats this in his *Tractatus Theologico-Politicus*: 'Everything is determined by universal laws of nature to exist and act in a certain and determinate way.'(Ch. 4) Spinoza accepts that this entails the denial of free-will. Nevertheless, an individual is free, not in the sense that his actions are undetermined, but in so far as they are self-determined (*Ethics*, Pt. 1, Definition 7). God himself is free only in this sense, for whatever he does is in accordance with his own nature.

It might be thought that this self-determined freedom is restricted to God alone, but Spinoza extends it to some, though not all individuals. There are some brave spirits, he contends, who have the capacity to fulfil their true nature against all the forces that oppose them. Some of these forces are external, but others are the passions which war against the life of reason. For Spinoza freedom comes from the mastery of the passions by the reason, but this does not lead to cold rationalism as his ideal; he believed that the individual reaches fulfilment when the reason and the passions come together in a fruitful union.

There are features here that were to inform George Eliot's fiction, but before considering these, two other figures demand further attention. These are Hegel and Herbert Spencer. The problem of free-will was not solved once and for all by Spinoza. Indeed, apart from Coleridge, few knew his work, which had not been translated into English. But he was increasingly known and admired in Germany where Kant and above all Hegel brought a new dimension to the problem of free-will.

Kant faced the dilemma of reconciling a material world run according to Newtonian laws and his conviction – summed up in his dictum 'I ought, therefore I can' – that the will is free. This conflict between a phenomenal world working according to physical laws, and a noumenal one which can be apprehended not by the pure reason, but only by the practical reason in its recognition of a moral imperative, presented a problem which Hegel thought he had solved. His proposed solution lay in a philosophy which saw history as a movement towards ever greater freedom. His notion of 'the freedom of necessity' can be dismissed as an attempt to reconcile two incompatibles, but the historical dimension Hegel gave to the problem was something new. Hegel's argument proceeded deductively, just as Spinoza's had; both worked from certain axioms to conclusions they thought were guaranteed by logical entailment. But now Herbert Spencer advanced a theory of evolution based on inductive reasoning and empirical evidence, which appeared to corroborate Spinoza and Hegel. Spencer saw evolution as a process which offered a greater number of choices to the individual as social and moral life became ever more complex.

As we have seen, Lewes's *History of Philosophy* had welcomed Hegel's *Philosophy of History* enthusiastically and in October 1842 Lewes had contributed a laudatory essay on Hegel's aesthetics to the *British and Foreign Review*. George Eliot also wrote a review article on 'The Antigone and its Moral' for *The Leader* in March 1856, which gave unstinting praise to Hegel's interpretation of Sophocles' tragedy. There can be little doubt that Hegel was a powerful influence on her, but it was Hegel and Spencer together who made such an impact on her thought and who inspired her fiction.

Kant's practical reason promised a foundation for a belief in 'God, freedom and immortality', but the often quoted passage of a conversation F. W. H. Myers had with her in the Fellows' Garden of Trinity College, Cambridge, records how she took the three great 'trumpet-calls of men, – the words God, Immortality, Duty, – pronounced, with terrible earnestness, how inconceivable was the *first*, how unbelievable was the *second*, and yet how peremptory and absolute the *third*'. Hegel had replaced God with an impersonal spiritual force working through history. Spencer had rejected God altogether, but offered a material, scientifically verifiable account of Hegel's historical process, which carried with it choice and belief in a moral law.[16] She and Spencer both saw evolution as development; not merely as process but as progress. For them, as for many other Victorians, it meant an evolution towards ever higher patterns of behaviour. Spencer's phrase 'survival of the fittest' meant for them the morally fittest, but this had no justification and it later became clear that it was a mere tautology; those survived who were fittest to survive. But when she started to write her novels, George Eliot felt that life offered the individual the possibility of greater freedom and the opportunity for growth and fulfilment. For Carlyle, history was advanced by the heroic qualities of great men, but George Eliot's fiction shows how these qualities can be shared by men and women in humbler walks of life who can also play their part in the progress of humanity.

It would be foolish to suppose that this sketch of George Eliot's intellectual development is sufficient to account for her achievement as a novelist. Her many gifts included not only a powerful mind, but a power of observation that cast a critical yet benevolent eye over human behaviour. She was interested not only in ideas but in people: their characters, their personal relationships, their place in the community, their motives, and the discrepancies between their beliefs and their actions. Her interest in ideas was never a cold and detached rationalism, but it would be wrong to ignore her intellectual life or to think it separable from her opinion of people and society. There is clear evidence that as her mind moved towards settled convictions this had its effect on her novels. Certainly the general view of her contemporaries was that her novels became increasingly novels of ideas and many regretted this change. Leslie Stephen divided her fiction into two parts: the first up to and including *The Mill on the Floss*, had 'the unmistakable mark of high genius', the later work showing 'a comprehensive and vigorous intellect' but leaving him 'regretting the loss of that early charm'.[17] Henry James made the point even more succinctly in writing about *Middlemarch*. *Silas Marner*, he writes, 'has a delightful tinge of Goldsmith – we may almost call it; *Middlemarch* is too often an echo of Messrs. Darwin and Huxley.'[18]

The early charm of *Adam Bede* had, nevertheless, been accompanied by a conviction that classical mythology was often a better source of wisdom and virtue than the Bible. Mr Irwine, the rector, is more often found reading classical texts than the Scriptures and his commitment to Christianity is a rather relaxed one. We are told that 'His mental palette, indeed, was rather pagan, and found a savouriness in a quotation from Sophocles or Theocritus that was quite absent from any text in Isaiah or Amos.'(Bk. 1, Ch. 5). In spite of this, perhaps because of it, Mr Irwine is a virtuous man who stands by Hetty Sorel and Adam Bede in their sorrows and George Eliot makes him one of the most attractive characters in the story.

The use of classical mythology becomes more important in *The Mill on the Floss* where it gives the narrative added depth and resonance. The community to which the Dodson sisters belong was a narrow and small-minded one.

> Their religion was of a simple, semi-pagan kind, but there was no heresy in it – if heresy properly means choice – for they didn't know there was any other religion, except that of chapel-goers, which appeared to run in families, like asthma . . . the vicar . . . was not a controversialist, but a good hand at whist. The religion of the Dodsons consisted in reverencing whatever was customary and respectable. (Bk. IV, Ch. 1)

The religion of Mr Tulliver, who marries one of the sisters, was little different, except that he showed a more robust scepticism towards the authority of the church: 'he considered that Church was one thing and common-sense another, and he wanted nobody to tell him what common-sense was'. And yet, in spite of the small-minded provincialism of Mr Tulliver, George Eliot sees in him a figure who recalls the story of Oedipus. Forced by circumstances to borrow money to meet his debts, Mr Tulliver is obliged to sign a bond for five hundred pounds and this marks the decline of his fortunes. 'Mr Tulliver had a destiny as well as Oedipus, and in this case he might plead, like Oedipus, that his deed was inflicted on him rather than committed by him.'(Bk. 1, Ch. XII)

One might think the comparison ludicrous and made with comic intent, but this can hardly be so since from this point on the story of Mr Tulliver becomes increasingly tragic. Indeed, the comparison has further implications for those who know their Greek tragedy, as most of her original readers would have done. Certainly George Eliot was aware of the implications for she had recently written her article on Hegel's essay on Sophocles' *Antigone*. Hegel sees in the story of Oedipus' daughter the perfect example of tragedy. *Antigone* recounts how a sister sacrifices her life for her brother and is united with him in death; a story very close to that of Maggie Tulliver. In her article George Eliot writes, 'Wherever the strength of a man's intellect, or moral sense, or affection brings him into opposition with the rules which society has sanctioned, there is renewed the conflict between Antigone and Creon.' We know that George Eliot had a warm affection for her own brother and felt lasting pain at his rejection when she decided to live with Lewes, and it is not difficult to detect the autobiographical element in the story of Maggie Tulliver, a latter-day Antigone.

The sufferings of insignificant people can be as tragic as those in a higher station in life. George Eliot tells us that even when she was a child 'there were passions at war in Maggie ... to have made a tragedy, if tragedies were made by passion only; but the essential *ti megethos* which was present in the passion was wanting to the action' (Bk. 1, Ch. X). The term *ti megethos* is taken from Aristotle's 'Poetics' and means that 'certain largeness or grandeur' which Aristotle considered necessary for tragedy. George Eliot denies the need for this and discerns in Maggie, even as a child, the seeds of the tragedy which was to overtake her. Maggie as much as Antigone must bear great suffering as a consequence of her actions and in a chapter devoted almost entirely to a discussion of tragedy, we are told that 'we need not shrink from this comparison of small things with great'. (Bk. 4, Ch. I) For Aristotle the tragic action is started by *hamartia*, an error of judgment which carries with it moral implications, although the consequences may be out of all proportion to any evil in the motive. Hegel sees tragedy as rather a conflict between two virtuous courses of action. Antigone is torn between her duty to her dead brother and to Creon, the ruler, and either way she is bound to meet a tragic end.

This clash of ideals accords with Hegel's notion of a dialectic in human affairs; although the individual may be caught up in a tragic conflict which brings great suffering this is a necessary step on the path of human progress. In this way the tragic hero or heroine becomes a victim, and this is how George Eliot regarded Mr Tulliver. A readiness to accept willingly one's tragic destiny may even turn the victim into a martyr and George Eliot was always temperamentally attracted by this idea of self-renunciation. This is most often encountered in those with religious faith but can be seen as an ideal by those with no religion. George Eliot, like Maggie Tulliver, found peace of mind at times of spiritual crisis in Thomas à Kempis's *Imitation of Christ*:

> Maggie turned from leaf to leaf, and read where the quiet hand had pointed. 'Know that the love of thyself doth hurt thee more than any thing in the world. . . . Both about and below, which

way soever thou dost turn thee, every where thou shalt find the cross: and everywhere of necessity thou must have patience, if thou wilt have inward peace and enjoy an everlasting crown.' (Bk. 4 Ch. III)

The truth of this for George Eliot went beyond Christian belief and was a feature of human experience which faced all her heroes and especially her heroines.

Nowhere is this more graphically illustrated than in *Romola*, where again there is an emphasis upon the consequences of one's actions and the retribution that follows the breaking of the moral law. A perceptive review in the *Westminster Review* in October 1863, the year in which the novel was published, makes the point:

> In the minute analysis of moral growth she has no equal; no one has so fully seized the great truth that we can none of us escape the consequences of our conduct, that each action has not only a character of its own, but also an influence on the character of the actor from which there is no escape. . . . To this deep moral maxim George Eliot constantly recurs, not in *Romola* only, but in *Romola* it forms the central idea to which all else is made subservient. (No. 80)

Romola acts nobly throughout but is betrayed by her treacherous husband, Tito, and is led by her own impulsive nature to make mistaken judgments which bring about her tragic isolation at the end of the book. But she achieves through her trials a self-knowledge that leads to self-sacrifice and finally to peace of mind.

In preparing to write *Romola* George Eliot travelled to Florence, the setting of her story, and also to Rome, and in both cities she and Lewes visited churches, libraries, and art galleries. The study of works of art she and Lewes made on this visit had a marked effect on her imagination which can be seen not only in *Romola* but in her later novels. The story she recounts in *Romola* is given iconographical form in two paintings which have a central place in the narrative.

Romola has been brought up in a cold and rationalist manner by her father, Bardo, a pedantic scholar not unlike Casaubon in *Middlemarch*. Bardo is bitterly anti-Christian and deeply mortified when his only son leaves home to become a monk and he himself is left in old age blind and dependent upon his daughter. There is tragic irony in the welcome he gives to Tito, the young Greek scholar whom he sees as a replacement for his son, an assistant in his scholarly work, and a husband for his daughter.

Bardo's blindness, which is matched by a spiritual blindness that is to bring disaster to Romola, is contrasted with the visionary powers of the artist, Piero di Cosimo. Before his marriage to Romola, Tito commissions Piero to execute a 'fantastic mythological design' which will depict him and his bride-to-be as Bacchus and Ariadne. Tito adds to Ovid's account of this myth by having Ariadne 'made immortal with her golden crown'. The miniatures of the couple are to be enclosed in a wooden case in the form of a triptych, a startling juxtaposition of pagan myth and Christian setting.

The work is meant to be a surprise for Romola and the question arises of how she can be made to sit for her likeness. Piero tells Tito that this can easily be arranged since he would like to use Romola and her father as models for a painting he has been asked to execute showing Antigone leading her blind father Oedipus at Colonus. The artist also reveals that he has already made a sketch of Tito, but when this is brought forward it shows Tito,

> his right hand uplifted, holding a wine-cup, in the attitude of
> triumphant joy, but with his face turned away from the cup with
> an expression of such intense fear in the dilated eyes and pallid
> lips, that he felt a cold stream through his veins. (Bk 1, Ch. XVIII)

The painter's visionary power enables him to see the fear that lies beneath Tito's insouciance; the fear of exposure that comes from the betrayal of his benefactor, Baldassare, and his callous abandonment of the innocent young contadina, Tessa, whom he has deceived by going through a mock marriage ceremony. The same power allows Piero to see Romola's future not as Ariadne, rejoicing in her married happiness, but as the tragic heroine Antigone.

For a sceptical humanist George Eliot gives a surprisingly large part to the visionary in *Romola*. Summoned by her dying brother whom she has not seen since he left home to become a monk, Romola hears him recount how he has seen her future three times in a vision and before he dies he begs her not to proceed with her marriage. At first she dismisses his warning as 'one of those visions she had so often heard her father allude to with bitterness' as mere superstition, but she is strangely moved by her brother's story of how he had come to distrust his rationalist upbringing and seek peace of mind elsewhere. 'I felt', he tells her,

> that there was a life of perfect love and purity for the soul; in
> which there would be no uneasy hunger after pleasure, no
> tormenting questions, no fear of suffering. Before I knew the
> history of the saints, I had a foreshadowing of their ecstasy. For
> the same truth had penetrated even into pagan philosophy: that

it is a bliss within the reach of man to die to mortal needs, and live
in the life of God as the Unseen Perfectness. (Bk. 1, Ch. XV)

Her brother's story remains fixed in Romola's memory as she carries
away with her the crucifix which he had clasped in his dying hands;
the same crucifix Tito on the day of his betrothal to Romola locks
away inside the triptych with the miniatures of Bacchus and Ariadne.
There is a wealth of symbolic meaning in this. In the original legend
Ariadne is joined with Bacchus after she has been delivered from
the labyrinth and Romola sees herself on her marriage as entering a
new life of freedom after the servitude of attending alone on her
father. When Tito locks away her brother's crucifix she welcomes
the action as a burial of the unpleasant past, but 'certain importunate
memories and questionings . . . still flitted like unexplained
shadows across her happier thoughts'. Only much later does she
understand that the shadows are a reminder that the crucified Christ
is a truer emblem than the figures in the triptych of that real
happiness which comes from self-sacrifice. But even in the early
days of her marriage she begins to realise that 'the crowned
Ariadne, under the snowing roses, had felt more and more the
presence of unexpected thorns'. Indeed, the golden crown Tito
had placed on her brows will be replaced with one made of thorns.

Later still, in a chapter entitled 'Ariadne Discrowns Herself',
when she has decided to leave her husband, Romola recalls her
brother's dying words and finds that she 'had lost her belief in the
happiness she had once thirsted for: it was a hateful, smiling, soft-
handed thing with a narrow selfish heart'. Before leaving Florence
and her husband she opens the triptych again and looks at 'Foolish
Ariadne! with her gaze of love, as if that bright face [of Tito], with
its hyacinthine curls like tendrils among the vines, held the deep
secret of her life!'(Bk. 2, Ch. XXXVII) Although she despises her
husband she still feels it would have been wrong to have broken
her engagement on the strength of her brother's vision, and even
now she dreads 'lest she should be drawn at last into fellowship
with some wretched superstition – into the company of the howling
fanatics and weeping nuns who had been her contempt from
childhood till now'. Nevertheless, she takes the crucifix from the
tabernacle and carries it away with her.

Until this point in the story she has been subject to her father,
her husband, and her brother. Her father and brother are dead and
she has just left her husband; now she feels free at last. But she now
encounters another and powerful influence in the person of
Savonarola, Fra Giralamo, the monk who is leader of the democratic

party in Florence. He has been told by God in a vision to interrupt her journey and direct her back to Florence to take up again the duties that wait her there. She is persuaded to return and so is caught up in the tumultuous events that lead to the condemnation and execution of Savonarola as a heretic. The execution is deliberately compared to the crucifixion of Jesus and Romola is filled with revulsion at the cruelty of the scene and with pity for the leader who has come to mean so much to her. Nevertheless, by this time she has developed serious reservations about Savonarola's mission with its call for a bonfire of the vanities and its excesses of spiritual zeal and here at the end of the novel her voice and George Eliot's merge into one.

Romola's doubts concerning Savonarola start with the question of why he did nothing to restrain and even condemn the false and hysterical visionaries who surrounded him and fed on his eloquent preaching, and claimed divine inspiration for their visions:

The answer came with painful clearness: he was fettered inwardly
by the consciousness that such revelations were not, in their
basis, distinctly separable from his own visions. (Bk. 3, Ch. LII)

If we cannot accept such visions as self-authenticating, how can we distinguish between the true and the false? Romola is torn between her new-found sympathy for Savonarola and his campaign for democracy and the worldly wisdom of her father and godfather.

She has become convinced that reason alone cannot find the truth and that deep feeling is needed for virtuous action, but feeling may degenerate into fanaticism just as reasoning may descend into the cynical *real-politik* of her godfather. After her disillusionment with Savonarola, Romola asks herself the question, 'What force was there to create for her that supremely hallowed motive which men call duty, but which can have no inward constraining existence save through some form of believing love?' (Bk. 3, Ch. LXI) The answer Romola finds to her question is that the dynamic behind the command of duty is love of one's fellows, compassion for the sufferings of others, and a readiness to sacrifice oneself. This is George Eliot's religion of humanity; a religion open to any spiritual insight which may be available from prophet, priest, and visionary, but one which requires no commitment to creed or dogma.

In preparing to write *Romola* George Eliot read Mrs Jameson's *Legends of the Monastic Orders*. In her entry for St Theresa of Avila, Mrs Jameson refers to the way in which St Theresa was shown in art as almost an erotic figure; the ecstasy of the saint depicted in a manner that suggested sexual passion, with the angel looking like Cupid as he shoots his arrow into the heart of the saint while she gazes up in rapture. Mrs Jameson mentions the Spanish painters as guilty in this respect, but she quotes as 'the grossest example – the most offensive – is the marble group of Bernini in the Santa Maria della Vittoria at Rome. The head of St Theresa is that of a languishing nymph; the angel is a sort of Eros; the whole has been significantly described as a 'parody of Divine love' '. We do not know whether George Eliot saw the Bernini sculpture when she was in Rome, and her Journal makes no reference to it, but given her interest in St Theresa she would almost certainly have done so.

Even so, it is highly unlikely that she had St Theresa in mind when she drew Camilla, the follower of Savonarola, with her wild and ecstatic visions, for she had too much respect for the saint to associate her with such excesses. It is Romola herself, with her acceptance of self-sacrifice and devotion to a high ideal, who is the St Theresa of the novel. Indeed, one can see all or most of her heroines as modern representatives of the saint, but above all, it is Dorothea Brooke, the heroine of *Middlemarch*, who is given this part. So much is made clear in the Prelude where George Eliot writes with compassion of those modern Theresas 'who found for themselves no epic life wherein there was a constant unfolding of far-resonant action; perhaps only a life of mistakes, the offspring of a certain spiritual grandeur ill-matched with the meanness of opportunity; perhaps a tragic failure which found no sacred poet and sank unwept into oblivion'.

Dorothea Brooke is a high-minded young woman who seeks to serve a cause by marrying the dessicated and pedantic Casaubon. Although Casaubon's study is mythology, he approaches it in a dry and rationalist spirit which fails to see it as a source of living wisdom and relevant for all times. During their honeymoon in Rome, Dorothea already experiences doubts about her marriage, as her husband disappears into the Vatican library, immersing himself in books and failing to satisfy her longing for love. It is then that Will Ladislaw sees her in the Vatican galleries 'where the reclining Ariadne . . . lies in the marble voluptuousness of her beauty'; she 'not shamed by the Ariadne, was clad in Quakerish grey drapery'. His German friend Naumann who accompanies Ladislaw, describes her, however, as 'a sort of Christian Antigone – sensuous force controlled by spiritual passion. ' (Bk. 2, Ch. XIX)

George Eliot brings together here two of her favourite images, Ariadne and Antigone. Dorothea has already sacrificed herself, not like Antigone for her brother, but for her husband. If he had lived, her sacrifice, too, would have led to her death, a living death, tied to one who had lived too long in the past to bring life to the present. Casaubon realises something of this himself when he confesses, 'I feed too much on the inward sources; I live too much with the dead. My mind is something like the ghost of an ancient, wandering about the world and trying mentally to construct it as it used to be'(Bk. 1, Ch. II). Fortunately Dorothea is delivered from this fate by her husband's death and from being Antigone becomes a modern Ariadne.

The contrast between Casaubon and Will Ladislaw, who becomes Dorothea's second husband, is the contrast between life and death. When the two men meet in the hotel in Rome Casaubon appears cold and lifeless, whereas Will is described as being like sunshine and 'his hair seemed to shake out light, and some persons thought they saw decided genius in this coruscation. Mr. Casaubon on the contrary stood rayless'. (Bk. 2, Ch. XX) This description of Will suggests not only Dionysus or Bacchus, who marries Ariadne, but also Apollo, the giver of light and life, of health and well-being. Apollo was also the god of music and as Will looks at Dorothea, 'The Aeolian harp again came into his mind.' The mixed imagery is, perhaps, a deliberate attempt by George Eliot to depict Will as one combining the qualities of both Dionysus and Apollo, a union of feeling and reason. He awakens the emotional part of Dorothea's personality and delivers her from the cold rationalism of life with Casaubon. Where Romola moves away from being cast in the part of Ariadne and takes on the role of Antigone, the reverse is true of Dorothea.

Her deliverance is not only from her unhappy marriage to Casaubon, but from seeing herself as a provincial St Theresa; an endeavour which leads to what George Eliot describes in her Prelude as 'perhaps only a life of mistakes'. Her upbringing had been narrow and Puritanical with a distrust of the passions which found even the pictures in her uncle's collection disturbing.

> To poor Dorothea these severe classical nudities and smirking Renaissance-Correggiosities were painfully inexplicable, staring into the midst of her Puritanic conceptions: she had never been taught how she could bring them into any sort of relevance with her life. (Bk. 1. Ch. IX)

Her visit to Rome marked a turning point, not only because it was there she began to appreciate the pleasure of looking at works of art and finding in them something that matched her needs, but because it was there she met Will and contrasted the happiness he brought her with the emptiness of her marriage. The situation is given an ironic twist when Casaubon is reluctant to accompany her to the Villa Farnesina[19] to see Raphael's frescoes. 'They are', he says,

> I believe, highly esteemed. Some of them represent the fable of Cupid and Psyche, which is probably the romantic invention of a literary period, and cannot, I think, be reckoned as a genuine mythical product. (Bk. 2, Ch. XX)

He seems unaware of, or disregards, the Christianizing of this pagan myth which interpreted it as the story of the angel of God seeking out the human soul and (of great importance for George Eliot herself) which treated human love as the shadow of divine love.

In describing this episode George Eliot would undoubtedly have recalled the Bernini sculpture in Rome which had so shocked Mrs Jameson. She realised, as Mrs Jameson did not, that Bernini in depicting St Theresa's ecstasy (when as the saint herself said, 'an angel of the Lord pierced her heart with a golden, flaming arrow, filling her with a mixture of pain and bliss') may have had the myth of Cupid and Psyche in mind. Even if Bernini did not, it is likely that George Eliot did when she saw the sculpture, either in Rome or reproduced pictorially. The sexual overtones would not have offended her for she knew that Dante and other poets saw earthly love as a reflection of the divine and that St Paul viewed marriage as an image of the love of Christ for his church. In Chapter III of *Adam Bede* after Seth has declared his love to Dinah, George Eliot writes, 'Love of this sort is hardly distinguishable from religious feeling. What deep and worthy love is so?' Her own union with Lewes was not recognised by either church or state, but she regarded it as a true marriage with a quasi-divine quality, for had not Feuerbach sanctified true marriage with his declaration that 'Love is God?' In *Middlemarch* her St Theresa finds fulfilment in the end by becoming Mrs Ladislaw.

In reading *Middlemarch* we should not make too much of George Eliot's scholarly interests, for there are places in the novel where she suggests that we learn most about life not from books or works of art, but from life itself. When Will Ladislaw tells Dorothea that Casaubon knows nothing of German scholarship and is only an amateur in the study of mythology, the author herself comments, 'Young Mr Ladislaw was not at all deep himself in German writers'. His ability to awaken Dorothea to a new awareness of life is not because of his scholarship, but because he is alive himself and his company life-enhancing. To compare Will and Dorothea with mythological figures is to risk seeing them as the personification of abstract forces rather than as creatures of flesh and blood. Attracted though she might have been by Coleridge's endeavour to make the supernatural natural, she was temperamentally more in sympathy with the Wordsworthian alternative of taking ordinary provincial life and, in the words of the Preface to *Lyrical Ballads* 'to excite a feeling analogous to the supernatural'. So she brings her characters down to earth by taking them back to provincial England, to their neighbours, and the duties that await them there. Nevertheless, the ancient myths saw humans in the context of supernatural forces and George Eliot believed that we are still subject to these and especially to the influence of good and evil. When Dorothea suspects Will of having an affair with Rosamund Lydgate, she sets out in spite of her emotional distress to give help to Rosamund, and indirectly to Lydgate and Will. Against all her own inclinations she feels an obligation laid upon her from outside. George Eliot provides her authorial comment at this point, 'The objects of her rescue were not to be sought out by her fancy: they were chosen for her. She yearned towards the perfect Right, that it might make a throne within her, and rule her errant will.'

In spite of all the constraints that hinder us we are free to make choices as Dorothea does, and these will bear upon the lives of those who come after us. At the very end of *Middlemarch* she looks back on the life of Dorothea and her two marriages. Though the second of these brings Dorothea happiness, her life has demanded self-denial and the service of others. In spite of this her actions have been limited by the society in which she lives; she has been denied the nobility of Antigone and remains a mute, inglorious St Theresa:

> Certainly those determining acts of her life were not ideally beautiful. They were the mixed result of young and noble impulse struggling amidst the conditions of an imperfect social state, in which great feelings will often take the aspect of error, and great faith the aspect of illusion. For there is no creature whose inward being is so strong that it is not greatly determined by what lies outside it. A new Theresa will hardly have the opportunity of reforming a conventual life, any more than a new Antigone will spend her heroic piety in daring all for the sake of a brother's burial: the medium in which their ardent deeds took shape is for ever gone. But we insignificant people with our daily words and acts are preparing the lives of many

Dorotheas, some of which may present a far sadder sacrifice
than that of the Dorothea whose story we know. (Finale)

The other and connected stories in *Middlemarch* are not given the
same mythological depth nor are their characters created in the same
heroic mould as Dorothea's. Mary Garth is an admirable young
woman who represents sense while Dorothea represents sensibility.
Mary refuses to give way to the tenderness of her feelings for
Farebrother, – 'And we can set a watch', she says, 'over our
affections and our constancy as we can over our other treasures. '
(Bk. 6. Ch. LVII). Fred Vincy is an amiable young man who accepts
her guidance and together they settle into married life and raising
a family. They preserve the traditional values of their society and
the ethics of 'my station and its duties'. Lydgate on the other hand
is one who wishes to advance society. He is a reformer, but his
idealism is undermined by his submissive and mistaken devotion
to his wife. He dies at the age of 50 with his hopes unfulfilled and
in weak subservience to her selfishness. He is not a tragic figure of
heroic proportions. Unlike St Theresa he does not sacrifice himself
to a cause, but to a shallow wife; unlike Antigone he is not caught
between conflicting duties, but only between his duty and weak
acquiescence. His failure is not the result of his emotions
overcoming his judgment, for he is a man of ideas and driven by
an arrogant intellect; it comes from an inability to understand
people and especially the failure to understand his wife, who has
her own needs and unsatisfied ambitions.

In a conversation between Will and Dorothea in which they
share their views on religion, Will says his religion is 'To love
what is good and beautiful when I see it', but Dorothea's is more
altruistic:

> That by desiring what is perfectly good, even when we don't
> quite know what it is and cannot do what we would, we are
> part of the divine power against evil. .... I have always been
> finding out my religion since I was a little girl. I used to pray so
> much – now I hardly ever pray. I try not to have desires merely
> for myself, because they may not be good for others, and I have
> too much already. (Bk. 6, Ch. XXXIX)

George Eliot would have approved of this and was probably
speaking for herself here.

If so, she would have meant by 'the divine power against evil',
not the God of the Bible, but the secularised historicism of Carlyle
and Hegel, supplemented by Comte's positivism and the emergent
evolutionary ideas of Spencer. This divine power, especially in

Hegel's philosophy, may place the individual in a morally ambiguous situation and call for self-sacrifice in the realisation of its purpose. In her review article on Hegel's essay on *Antigone*, George Eliot declared that the individual may find himself in

> the struggle between elemental tendencies and established laws by which the outer life of man is gradually and painfully being brought into harmony with his inward needs. Until this harmony is perfected, we shall never be able to attain a great right without also doing a great wrong. Reformers, martyrs, revolutionists, are never fighting against evil only; they are also placing themselves in opposition to a good.

This is illustrated in *The Mill on the Floss*, *Romola* and *Middlemarch*, but nowhere is it given greater depth than in *Daniel Deronda*. *Daniel Deronda* is concerned with reformers and revolutionaries of a visionary rather than a political kind, but as in *Middlemarch* the freedom of action for modern men and women is circumscribed, even when, like Daniel Deronda himself, they are prepared to sacrifice themselves for a great cause. Hegel saw history as an ever increasing realisation of human freedom, but this entails for some heroic spirits a tragic destiny. As one might expect in a novel largely taken up with Judaism, there is far less of an attempt by George Eliot to depict her characters in terms of Greek drama, but she does invoke the *Prometheus Bound* of Aeschylus when she describes Mordecai, the Jewish nationalist and visionary. 'There be', she writes, 'who hold that the deeper tragedy were a Prometheus Bound not *after* but *before* he had well got the celestial fire . . . thrust by . . . instituted methods into a solitude of despised ideas, fastened in throttling helplessness by the fatal pressure of poverty and disease' (Chapter XXXVIII). Mordecai's sufferings are not his alone, but of his whole race; he is 'a frail incorporation of the national consciousness' and what is true of him is true of the Jewish people.

George Eliot views the history of the Jews as one long tragedy. At the beginning of Chapter XXXXII of her novel she quotes Leopold Zunz, the nineteenth-century Zionist and founder of 'the Science of Judaism':

> If there are ranks in suffering, Israel takes precedence of all the nations – if the duration of sorrows and the patience with which they are borne ennoble, the Jews are among the aristocracy of every land – if a literature is called rich in the possession of a few classic tragedies, what shall we say to a National Tragedy lasting for fifteen hundred years, in which the poets and the actors were also the heroes?

We are told that 'Daniel Deronda had lately been reading that passage of Zunz.' He is on his way to join Mordecai who takes him to a working-men's club where they meet to debate and exchange ideas. As they enter this small group they hear one of the members quote Shelley's 'Prometheus Unbound':

As thought by thought is piled, till some great truth
Is loosened, and the nations echo round.

The quotation is pregnant with meaning for the Jews who are present, for it seems to promise liberation for their people.

When Mordecai addresses the meeting, he reminds them that already, centuries before, Spinoza 'saw not why Israel should not again be a chosen nation'; and he continues in a manner that explains why George Eliot no longer draws on Greek mythology in this her last novel. 'Who says that the history and literature of our race are dead? Are they not as living as the history and literature of Greece and Rome . . . ? These were an inheritance dug from the tomb. Ours is an inheritance that has never ceased to quiver in millions of human frames.'

Daniel Deronda is concerned not only with the fate of nations but of individuals who are caught up in these national events. Not to see the interrelatedness of the two is to miss the point of the novel, but it is a mistake made by those critics who consider the work an artistic failure, notably F. R. Leavis in *The Great Tradition*. Certainly George Eliot's novel was experimental and tried to achieve something never attempted before, but even if its success is less than perfect some have criticised it for the wrong reasons. They perceive what they think is an unbridgeable gap between the story of Gwendolen Harleth's marriage to Grandcourt and her relationship with Daniel Deronda, between the picture of English society and the Jewish community that was hardly recognised by that society; and, even worse in their eyes, between a love story and a dissertation about the historical destiny of the Jewish race. What they fail to see is that all these are brought together in a pattern governed by George Eliot's belief that the life of the individual is part of a historical process.

There is, no doubt, a certain idealisation of the leading Jewish characters in the novel, and while this can be explained as necessary to the satirical comparison she draws between them and the nominally Christian society of upper-class Victorian England, it leads at times to a degree of sentimentality. The contrast between the acutely observed, narrow-minded, venal, and cynical English characters and their idealised Jewish counterparts may invite criticism, since the English characters come from the tradition of novel-writing seen in Trollope, whereas the Jewish ones conform to Henry James's comment on her fiction. In his review of Cross's *Life* James maintained that for her the novel 'was not primarily a picture of life . . . but a moralized fable, the last word of a philosophy endeavouring to teach by example'. This describes very well the Jewish part of *Daniel Deronda* even if it applies less directly to the English one.

What made George Eliot so sympathetic towards the Jews and Zionism? This was a question that puzzled many of her contemporaries who had never had any dealing with Jews and knew next to nothing of their history. They were interested in and admired the English part of the story and thought she should have concentrated on this and entitled her novel *Gwendolen Harleth* instead of *Daniel Deronda*. Certainly Gwendolen is the best drawn character; she is a lively young woman who wins our sympathy as she advances in self-knowledge. Like Maggie Tulliver, Romola, and Dorothea Brooke, she is brought up in a restricted environment, but in spite of a more nervous disposition than theirs, progresses with determination to confront the challenges that face her. Her marriage to Grandcourt, undertaken not for love but for position and to save her mother and sisters from destitution, exposes her to her husband's brutalizing treatment, harsher than anything these other heroines endure. Her love for Daniel Deronda, which promises her happiness and fulfilment, ends in bitter disappointment and a lonely future on which she embarks with courage. Mirah, who wins Daniel Deronda's love, is an insipid figure in comparison. It is Gwendolen's story which seized the attention of her contemporaries and still does with readers today.

Perhaps her failure to create in Deronda a character as well-drawn as Gwendolen accounts for the dissatisfaction felt by some readers. Leslie Stephen was only one of several critics who suggested that George Eliot was incapable of portraying a convincing male character, but this is not entirely true and does not meet the point about her portrait of Deronda, for Grandcourt himself is far more convincing. Virtuous characters are notoriously more difficult to depict than vicious ones and Deronda is a saintly figure who is too good to be true and yet he has to carry the main weight of what George Eliot sets out to do in her novel.

Deronda is the bridge between the English part of the novel and the Jewish one. He has been brought up to be an English gentleman, but then discovers his Jewish identity. Unlike Gwendolen, who marries unhappily to satisfy her mother's ambitions, he rejects his mother's desire to repudiate his Jewish ancestry and marries Mirah, the sister of Mordecai. But the question remains: Why give Deronda this importance? The answer is twofold. We have seen George Eliot's admiration for Spinoza and for St Theresa, a Christian saint but of Jewish blood, and this admiration for Jews grew as she came to know them and to assess their achievements in scholarship and spirituality. Her personal regard was strengthened by the friendship she and Lewes formed with Emanuel Deutsch, a German Jew who worked at the British Museum and who taught her Hebrew. Deutsch had visited Palestine and become a fervid Jewish nationalist and he convinced her of the justice of this cause and of the possibility of a national home for the Jews.

The second part of the answer to the question of why George Eliot incorporated the cause of Zionism in her novel was her conviction that the Jewish diaspora illustrated the Hegelian idea of history. This should not surprise us since Hegel's philosophy of history was a secularised version of the Biblical story. It saw history as the realisation of an immanent mind or spirit working in human affairs until its consummation in the nation-state. According to Hegel each nation has its own spirit which creates its peculiar history, but each nation-state is related to other states and in each the spirit will cause it to grow until the final consummation of a world-state. For George Eliot the Jews were only one example of this historical process, but they illustrated it more graphically than the so-called Christian society in which she lived. She would have approved of Coleridge's comment about his Jewish friend, Hyman Hurwitz, the professor of Hebrew in London University, and would have considered it appropriate to Emanuel Deutsch,

that a learned, unprejudiced, & yet strictly orthodox Jew may be much nearer in point of faith & religious principles to a learned & strictly *orthodox* Christian, of the Church of England, than many called Christians.[20]

The Christian teaching that self-realization is achieved by self-sacrifice finds its counterpart in Hegel in his notion of an opposition between the natural self and the non-self and his belief that the death of the natural self opens the way to the birth of a higher self. George Eliot had placed this at the centre of her previous novels, but in *Daniel Deronda* we see it illustrated not only in the lives of individuals but in the collective lives of the Jewish people. The destiny that shapes men's lives orders also the ends of society and nations. It is not necessary to be a Jew to accept this for all can identify with and serve a noble purpose and all can rise above the circumstances that hedge us in. It is true that Gwendolen seems to be a prisoner of her upbringing and because of this her tragic error in marrying Grandcourt should not be judged harshly. In Chapter XXIX Gwendolen discusses with Deronda the ethics of gambling and says, 'But you do admit that we can't help things . . . I mean that things are so in spite of us; we can't always help it that our gain is another's loss.' To which he replies, 'Clearly. Because of that, we should help it when we can.' Nevertheless, our desire to be free should not be at the expense of others if we can possibly avoid it, and this means that we may be called upon to sacrifice our own happiness for the good of others. At the end of Chapter LII Mordechai says to his sister, 'We must take our portion Mirah. It is there. On whose shoulder would we lay it, that we might be free?'

At the end of the novel Gwendolen achieves some freedom, but she pays a high price for it. Deronda and Mirah are brought up in circumstances that might easily have led them to renounce their Jewish identities but they choose to accept their destiny and leave England for an unknown future in the Holy Land. Their faith is in the future rather than any expectation of the coming of the Messiah for, like George Eliot's Jewish friends, they were liberal Jews who sat loosely to orthodox Judaism. There is self-sacrifice in Deronda's decision for he leaves behind the comfort of English society and the love of Gwendolen but his is hardly a tragic choice; there is little struggle and not a shadow of doubt in his mind as he makes his decision. F. R. Leavis goes so far as to describe this as self-indulgence rather than self-sacrifice and there is some truth in this. Most readers find Gwendolen the really tragic figure.

Daniel Deronda demonstrates once again the religion of humanity to which George Eliot subscribed. Without any belief in a personal God and without any hope in a future life, she acknowledged the moral imperative that lays upon us the obligation to serve others even at the cost of our own happiness. One can see her, as Spinoza was seen, either as a God-intoxicated person (although her God like his was impersonal) or as Lord Acton described her, an atheist. But even he declared of her novels that 'there are few works in literature whose influence is so ennobling'. Certainly her fiction had an enormous influence on the religious life and thought of the nineteenth century.

Her admirers included churchmen as well as freethinkers and writing in his most caustic vein to Leslie Stephen in 1902, Meredith recalled the gatherings when George Eliot and Lewes were at home to their friends, and described the 'comic scenes' with 'Bishops about the feet of an errant woman'.[21] This is manifestly unfair, but it witnesses to the regard she received from many who respected her religious opinions even when they did not share them and the acceptance of humanism by the establishment. Meredith was expressing the kind of criticism which became more frequent with a later generation. Commenting on this letter to her father, Virginia Woolf remarked that George Eliot 'became one of the butts for youth to laugh at, the convenient symbol of a group of serious people who were all guilty of the same idolatry and could be dismissed with the same scorn'.[22]

Even in her own lifetime there were those who considered her fiction too serious and overburdened with philosophy, and who preferred the more popular appeal of Dickens. A year after Dickens's death, Lewes wrote an essay in the *Fortnightly Review* for 1872, of which Forster in his *Life of Dickens* said 'the trick of studied depreciation was never carried so far or made so odious.' One can assume that George Eliot herself agreed with Lewes's criticism that

> sensations never passed into ideas. Dickens sees and feels, but the logic of feeling seems the only logic he can manage. Thought is strangely absent from his works. I do not suppose a single thoughtful remark on life or character could be found throughout the twenty volumes.

According to Lewes, Dickens created 'fun' rather than humour and his characters were mere puppets, all 'monstrous failures' who act upon reflex like decorticated frogs. But in this severe criticism of Dickens there is one interesting and suggestive remark. 'We do not turn over the pages', he writes, 'in search of thought, delicate psychological observation, grace of style, charm of composition; but we enjoy them like children at a play, laughing and crying at the images which pass before us.'

If George Eliot's novels are used as a yardstick then clearly Dickens's achievement falls below hers. But is the comparison a fair one? Certainly Lewes is right when he says that Dickens's characters are generally portrayed from the outside without the psychological analysis of motives and behaviour that George Eliot brings to her fiction. But then Dickens's novels are dramatic, and Lewes's remark about 'the images which pass before us' reminds us that they translate easily into television serials. We become absorbed in his stories and can understand the eager anticipation that awaited each instalment when his novels were first published in periodical form, and sympathise with those who appealed to their author not to let Little Nell die as *The Old Curiosity Shop* neared its end.

G. K. Chesterton and others have remarked on the fairy-story quality of Dickens's novels and Lewes was right to compare the pleasure they give us to the experience of our childhood reading. Many have linked this appeal to Dickens's own childhood and the trauma he suffered when he was put to work in the blacking factory. There can be no doubt of the humiliation and insecurity he felt at the time and his writing can easily be seen as both compensation and therapy. The fictional world he created is very much that of the child, with its fears, its swift transitions from laughter to tears and back again, its division of people into goodies and baddies. The most dominant image of his novels, sometimes actual but often only implied, is the cosy domesticity of the family gathered around the fireside, with the curtains drawn, and outside the cold, hostile world that awaits any forced to leave this happy circle; an image that haunts the mind of the child with its picture of happiness and its threat of insecurity.

One should not belittle this quality in Dickens's work. Some of our greatest literature is rooted in childhood memories as we see in Blake, Wordsworth, and also the early work of George Eliot. Some of the best novels tell the story of a hero or heroine who grows up, leaves home and undergoes great trials before a happy return. This is the archetypal story of the Prodigal Son which is itself a version of mankind's fall and redemption as recounted in the Bible. In a well-known essay in *The Dyer's Hand*, Auden sees *Pickwick Papers* as an example of this archetypal pattern, when he says that 'the real theme of *Pickwick Papers* . . . is the Fall of Man', and that Mr Pickwick falls not from innocence into sin, but 'from an innocent child into an innocent adult'. This, too, is the journey Blake's poetry makes from innocence through experience to another and more mature innocence; to a deeper and wiser happiness which those Church Fathers had in mind who spoke of a happy Fall.

The happy ending in fiction is often brought about by marriage and Christian writers from St Paul onwards have used it as an image of a heavenly union. But it can also come through death, and in *Pilgrim's Progress*, for instance, it comes at the end of the hero's earthly life and his arrival at the heavenly city. In Dickens we encounter death and marriage frequently and they are invariably given a religious dimension. His death scenes which offend or embarrass many modern readers are rarely tragic since death comes as a release from the sorrows of this world and brings the hope of a happier life beyond. Even his villains are left to be dealt with by a merciful providence.

Some have argued that Dickens's fiction shows little indication of real Christian belief, but those who use the comic nature of his work to support their argument forget that Christianity is a divine comedy. Others have conceded this but maintain that his religion is little different from secular humanism and, more plausibly, the suggestion is often made that Dickens invented the modern and sentimentalised Christmas with its dilution of the Christian message. But this has also been said about Prince Albert and with the same degree of exaggeration. It is always difficult to know whether Dickens changed public taste or whether he only reflected it; it can count either way that the first Christmas card and *A Christmas Carol* appeared in the same year. Certainly this novel has remained his best known and most popular work and has undoubtedly affected the way in which we celebrate the feast of Christmas today. This has led to the dubious charge that Dickens holds up everywhere the image of Christmas but attaches little importance to Easter. Since Dickens, unlike George Eliot, rarely reveals his deepest beliefs in an authorial voice, we have to let his novels speak for him here.

In *The Dickens World*, Humphry House makes a strong case for the view that Dickens everywhere upholds Christian ethics but is silent about Christian doctrine. House quotes several contemporary writers who objected to his portrayal of Christianity. But these were mostly Evangelicals in the Church of England and the Free Churches who resented the treatment they had received from Dickens. One can understand the resentment, for the figures of Mr Stiggins in *Pickwick Papers* and Chadband in *Bleak House* are far from flattering; they are religious frauds and show Dickens's hatred of cant, humbug and hypocrisy. With Pecksniff in *Martin Chuzzlewit* his dislike is turned against pharasaism and self-righteous scruples, and with Mrs Clennam in *Little Dorrit* against the neurotic sensibility of a woman whose self-hatred reduces her to invalidism and consigns the rest of mankind to perdition.

He is equally hostile to what he considers the extremes at the other end of the religious spectrum. Evangelicalism was followed in the Victorian period first by the Oxford Movement and then by the establishment of the Roman Catholic hierarchy in England. Dickens was in favour of Catholic emancipation and in *Barnaby*

Rudge showed sympathy for persecuted Catholics, but for Roman Catholicism itself he had nothing but the contempt of the xenophobic Protestant Englishman. When he visited Italy, unlike George Eliot, he found little to admire and considered the liturgy of the Roman church as mere superstition. He was disappointed in Rome and unmoved by the buildings and paintings he saw. His famous attack in 1850 on Millais's *The Carpenter's Shop* found its counterpart in his dislike of the Puseyites whom he regarded as the Pre-Raphaelites at prayer. The most notable example of this is Mrs Pardiggle in *Bleak House* who named her sons after the saints and martyrs of the primitive church, attended mattins at a very early hour and described the service as 'very prettily done'.

In middle age Dickens left the Church of England in which he had been brought up and attended a Unitarian chapel in Little Portland Street, where the minister, Edward Tagart, became a close friend. This change owed something to his visit to America during which he was lionized, especially in Boston, the centre of Unitarianism, where he met the famous preacher, William Ellery Channing, with whom he formed a warm friendship. In his *Dickens and Religion* Dennis Walder perceptively remarks that

> the common view was that Unitarianism and its offshoots were coldly rational, sterile; whereas in fact Unitarianism, especially the American variety, had by the 1840s, if not earlier, shuffled off the severe rationalism of its eighteenth-century forebears, such as Joseph Priestley, and had taken on a warmer, more Romantic look, derived from Kant and Goethe, Wordsworth, Coleridge and Carlyle.[23]

Although he may have found the Emersonian Transcendentalism of American Unitarianism attractive, it was probably its emphasis on the ethical teaching of Jesus rather than its theology that evoked Dickens's sympathy, and when the influence of the Broad Church and the growth of liberalism in the Church of England gathered force he was glad to return to the established church. The leaders of this movement published their views in *Essays and Reviews* (1860), which sought to accommodate Christian theology to contemporary science, philosophy and Biblical criticism. The book created a furore amongst churchmen and its reception was largely hostile, but Dickens welcomed its publication. Writing to his Swiss friend de Cerjat in 1863, he referred to the essays' 'timely suggestions' and his hope that 'the Church should not gradually shock and lose the more thoughtful and logical of human minds; but should be so gently and considerately yielding as to retain them, and through them, hundreds and thousands'.[24]

All that we have considered so far might suggest that Dickens's religion was a liberal kind of Christianity not all that far removed from Unitarianism, and it may come as a surprise to some to be told in an essay by Angus Wilson that 'Two of the most important foreign writers who were influenced by him, namely Dostoevsky and Tolstoy, both speak of him as 'that great Christian writer' '.[25] But there is, indeed, truth in this claim.

Where George Eliot's concern is with conscience and the struggle between right and wrong, Dickens's concern is with the struggle between good and evil. George Eliot's recourse to mythology gives her novels a universal quality, but her use of classical mythology can only illustrate the operation of a moral law. Her characters play their part in the historical process and affect the lives of their contemporaries and of generations still to come, but the religion of humanity is a religion of morality only and however noble this may be, it lacks any transcendental dimension. Dickens sees the struggle between good and evil worked out in his characters and is concerned with conduct, but his characters are also actors in a drama set in a context which is *sub specie aeternitatis*. His vision is a religious one and his novels can rightly be claimed as Christian.

His Christianity was certainly influenced by Carlyle and Dickens's sister-in-law told Carlyle that 'there was *no-one* for whom he had a higher reverence and admiration'. Carlyle's vision of human history as a great drama working towards its fulfilment in the lives of individuals was one that owed much to the Bible. For Dickens the drama was not over but belonged to the present and in this he was at one with George Eliot and those other Victorians who had been influenced by Carlyle. In the Bible the sins of one generation are visited upon the next and this is true of Dickens's novels where the fate of the characters is often governed by the actions of those who have gone before. The sense that human destiny depends upon outside forces is common to him and George Eliot and gives their work a depth and height which remove it from the world of Trollope and Thackeray. However, Dickens's novels take a religious view of life, a belief in eternity and a personal God which separates them from hers. It also removes them from the world of Carlyle, for in spite of the similarities there is an important difference between Dickens and Carlyle. Dickens has a concern for the little man and this gives his fiction a quality absent from Carlyle; a quality it shares with the films of Charlie Chaplin, who like Dickens experienced at first hand the life of London's poor. Dickens's novels and Chaplin's films both exhibit pathos, pity, and compassion, together with the comic; a combination which is at the centre of Christianity.

Dickens's compassion for the down-and-out, for the dispossessed, the handicapped, the failures, and the casualties in life's battles is one of the things that relate his fiction to that of Dostoevsky and Tolstoy. In no other of our novelists is there such a roll-call of characters who arouse our pity. But his novels arouse fear as well as pity; a feeling that we live in an unpredictable world in which misfortune can overtake us overnight. This is felt especially by his child characters. Sometimes the change of fortune is upwards rather than down, as with Pip in *Great Expectations*, but even here the change is not what it seems and brings evil rather than good. Often, as with Oliver Twist, the turns of fortune depend upon coincidence. This device is used frequently by Dickens and has met with hostile criticism, although it is found in Shakespeare and other great writers and is what one might expect in a world where the supernatural and miraculous have a place.

The coincidences in Dickens are often the means of giving his stories a happy ending. The difference between tragedy and comedy, in life as in literature, is often the result of chance, but this is forgotten by those who contend that Dickens's main fault as a novelist is that he contrives to bring about a happy ending against all the odds. The argument that comedy is the most appropriate literary form for the expression of Christian belief has met with the retort that Dickens achieves his happy endings too easily and at little cost to his protagonists. Even when his characters meet an early death, it is argued, they are promised the reward of eternal bliss. Certainly there seems to be a preoccupation with sentimentalised death-bed scenes on Dickens's part, the most famous (or infamous) being those of Little Nell and Jo, the crossing-sweeper in *Bleak House*, but here he was reflecting contemporary taste. The Victorians loved their elaborate funerals with hired mourners and the extravagant sculpture which still adorns their cemeteries. The same taste, or lack of it, can be found in the popular paintings and poetry of the period and while we may not share it, at least it shows a readiness to contemplate death rather than our own reluctance to discuss it at all.

To argue that his characters achieve happiness in death too easily, and what the Burial Service in the *Book of Common Prayer* calls the 'sure and certain hope of the Resurrection to eternal life', without undergoing great suffering, is to disregard all the evidence to the contrary. Little Nell, leading her old father on their journeys, Little Dorrit, waiting upon her ungrateful father in the Marshalsea, Lucie Manette, who nurses her old father back to sanity after his release from the Bastille, are all in their devoted service as close to Antigone as George Eliot's Romola. Lady Dedlock is a spirited woman who pays dearly for her youthful indiscretion and after great suffering meets her end with dignity and courage. She bears comparison with George Eliot's Gwendolen Harleth, even if one has to admit that she is unusual amongst Dickens's women characters, who are generally more docile and self-abasing. As for his heroes, many of them, and one thinks at once of David Copperfield, Nicholas Nickleby, and Pip, achieve happiness only after undergoing great trials and many misfortunes.

The novel which displays self-sacrifice most strikingly is, of course, *A Tale of Two Cities*, which has often been seen as the embodiment of Dickens's Christian faith, although some have suggested that *Little Dorrit* or *Our Mutual Friend* illustrate this more clearly.[26] Angus Wilson in *The World of Charles Dickens* notes in all the last novels a more explicit Christian theme:

> Renunciation, redemption, resurrection – we are in these last novels well into the world of Tolstoy in his late works, or in that of Dostoevsky's *Crime and Punishment*. . . . It is essentially a Christian New Testament world, with transcendental overtones. Sidney Carton, who actually gives his life, should surely preach the most Christian of all sermons.[27]

At the end of the novel when Carton faces the guillotine we hear a voice, whether Carton's or the author's is not clear, reciting the opening sentences of the Burial Service in the *Book of Common Prayer*, verses which are taken from St John's gospel: 'I am the Resurrection and the Life, saith the Lord: he that believeth in me, though he were dead, yet shall he live: and whosoever liveth and believeth in me shall never die.'

Knowing that Dickens admired Carlyle so much leads one to ask whether this compromises the Christian content of *A Tale of Two Cities*. When he was writing his novel Dickens was in close touch with Carlyle who arranged for a cart-load of books on the French Revolution to be sent to him from the London Library. It was Carlyle's *The French Revolution* which inspired him to write his novel and in the Preface he pays tribute to 'the philosophy of Mr Carlyle's wonderful book'. Carlyle's account of the French Revolution is not a sober record of the historical facts. His vision of human history as a struggle between good and evil, led him to see the events in France as another act in the unfolding story of human destiny. The struggle takes place in every human heart and because of men's wickedness there are many setbacks, but he believed that in spite of this good would triumph in the end. Indeed, even evil itself produces good, just as in *Faust* Goethe's Mephistopheles describes himself as 'Ein Theil von jener Kraft || Die stets das Bose will und stets das Gute Schafft. ' (A part of that power which always produces good, while constantly devising evil.) So Carlyle viewed the conflict between the *ancien régime* and the revolutionaries as a clash between demonic forces, destructive in their purposes and yet giving birth to a new order. He regarded the Reign of Terror not simply as a struggle between ordinary good and bad men, but as a Titanic battle,

> the black desperate battle of Men against their Whole Condition and Environment, – a battle, alas, withal, against the Sin and Darkness that was in themselves as in others; This is the Reign of Terror. . . . Despair pushed far enough, . . . becomes a kind of genuine hope again.[28]

For Carlyle, history is moved on by great men and at times he writes in terms that almost anticipate Nietzsche's notion of the Superman. The tragedy of the French Revolution for him was that no great leader emerged from the Terror. He regarded Napoleon as a flawed hero, one who had great qualities but who was partly a charlatan. Nevertheless, he believed that from the excesses of the Revolution good would come and he does not blame those who brought it about since they were faced with corruption, greed, and injustice. The lesson for his countrymen is not to condemn the revolutionaries, but to remedy the injustices of their own society.

The framework of Dickens's story owes much to Carlyle. The famous opening of the novel, 'It was the best of times, it was the worst of times . . . it was the spring of hope, it was the winter of despair.', lists the ambiguities which underlie Carlyle's vision of history. The last chapter, too, looks as Carlyle did, to the Apocalypse of St John. Carlyle's view of history was a variant of the Biblical narrative and he describes the events of recent times, just as the radicals of the seventeenth and eighteenth centuries had done, in terms that recall Armageddon, the final battle between good and evil. Dickens gives this vision even greater power when at the end of *A Tale of Two Cities* and before his execution, Sidney Carton sees the New Jerusalem established on earth and the battle won:

> I see a beautiful city and a brilliant people rising from this abyss,

and, in their struggles to be truly free, in their triumphs and defeats, through long, long years to come, I see the evil of this time and of the previous time of which this is the natural birth, gradually making expiation for itself, and wearing out.

Nevertheless, there are significant differences between Dickens's version of the Revolution and Carlyle's account. The story of Sidney Carton, the hero of the novel, is not the story of a great man according to Carlyle's notion of greatness. Carlyle's hero is Napoleon, who for all his faults had a certain grandeur because he had an *idea*, that prerequisite of greatness according to Carlyle. Sidney Carton acted as he did not because of any driving intellectual or political idea; his motive was love, a belief in personal relationships and a regard for family life. He would hardly have been included in Carlyle's hall of fame. Dickens's hero played an inconspicuous part in the momentous events of the Revolution, but his creator shows him taking up his cross and giving his life for another. The message this gives us is clear: if we were all prepared to follow this pattern of self-sacrificial love it would do more to bring about the New Jerusalem than the great men in whom Carlyle placed his faith. Dickens believed in the little man; with George Eliot he thought the heroic virtues, especially heroic self-sacrifice, could be found in the humblest setting. His novels, and especially the later ones, reveal his belief that this is best seen in those who seek to make their lives an imitation of Christ.

The impact of Dickens as a Christian writer was lessened by his anti-clericalism. There had been a long literary tradition, stretching from Chaucer to Trollope, which satirised the church for failing to live up to its own gospel, but in spite of this Dickens was treated harshly by the many Christian periodicals that flourished in the Victorian period. His satire was mostly at the expense of both extremes of the religious spectrum and these were united in their dislike of the middle ground on which he stood. Moreover, he had a general distrust of those who made a profession of the ministry of the church and shared St Paul's belief that we have our treasures in earthen vessels. Of the many clerical figures who appear in his pages the only really sympathetic character is the Rev Frank Milvey in *Our Mutual Friend*, who sat loosely to the Thirty-Nine Articles and could not bring himself to accept the possibility of eternal damnation. This may have been suggested to Dickens by the dismissal, not many years before, of F. D. Maurice from his chair at Kings College, London, for refusing to subscribe to such a doctrine. Writing to de Cerjat on 5 October 1864, he expresses his despair at the state of the church:

> As to the Church, my friend, I am sick of it. The spectacle
> presented by the indecent squabbles of priests of most
> denominations, and the exemplary unfairness and rancour with
> which they conduct their differences, utterly repel me.... How
> our sublime and so-different Christian religion is to be
> administered in the future I cannot pretend to say ... the Master
> of the New Testament put out of sight, and the rage and fury
> almost always turning on the letter of obscure parts of the Old
> Testament ... these things cannot last. The Church that is to
> have its part in the coming time must be a more Christian one,
> with less arbitrary pretensions and a stronger hold upon the
> mantle of our Saviour, as He walked and talked upon this earth.[29]

As the Victorian period advanced Dickens found a growing
convergence between his own religion and the liberal opinions
coming from the Church of England. His influence on theology
would have been slight and indirect, of course, but his fiction
popularised the changes in religious thought that were coming
about. Certainly a great deal of religion today approximates more
and more to his idea of Christianity. His emphasis on ethics rather
than doctrine, on the New Testament rather than the Old, on God's
mercy rather than his wrath, on ecumenism rather than authority,
are all in accordance with the religious sensibility of today.

IV

Tennyson and Browning

Most discussions of Tennyson's religion concentrate on *In Memoriam* and they are probably right to do so if they are concerned with his public image and his influence on his contemporaries. But to regard it as the key to his religious beliefs is to overlook the importance of the rest of his poetry and especially the poems he composed when writing the first of the pieces which grew into *In Memoriam*.

Arthur Hallam died in Vienna in September 1833, and his body was brought back by sea from Trieste and buried on 3 January 1834, in the parish church of Clevedon, overlooking the Bristol Channel. Most readers think of *In Memoriam*, or at least some sections of it, as the expression of Tennyson's grief at the loss of his friend, but in a conversation he had later when he read the poem to James Knowles, he qualified this by saying:

> There is more about myself in 'Ulysses', which was written under the sense of loss and that all had gone by, but that still life must be fought out to the end. It was more written with the feeling of his loss upon me than many poems in *In Memoriam*.[1]

For the initial reaction to his bereavement, then, we should look not at *In Memoriam* but at 'Ulysses', which was written in October 1833. Tennyson mentioned the *Odyssey* and Dante's *Inferno* as the sources of his poem and both relate how Ulysses after his return home set out again on his final voyage. Tennyson's voyager desires to escape the monotony of existence and to seek new adventures, coupled with a desire for death and after this a new life which he will share with his old comrades:

for my purpose holds
To sail beyond the sunset, and the baths
Of all the western stars, until I die.
It may be that the gulfs will wash us down:
It may be we shall touch the Happy Isles,
And see the great Achilles, whom we knew. (*P. T.*, 565)[2]

The imagery of 'Ulysses' is perhaps deliberately ambiguous, for it leaves one wondering whether the speaker's faint hope of a reunion with his friends in a future life is as strong as the simple desire for death and whether this reflects Tennyson's own state of mind.

In Memoriam was not published until 1850, but already in 1833 Tennyson had begun to write 'the earliest jottings of the 'Elegies' ' which started him off on its composition. We know this from the *Memoir* Hallam Tennyson published in 1897, after his father's death, but the *Memoir* is wrong when it claims that 'The Two Voices' 'was also begun under the cloud of his overwhelming sorrow after the death of Arthur Hallam'.[3] Tennyson may have altered 'The Two Voices' after news of his friend's death reached him in October 1833, for the poem was not published until 1842, but we now know that Tennyson had started it before Hallam's death.[4] There are verses in *In Memoriam* similar to parts of 'The Two Voices', but 'the conflict in a soul between Faith and Scepticism', which Hallam Tennyson refers to, takes on a despairing note which differs from the larger hope expressed in *In Memoriam* and leads to serious thoughts of suicide rather than a simple longing for death.

We should not assume that the speaker in a poem represents the poet himself, but the persistence of certain themes, among them a preoccupation with death, in so many poems Tennyson wrote or started in the 1830s, suggests a confessional element that can hardly be ignored. This is hinted at in the title 'Supposed Confessions of a Second-Rate Sensitive Mind Not in Unity with Itself', a poem published in the 1830 volume, where Tennyson makes little attempt to deny that the narrator's voice is his own. Here he looks back to the lost religious certitude of his childhood, which would comfort him now as he faces the reality of death:

How sweet to have a common faith!
To hold a common scorn of death!
And at a burial to hear
The creaking cords which wound and eat
Into my human heart, whene'er
Earth goes to earth, with grief, not fear,
With hopeful grief, were passing sweet! (*P. T.*, 198)

The poem ends without this consolation; only with doubt and perplexity.

The conflict in his mind becomes a duologue in 'The Two Voices', which is a more considerable poem with a greater range of ideas and deeper feelings than those in 'Supposed Confessions'. One of the voices in the poem is that of a tempter, who observes that although the Bible sets man over nature, he is insignificant in the infinitude of the universe. If this is true of mankind, the life of the individual must be even less important. The voice speaks of one recently dead who now is nothing 'But long disquiet merged in rest'. The narrator retorts that the human mind has an idea of perfection unknown in nature which must be an intimation of immortality:

> That type of Perfect in his mind
> In Nature can he nowhere find.
> He sows himself on every wind.
>
> He seems to hear a Heavenly Friend,
> And through thick veils to apprehend
> A labour working to an end.

The argument ranges over pre-existence, the transmigration of souls, reincarnation, the possibility of escape from despair by engaging 'In some good, not in mine own', and mystical states 'Such as no language may declare', but none of these dismisses the insistent temptation the narrator feels to end his own life. The tempter reminds him in a scornful voice that 'it is the Sabbath morn' and the narrator opens the window to hear the church bells and see people making their way to worship. The scene recalls the end of 'The Ancient Mariner' and the narrator here is also moved by a feeling of love in his heart and by a new and hitherto silent voice, 'Like an Aeolian harp'

> So heavenly toned, that in that hour
> From out my sullen heart a power
> Broke, like the rainbow from the shower,
>
> To feel, although no tongue can prove,
> That every cloud that spreads above
> And veileth love, itself is love.

This has its counterpart in *In Memoriam* which wisely omits the picture of the husband with his wife and child as they walk to church, a subject favoured by the more sentimental painters of the Victorian period:

> The prudent partner of his blood
> Leaned on him, faithful, gentle, good,
> Wearing the rose of womanhood.
>
> And in their double love secure,
> The little maiden walked demure,
> Pacing with downward eyelids pure.

Far darker images are taken up in the poems that followed. This is seen in 'Locksley Hall', probably written in 1837-8 and influenced by his unhappy courtship of Rosa Baring, the daughter of a wealthy family who were neighbours of the Tennysons in Lincolnshire. Whatever the facts of the relationship (some have written about it as an engagement, others as merely a flirtation), when it was over Tennyson felt hurt and humiliated.

He had a fierce pride which compensated for an inner diffidence and his rejected love quickly turned to dislike. After writing some dozen or more poems either to or about Rosa, he ended with a wounding criticism of her shallowness:

A hand displayed with many a little art;
An eye that glances on her neighbour's dress;
A foot too often shown for my regard;
An angel's form – a waiting-woman's heart;
A perfect-featured face, expressionless,
Insipid, as the Queen upon a card.[5]

One critic has connected 'Locksley Hall' with Teufelsdröckh's unfortunate love affair in *Sartor Resartus*[7], and while there is little evidence to support any direct influence, the poem marks a spiritual crisis in Tennyson's life not unlike the one Carlyle experienced. The hero of the poem, who has much of Tennyson in his make-up, attempts to give an Everlasting Yea to life, but his confidence falters and he remains a minor Hamlet-like figure whose capacity for action is always threatened by self-doubt.

Although a personal poem, 'Locksley Hall' reflects the spirit of the age. Britain was now entering a period of prosperity and the Reform Bill heralded a mood of political optimism, which was accompanied by the pursuit of wealth and material gain. Jilted by his cousin Amy, who is pressed into marriage with a richer man, the hero turns his back on the competitive values of the time and looks for an escape to the Far East or a tropical island, where a simpler life may be found. This desire for a new life is similar to the discontent and restlessness of 'Ulysses' and not unlike the challenge which faces Sir Bedivere when left alone on the death of the king in 'Morte D'Arthur', a poem written at about the same time as 'Locksley Hall'. In the end the hero of 'Locksley Hall' dismisses this dream of escape as a retreat from his responsibilities and looks to the future and its challenge:

Not in vain the distance beacons. Forward, forward
    let us range,
Let the great world spin for ever down the ringing
    grooves of change.
Thro' the shadow of the globe we sweep into the

younger day:
Better fifty years of Europe than a cycle of Cathay.
Even so, he feels he can help his country best by taking up the white man's burden and serving the Empire abroad; a duty that will last until universal peace has been established.

The notion of finding fulfilment in a just war, seen in 'The Two Voices' and repeated in 'Locksley Hall', takes on a more jingoistic and even an hysterical note in *Maud*. Although Tennyson claimed that *Maud* was in no way autobiographical, his denial is clearly disingenuous. The hero of the poem may be an overwrought version of his own personality, but the feelings and motives that drive him, and the concerns that fill his mind, are those found in 'The Two Voices' and 'Locksley Hall' and which preoccupied Tennyson himself when he was writing the poem. Although not published until 1855, we know that he started it soon after the death of Hallam and that like *In Memoriam* it was produced by a process of accretion. Hallam Tennyson's account of the poem, although not meant to encourage any biographical speculation, reveals the similarities between Tennyson and his fictional character:

> This poem of *Maud or the Madness* is a little *Hamlet*, the history of a morbid, poetic soul, under the blighting influence of a recklessly speculative age. He is the heir of madness, an egoist with the makings of a cynic, raised to a pure and holy love which elevates his whole nature, passing from the height of triumph to the lowest depth of misery, driven into madness by the loss of her whom he has loved, and, when he has at length passed through the fiery furnace, and has recovered his reason, giving himself up to work for the good of mankind, through the unselfishness born of a great passion.[8]

Not all of this is literally true of Tennyson and there are plenty of literary influences that coloured the poem, but some of it is very close to his own situation.[9] His love had been rejected because his lack of means made him an unsuitable match. His father was a man of violent temper and at times mentally unstable and had become an alcoholic after losing his inheritance. Tennyson, too, suffered from the melancholia which afflicted several of his family and had a fear of the epilepsy which his father, his uncle Charles, and his cousin George had all inherited. He himself had several emotional breakdowns and undertook the 'water-cure' at various establishments in the 1840s. It is little wonder that like the hero of *Maud* he experienced fear, depression, and disappointment, and the feeling that the times were out of joint. Some readers of *Maud* have thought the hero's fear and hatred hysterical, especially when they extend to the whole of life, but the ruthless struggle for survival he discerns in nature is no different from that in *In Memoriam*:

> For nature is one with rapine, a harm no preacher
> can heal;
> The Mayfly is torn by the swallow, the sparrow
> speared by the shrike,
> And the whole little wood where I sit is a world of
> plunder and prey. (P. T. , 1049)

Hallam Tennyson reassures his readers that after the hero has 'passed through the fiery furnace, and has recovered his reason', he devotes himself to the service of mankind, but for many the end of the poem becomes a glorification of war. Yet this, too, is to mistake its meaning. *Maud* tells the story of a young man whose freedom is frustrated by social and family constraints: his father has committed suicide because of a business failure brought about by Maud's father and brother, and she is being forced to marry a rich young lord. When her brother discovers her with the hero in the garden at midnight, they fight a duel in which the brother is killed. Maud dies and the hero descends into madness, but recovers his sanity by recalling Maud's love for him and resolves to atone for his crime by going to the Crimea to fight in what he regards as a just war. This crude outline makes the poem seem no better than many of the romantic novels of the time, but a closer reading suggests that that it is nearer to one of the Arthurian legends. The war at the end of the poem becomes a crusade against the commercial greed and exploitation of an acquisitive society and at the same time a means of regeneration for the hero. Already in Part 1 where he hears Maud singing there is a scene which recalls stories of knights being charged by their ladies with some great enterprise:

> She is singing an air that is known to me,
> A passionate ballad gallant and gay,
>
> Singing of men that in battle array,
> Ready in heart and ready in hand,
> March with banner and bugle and fife
> To the death for their native land.
>
> Singing of Death, and of Honour that cannot die,
> Till I well could weep for a time so sordid and mean,
> And myself so languid and base. (P. T. , 1052)

This belief in a righteous war as a means of personal and social regeneration is found in some of Tennyson's other poems such as 'Riflemen Form!', 'Jack Tar', and 'Rifle Clubs', but what distinguishes *Maud* is the vehemence of its violence, despair, fear, and madness. Just as Dickens had an obsessional need to give public readings of his work, and especially *Oliver Twist* with its mixture of childhood innocence and violence, so Tennyson had a compulsive desire to read *Maud*, as an outlet for the feelings that ran deep in his forceful character.

The poems discussed so far show the two poles of Tennyson's personality: the fear and insecurity which dogged him throughout his life, even when he had found fame and success, and his attempt to overcome these by becoming a poet of heroic action rather than thought. These two impulses found expression in the two great poetic achievements which occupied so many years of his life, *In Memoriam* and the *Idylls of the King*. Both of these transmuted his own personal concerns into poems with a public and national significance. *In Memoriam* moved from doubt to an affirmation of faith which expressed the feelings and met the needs of the great majority of his countrymen, while the *Idylls of the King* held up Arthur as the ideal man, an example which could deliver them from the greed, selfishness, and corruption which threatened their society.

In turning what had been private into a subject of public interest Tennyson gave his poems a Christian foundation. An enthusiastic review written by Gladstone for the *Quarterly Review* (October 1859) declared that Arthur was not only a national but a Christian hero, and that the poem 'raises the character and the hopes of the age and the country which produced it'.[10] In a famous declaration which has haunted Tennyson studies ever since it was first made, T. S. Eliot maintained that *In Memoriam* 'is not religious because of the quality of its faith, but because of the quality of its doubt',[11] but even Eliot acknowledged that it was welcomed by its Victorian readers as a message of hope.

The *Idylls of the King* had their origin in 'Morte d'Arthur', which Tennyson wrote after receiving news of Hallam's death, and the portrait of King Arthur owes much to Tennyson's memory of his friend. Milton had seriously considered Arthur, 'Begirt with British and Armoric Knights' as an alternative to the Biblical story which he chose as the subject of *Paradise Lost* and it may be that this inspired Tennyson to embark on what he originally planned as an epic poem in twelve books and which he thought would take him twenty years to complete. 'Morte d'Arthur' was published in 1842 and received some hostile reviews. It was one of these by John Sterling in the *Quarterly Review* in September 1842, which especially undermined Tennyson's confidence in a poem which harked back to the legends of a legendary king and his knights, who might be thought to have little relevance to the nineteenth century. In spite of this he felt that such criticism failed to recognise the universality of the Arthurian legend which for him held up an ideal vision of what society was meant to be.

Instead of the twenty years he thought the poem would take, the task remained with him for the rest of his life and was one he returned to again and again as he altered or added to what he had written. Instead of the epic he had planned, with Arthur as the hero throughout, it developed into a series of poems about the individual knights of the Round Table, with Arthur as the central but rather shadowy figure who linked them together. After the first poem, Tennyson reflected on the project and it was not until 1859 that he published further instalments. These received warm praise from the public and many of the critics. One has to realise, as Kathleen Tillotson has pointed out, that King Arthur was a subject unfamiliar to most in the nineteenth century and that Tennyson had to create the taste an appreciation of the poems demanded. Gratified by the growing recognition of his achievement, Tennyson pressed on with what Hallam Tennyson described as 'a more or less perfected scheme' of how the whole poem might be shaped; a claim that seems more conjecture than fact. After another ten years Tennyson published in 1869 four more instalments: 'The Coming of Arthur', 'The Holy Grail', 'Pelleas and Ettare', and 'The Passing of Arthur', this last consisting of the original 'Morte d'Arthur' but with a new beginning and a new end which gave an account of the last great battle. The final version in twelve books, with all the revisions and rearrangement of the preceding instalments, was not published until 1885, more than fifty years after it was first conceived.

The reception of the poem by the general public was increasingly enthusiastic, but the reviewers and critics were mixed in their reactions. Some agreed with Gladstone, but others were less certain and some outspokenly hostile. Swinburne protested that Tennyson had distorted the historical element in Malory's account by making 'the ideal cuckold his type of the ideal man'. Tennyson had dedicated the earlier of the poems to the memory of the Prince Consort, who had recently died, and his wife persuaded him to write an Epilogue to the completed work addressed to the Queen. Swinburne mischievously suggested that an alternative title for the poems should be 'The Morte d'Albert, or Idylls of the Prince Consort'. Elizabeth Barrett Browning thought there were 'exquisite things' in the *Idylls* but that the general effect was devoid of vitality. This was the judgement of many, including George Eliot and Carlyle who, writing in 1867 declared the poems to have 'finely elaborated execution' but 'an inward perfection of vacancy' and complained that they treated their readers as 'so very like infants, though the lollipops were so superlative'.[12]

What many critics failed to realise was that Tennyson was neither telling a historical story nor constructing an allegory in which all the details had an exact meaning. He was irritated by enquiries such as that from the Bishop of Ripon, who asked him whether the three Queens who accompanied Arthur on his last voyage, represented Faith, Hope, and Charity, to which he replied, 'They mean that and they do not. They are three of the noblest of women. They are also those three Graces, but they are much more. I hate to be tied down to say, 'This means that and they do not'.'

Nevertheless, he gave Hallam Tennyson a much more positive account of what his intention had been. Although he accused some critics of explaining 'some things too allegorically', he admitted that 'there is an allegorical or perhaps rather a parabolic drift in the poem'. Quoting his father in the *Memoir* Hallam writes,

'The whole is the dream of a man . . . ruined by one sin . . . It is not the history of one man or of one generation but of a whole cycle of generations'. . . My father said on his eightieth birthday, 'My meaning in the *Idylls of the King* was spiritual. I took the legendary stories of the Round Table as illustrations. I intended Arthur to represent the Ideal Soul of Man coming into contact with the warring elements of the flesh.'

Hallam Tennyson tells us that his father found justification for this idealisation of Arthur in Joseph of Exeter, who had declared, 'The old world knows not his peer, nor will the future show us his equal'. But he adds, 'my father thought that perhaps he had not made the real humanity of the King sufficiently clear in his epilogue; so he insisted in 1891, as his last correction, 'Ideal manhood closed in real man,' '

Tennyson often spoke of Arthur as a kind of second Adam, who in the words of Newman's famous hymn, 'to the fight and to the rescue came'. But Newman, of course, was writing of Jesus and one wonders what Tennyson had in mind when he described

Arthur in this way. He avoids identifying Arthur with Christ and even the initial suggestion that Arthur is a supernatural being whose return will usher in the reign of God gives way as the poem develops. Indeed, there is deep disappointment as the bright hopes fade. The adultery of Lancelot and Guinevere is the central example of the infidelities that spread through the other *Idylls* and is symbolic of the forces that bring down Arthur's court. The king himself is revealed as more like the first Adam, the representative of a fallen race, than the restorer of a new age.

This reflects Tennyson's pessimism which grew with the years and had its effect on the poem. In one of the best of the discussions of the *Idylls*, J. H. Buckley[13] shows how the image of musical harmony runs through the poem and how at the Last Tournament this harmony has been disrupted and silence begun to fall:

It is the little rift within the lute,
That by and by will make the music mute,
And ever widening slowly silence all.

Buckley might have added that Tennyson was drawing here on a long tradition which he would have met, if not elsewhere, in Milton's 'At a Solemn Music', which brings together Plato's discourse on harmony in the *Republic* and St John's vision in Revelation of the redeemed singing a 'new song before the throne' of God (Rev. 14, 3-4). This tradition taught that mankind was once part of this harmony, but now sin has silenced the music until Milton's prayer is answered:

That we on Earth with undiscording voice
May rightly answer that melodious noise;
As once we did, till disproportion'd sin
Broke the fair music that all creatures made
To their great Lord.

The hope of the earlier *Idylls* for a new age of justice and peace gives way to a fear that society will revert to the animal world from which it emerged; a vision as bleak as Lear's. The fresh springtime which heralded the coming of Arthur has changed to the bleak midwinter which sees his passing. Bedivere, who even at this solemn and sad time disobeys his King, watches as the dying Arthur is carried away on the barge accompanied by the three wailing Queens:

But when that sad moan had past for evermore,
The stillness of the dead world's winter dawn
Amazed him, and he groaned, 'The King is gone.'

Tennyson never completed the poem with the expected 'Return

of the King' and Bedivere is left to contemplate the future only
with doubt and anxiety:

'He comes again; but - if he comes no more – ?'

The poem ends not with the return of Arthur, but with the resumption
of the old order in which things are left much as they were. The last
line, 'And the new sun rose bringing the new year', may seem to
suggest a new beginning, but one is left only with the old
uncertainties.

However pessimistic the end of the *Idylls* may be, Tennyson
embarked on his project with a sense of dedication. It was meant
to form a major part of his poetic achievement and one which
demanded the almost religious vocation Milton and Wordsworth
brought to *Paradise Lost* and *The Prelude*. In his lecture on the
Hero as Poet, delivered in 1840, Carlyle had advanced the notion
that poetry was best suited of all human achievements to penetrate
the appearances of things and apprehend ultimate reality, because
reality itself is a cosmic harmony:

> The Greeks fabled of Sphere-Harmonies; it was the feeling they
> had of the inner structure of Nature; that the soul of all her
> voices and utterances was perfect music. Poetry, therefore, we will
> call *musical Thought*. The poet is he who *thinks* in that manner.[14]

In his lecture on the Hero as a Man of Letters he declares that the
poet is 'our most important modern person' and follows Fichte in
calling the poet a Priest who views the world 'as a vesture for the
'Divine Idea' ', one who guides it 'like a sacred Pillar of Fire, in
its dark pilgrimage through the waste of Time'.

This is the language of Romanticism and the last of these
phrases, which recalls Coleridge's *Biographia Literaria*, reminds
us that Tennyson owed much to Coleridge and his followers; not
only his views on poetry, but those on religion as well. At
Cambridge Tennyson had belonged to the Apostles, whose members
had included Hallam and others who remained his life-long friends.
A leading light in the Apostles was F. D. Maurice, a devoted disciple
of Coleridge, who in 1828, when Tennyson was still an
undergraduate, had advanced the high idea of the poet as a religious
visionary:

> The mind of a poet of the highest order is the most perfect mind
> that can belong to man . . . his mind is a mirror which catches and
> images the whole scheme and working of the world. . . He cannot
> be untrue, for it is his high calling to interpret those universal truths
> which exist on earth only in the forms of his creation.[15]

Encouraged by his fellow Apostles, Tennyson came to see himself in this way, not only in his youth, but increasingly throughout his life, as a reviewer of *The Memoir* recognised:

> No poet, perhaps, has ever come so close to the type of the Seer-prophet of the Old Testament ... none was ever so penetrated through and through as he was with the sense of the divine source of the gift of poetry. . . . He told me that this sense was *almost awful* to him in its intensity, because it made him feel as a priest ... whose every word must be consecrated to the service of Him who had touched his lips with the fire of heaven ... to speak in God's name to his age ... all through his life as a poet, Tennyson felt that he had a divine purpose to follow.[16]

This is of the greatest importance for understanding Tennyson's poetry and his religion, and like Wordsworth, he saw these as intimately related. Indeed, the two men had much in common. Both of them felt religious experience more important than theology, but were ready to accept the support for their beliefs theology could provide. Tennyson, like Wordsworth, was led to accept an idealist philosophy, for like Wordsworth he thought this explained the trance-like states he experienced in which he felt sensory objects existed only in his own mind and that he existed in the mind of God. James Knowles in his *Nineteenth Century* article tells us that 'He was disposed to doubt the real existence of a material world, and frequently adduced the infinite divisibility of matter as a difficulty which made it unthinkable', and added, 'He leaned to the idealism of Berkeley.' Tennyson recounts the nature of these experiences in the early lines entitled 'Armageddon':

> I was a part of the Unchangeable,
> A scintillation of Eternal Mind,

but gives it a more sophisticated and philosophical form in the better-known 'Flower in the crannied wall' which was not published until 1869:

> Flower in the crannied wall,
> I pluck you out of the crannies,
> I hold you here, root and all, in my hand,
> Little flower – but *if* I could understand
> What you are, root and all, and all in all,
> I should know what God and man is.

One writer[17] has linked these lines to the philosophical theory known as the doctrine of internal relation which holds that a truth about, say, Mr Gladsone, is a truth about the whole universe, since every thing or person is logically related to every other thing or person; a doctrine advanced by Hegel and his British disciples.

This is possible, for although Tennyson never professed much interest in philosophical speculation, he was more widely read than is often thought and his membership of the Metaphysical Society (although he attended only eleven times in ten years) might have led to his hearing such subjects discussed. It is more likely, however, that he was drawing on the old tradition already referred to and found in 'At a Solemn Music', where Milton ends his poem with the image of mankind forming part of the heavenly harmony:

O may we soon again renew that Song,
And keep in tune with Heav'n, till God ere long
To his celestial concert us unite.

One of Milton's editors observes that 'Milton's audience was familiar with the principle that the universe from sand-grain to sun and from grass-blade to seraph, is one mighty, sweet-toned instrument'.[18] Kindred to this is the equally traditional notion of the Great Chain of Being, which Tennyson may have had in mind in the lines he gives to Arthur, who at his passing asks for the prayers of Bedivere:

If thou shouldst never see my face again,
Pray for my soul. More things are wrought by prayer
Than this world dreams of . . .
For so the whole round earth is every way
Bound by gold chains about the feet of God.

Writing of the *Idylls of the King*, Hallam Tennyson tells us in his *Memoir* that 'the completed poem, regarded as a whole, gives his [Tennyson's] innermost being more fully, though not more truly than *In Memoriam* '. This may seem surprising, but *In Memoriam* was written alongside the earlier *Idylls* and both were written over several years. It would be surprising, therefore, if the two poems did not interact on each other, even if there is little formal similarity between them. The *Idylls* do not form the epic Tennyson had in mind when he started to write them and he denied that Arthur was the national figure an epic demands. What they consist of is a series of tableaux, behind which stands the shadowy figure of Arthur whose mission is thwarted by the shortcomings of his companions. *In Memoriam* can be seen as an elegy belonging to the same tradition as Milton's 'Lycidas', and the first provisional and private title he gave it was *Fragments of an Elegy*, but it is too long for the proper elegiac form. Although different in many respects from Pope's *Essay on Man*, it expatiates freely 'o'er all this scene of man' and in places comes close to being a theodicy. It is none of this, however, which brings the two poems together, but the idealised figure of King Arthur in the one and of Arthur Hallam in the other; and the two were closely identified in Tennyson's imagination

Hallam's death was a great personal blow for Tennyson. Hallam had given him friendship and a growing confidence in his own worth as a poet, and Hallam's engagement to his sister had brought him into a wider family circle. His loss was deeply felt by Tennyson and his bereavement a heavy burden to carry. As T. S. Eliot recognised, *In Memoriam* can be seen as the diary of how Tennyson sustained and recovered from his loss.[19] Although its composition was spread over seventeen years, the poem covers only three, each punctuated by a Christmas and each marking a stage in the process of recovery, and all suggesting the healing power of time and nature. In spite of the way it was composed, the poem has a certain unity and Tennyson indicated the nature of this when he told Knowles that *In Memoriam* was

> rather the cry of the whole human race than mine. In the poem altogether private grief swells out into thought of, and hope for, the whole world. It begins with a funeral and ends with a marriage – begins with a death and ends in promise of new life – a sort of Divine Comedy, cheerful at the close. It is a very impersonal poem as well as personal.[20]

This is in accordance with the elegiac tradition. 'Lycidas', for instance, is more than a lament for the death of Edward King; it is as much about Milton as King and the personal element is incorporated in a larger public theme. 'Lycidas' like *In Memoriam* calls for Christian dedication and ends hopefully with the assurance that Lycidas is not dead and that 'all the Saints above' 'wipe the tears for ever from his eyes'. The note of personal loss in *In Memoriam* is more insistent, for Tennyson's relation to Hallam was far closer than Milton's to King. The flowers which Milton calls to be strewn on 'the Laureate Hearse where Lycid lies' sound like a literary tribute rather than the real ones of *In Memoriam*. Before Tennyson realised that Hallam's body was buried in the church and not the churchyard at Clevedon, he wrote the lines:

> 'Tis well; 'tis something; we may stand
> Where he in English earth is laid,
> And from his ashes may be made
> The violet of his native land. (XVIII)

This was more than a conventional sentiment, for Clevedon was well known for its violets, and when the railways came they were taken by special train to the London markets and regular supplies made to the Queen. Similarly the family gatherings and the landscapes of the country around Somersby are described with detailed realism. Above all, no-one can doubt the anguish of Tennyson's grief nor fail to realise that the larger questions of faith in the poem originate in what was felt as a personal calamity.

The ambiguity with which Tennyson leaves the reader at the end of 'Ulysses' is scarcely felt here. The longing for reunion with his dead friend in a future life is a constant theme running through the poem, but the feelings of doubt and despair, disturbing as they are, hardly allow room for thoughts of self-destruction. In his conversation with James Knowles, Tennyson said of *In Memoriam*, 'It's too hopeful this poem, more than I am myself.' But when he turned his private grief into a poem which addressed larger and public issues he did his best to moderate his melancholy and doubt, not by suppressing them altogether but by treating them as part of a process which led to belief. This is why he described his poem as a Divine Comedy, for it led from an Inferno of desolation, through a Purgatory of recovery, to a Paradiso of a new life, symbolised in the wedding of his sister Cecilia to his friend Edmund Lushington.

In Memoriam is both a religious poem in the sense that it relates its author's personal journey from doubt to faith, and also a theological and philosophical one which sets this in a framework of metaphysical thought. Jowett, who was a close friend of the poet, understood these two sides of Tennyson's achievement. In the Recollections he gave Hallam Tennyson for his *Memoir* he wrote, 'It was in the spirit of an old saint or mystic, and not of a modern rationalist, that Tennyson habitually thought and felt about the nature of Christ'.[21] But Jowett also told Tennyson in a conversation that mentioned *In Memoriam*, 'Your poetry has *an element of philosophy more to be considered than any regular philosophy in England.* It is almost too much impregnated with philosophy, yet this to some minds will be its greatest charm.'[22]

The philosophy Jowett had in mind, 'one more to be considered than any regular philosophy in England', was undoubtedly Hegel's. Jowett was one of the leading exponents of Hegel in Britain and in 1858 he sent Tennyson a parcel of books containing Hegel's *Philosophy of History*, 'which', he wrote in the accompanying letter, 'is just 'the increasing purpose that through the ages runs' buried under a heap of categories. If you care to look at it will you turn to the pages I have marked at the beginning?'[23] It is doubtful whether Tennyson ever took up this suggestion, for writing in 1874 to Benjamin Paul Blood, an American philosopher, to thank him for sending him a copy of his *The Anaesthetic Revelation* and the *Gist of Philosophy*, he gives us some idea of the extent and limits of his philosophical reading:

> But what need you my praise, when you have secured the approval of him who is by report our greatest, or one of our greatest Hegelians [Jowett], whereas I, though I have a gleam of Kant have never turned a page of Hegel, all that I know of him having come to me obiter, and obscurely through the talk of others; nor have I ever vigorously delivered myself to dialectics.[24]

Tennyson tells Blood that he has never had any revelations 'through anaesthetics' but admits to having had ' 'a kind of waking trance'. . . from boyhood when I have been alone'.

It is not difficult to see why Jowett should have thought of Tennyson as a Hegelian, for there are several passages in *In Memoriam* and his other poems which seem to support this. These all relate to Hegel's philosophy of history and this is hardly surprising since the notion of evolution and progress, which is the central feature of this philosophy, was common in Victorian thought. *In Memoriam* was written before Darwin's *Origins of Species* appeared, but Tennyson had read Lyell's *Principles of Geology* and Chambers's *The Vestiges of Creation* and had a very good grasp of contemporary science. Although the geological and zoological investigations of the scientists raised questions for religion, and especially the authority of the Scriptures, it was still possible to see evolution as part of a divine purpose and not, as Darwin was later to suggest, merely chance. But this divine purpose still remained a matter of faith when faced with the findings of science and so Tennyson is forced to ask the fundamental questions:

> Are God and Nature then at strife,
> That Nature lends such evil dreams?
> So careful of the type she seems,
> So careless of the single life;
>
> 'So careful of the type?' but no.
> From scarped cliff and quarried stone
> She cries, 'A thousand types are gone:
> I care for nothing, all shall go.

What of man, nature's 'last work, who seem'd so fair'? Is man's faith in a God of love, and in love as 'Creation's final law', a wild fancy, since man seems no more than the product of a natural order 'red in tooth and claw'? Tennyson's answer is put tentatively in the form of a question: how did we come to have the idea that our life transcends the natural order and that we shall survive physical dissolution? May our highest hopes and aspirations themselves point to a supernatural origin?

> The wish, that of the living whole
> No life may fail beyond the grave,
> Derives it not from what we have
> The likest God within the soul?

If there is something of the divine in man, then perhaps we can 'trust that somehow good /Will be the final goal of ill'. Evolution may be the story not of the descent of man but of his ascent. Man may be 'the herald of a higher race', by which Tennyson meant man raised to the fulfilment of his potential.

This seems close to Hegel's notion that religion is really the history of man's developing thought about the Absolute. For Hegel, God becomes realised in man, as man becomes conscious of God in himself. In *The Philosophy of Religion* Hegel speaks of our knowing God through revelation, but the revelation is an on-going process which will be consummated when this unity of consciousness has been fully achieved. This raised the problem of whether the Incarnation is the central event in human history or merely one event in a history that goes back to before man existed. Is the Incarnation a full revelation of God in Christ or is revelation a continuing process? *In Memoriam* speaks of 'the one far-off divine event to which the whole creation moves', but does not say whether this is the end of the evolutionary process or the coming of the millenium. Tennyson would have thought of them as the same, as the raising up of man to the perfection which was God's purpose.

Tennyson rightly insisted that *In Memoriam* was a poem and not a philosophical treatise, but it certainly advances philosophical ideas, some of which he may have owed not to Hegel directly but to Jowett, the most Hegelian churchman at the time. Jowett believed that God's self-revelation to mankind was continuous and not restricted to the Bible or the church. In the essay 'On the Interpretation of Scripture' which he contributed to *Essays and Reviews* (the volume which caused so much controversy and brought some of its authors before the Court of Arches on a charge of heresy), Jowett argued that 'the Interpreter of Scripture . . . feels that the growth of revelation which he traces in the Old and New Testament is a part of a larger whole extending over the earth and reaching to another world'. Then quoting 'Locksley Hall', he says that to the careful reader of the Bible 'the sense of 'the increasing purpose which through the ages ran' is present to him'.

It is likely, however, that Tennyson owed far more to F. D. Maurice, a friend ever since his Cambridge days, whom Tennyson once described as 'the truest Christian he knew in the world', and who was Hallam Tennyson's godfather.[25] Maurice's dismissal from his chair at King's College, London, for refusing to accept the doctrine of everlasting damnation, angered Tennyson and caused him to write the polished Horatian ode, the opening lines of which invited Maurice to visit the poet's home at Freshwater:

> Should eighty-thousand college councils
> Thunder 'Anathema', friend, at you;
> Should all our churchmen foam in spite
> At you, so careful of the right,
> Yet one lay-hearth would give you welcome;
> (Take it and come) to the Isle of Wight.

Maurice believed that God lives in man and by what the Cambridge Platonists called 'the candle of the Lord', provides a light which illumines every man's mind. In *The Kingdom of Christ* he defended the Quaker belief in this Inner Light and the possibility that we may apprehend God in what is loosely described as mystical experience. But he also believed that God is transcendent as well as immanent and criticised those like Hegel whose teaching was ambiguous on the point:

> The Parmenidean 'One', the 'Being' of Spinoza, the 'Absolute' of Hegel, if they are only conceptions of the intellects of those men, are horrible ghastly self-contradictions. If they are recognitions by the intellect, of that which the intellect cannot conceive, of a God who must make Himself known, they are blessed and glorious testimonies to truths which are not theirs but universal.

In other words their doctrines were either novel and false, or true and unoriginal. Moreover, Hegel's God was an impersonal force that imposed itself upon the human mind rather than the living God of the Bible, a personal God who cares for every individual as well as the progress of mankind.

For Maurice the world was independent of a perceiving mind. His son writes that for Maurice, 'Every discovery made by Mr Darwin or Mr Huxley was a discovery of a truth which had been true in itself, ages before it was discovered ... He believed the thing itself to be, when discovered, just in so far as it was true, a revelation to man by God whether the discoverer accepted it in that sense or not.'[26] It follows from this that the whole history of mankind and not only science, is a progressive revelation, including 'the emancipation of women, the abolition of slavery, the gradual substitution of law for arbitrary will'. One might ask where this leaves the Incarnation. Running throughout Maurice's writings is his conviction that the revelation of God in Christ is complete, but although complete it still works out its purposes and seeks to develop man to his full potential as a child of God. Christ is the mirror in which man can see himself perfected; a rather Platonic notion but one supported in the Gospel of St John and the Epistles of St Paul. The perfection of man for Maurice and for Tennyson is 'the one far off divine event to which the whole creation moves'.

Is this a matter of knowledge or only faith? Maurice believed that we can know God, but that this knowledge is knowledge by acquaintance; it is not notional but the knowledge we speak of when we say we know a person. We know God not through the speculative intellect but as the response to a person whom we love and trust. Hegel, although he never contended that religion was a matter of reason alone but depended upon the feeling of God's 'immediacy', nevertheless taught that religion would give way to philosophy as the fullest way of apprehending the Absolute. Maurice, on the other hand, taught that God is known to us as a person, to whom we respond through our emotions, our moral consciousness, our reason, and our will; religion is not talk about God, but believing in a living Presence. This did not mean that Maurice cared little for doctrine or the church. He believed that the Bible when properly interpreted and the on-going life of the church provided a body of doctrine which could satisfy the intellect and guide men in the conduct of their affairs, but that reason alone without revelation was insufficient. But, as we have seen, revelation for him meant that no branch of the church, nor indeed the church itself, had a monopoly of the truth. The church is an anticipation of the kingdom of Christ, but it has not yet reached that fullness of truth and life that will be realised only with the coming of the kingdom.

This then is the theological background of *In Memoriam*. It did not give Tennyson the systematic theology of the kind Thomism gave Dante, but it informs the whole poem and is seen in the Prologue which was written when the rest had been completed, and especially in the following stanzas where the divine initiative and man's response meet:

Strong Son of god, Immortal Love,
Whom we, that have not seen thy face,
By faith, and and faith alone embrace,

Believing where we cannot prove;
Thou seemest human and divine,
The highest, holiest manhood, thou:
Our wills are ours, to make them thine.

And taking in the image of the heavenly harmony which has been lost, he sees it found again in the fulfilment of God's purpose:

Let knowledge grow from more to more,
But more of reverence in us dwell;
That mind and soul, according well,
May make one music as before,

But vaster.

In reading *In Memoriam* one is conscious that behind this confident ending lie other forces: his insecurity, his fear of death and physical dissolution, his sense of alienation in an indifferent universe. He had told James Knowles that his poem was more hopeful than he himself was and this was undoubtedly true. It may have declared that 'There lives more faith in honest doubt, / Believe me , than in half the creeds', but the doubt Tennyson had to wrestle with was not primarily a matter of the intellect, but a product of a melancholic and at times morbid personality. Carlyle, who knew Tennyson well and had spent long hours talking to him or sitting in silence as they smoked their pipes, understood this, and writing to Emerson he made the perceptive remark that Tennyson carried about inside himself 'a bit of chaos'.

The nightmare of chaos runs through a good deal of Tennyson's poetry and counters the vision of a harmonious cosmos which the rest of it aspires to. But the nightmare became more insistent as he grew older. Nothing brings this out more clearly than a comparison of the two 'Locksley Hall' poems. The earlier poem ends by looking forward to the future with optimistic hope. In 'Locksley Hall, Sixty Years After', written when Tennyson himself was aged seventy-seven, the youthful narrator of the earlier poem is now an old man of eighty. As he looks back he sees little to justify his youthful confidence. Man still seems to be at the cross-roads; in one direction lies the promise of progress, order and cosmos, the other points to a descent into chaos. This has been the choice throughout the ages:

Chaos, Cosmos! Cosmos, Chaos! who can tell how all will end?
Read the wide world's annals, you, and take their wisdom for
your friend.

Gladstone, who reviewed the later poem in *The Nineteenth Century*, was dismayed by what he considered its reactionary opinions, but he foresaw the future less accurately than Tennyson. The optimistic belief in progress of the Victorian period, whether it manifested itself in unbridled capitalism or later in Marxism, is now seen to be ill-founded. Tennyson does not deny the need for progress, but realises that it is hard to achieve:

> Forward then, but still remember how the course of Time
> will swerve,
> Crook and turn upon itself in many a backward streaming
> curve.

Evolution, greeted with a degree of fear in the earlier decades of the century, had later become a popular slogan, synonymous with progress, but Tennyson warns against its facile use:

> Is there evil but on earth? or pain in every peopled sphere?
> Well be grateful for the sounding watchword 'Evolution'
> here,
> Evolution ever climbing after some ideal good,
> And reversion ever dragging Evolution in the mud.

As for the dream of a world at peace, this grew ever less likely as the century advanced:

> . . . who can fancy warless men?
> Warless? war will die out then. Will it ever? Late or soon?
> Can it, till this outworn earth be dead as yon dead world
> the moon?
> Man is what he has always been, half an ape and half an angel.

In Memoriam offered consolation and hope to many in his and later generations with its belief in a religion based on the primacy of human experience; a religion which accepted doubt as an element in that experience and welcomed new knowledge as part of God's revelation. But the darker side of his poetry anticipated concerns which Victorian optimism ignored or kept at bay and of which many were scarcely aware. These have become all too familiar to us in the present century: the fear of over-population; of commercial competition and exploitation; of world wars which could bring about a new barbarism; the angst of men living in a post-religious society and what seems an indifferent universe. Tennyson was impatient with contemporary churchmen who failed to realise the importance of these concerns and who preferred to quarrel about points of ritual, such as candles, vestments, and incense. *In Memoriam* for its part endeavoured to meet the fears and answer the deep-seated needs of his contemporaries, even if the assurance it offered was something he himself hoped for rather than fully shared.

Tennyson's reputation has grown in our day and even his standing as a religious poet has enjoyed something of a revival; T. S. Eliot's curt dismissal of the theology of *In Memoriam* no longer seems so impressive to a generation that shares Tennyson's suspicion of dogma. The same can hardly be said of Browning. It is difficult now to understand the immense following he had at the end of his life and the respect given to his poetry in the years immediately after his death, when Browning societies studied his work as that of a philosopher and sage. Indeed, few today know his poetry apart from the anthology pieces such as 'The Pied Piper of Hamelin', 'Home Thoughts from Abroad', and 'How they Brought the Good News from Ghent to Aix'. More people are interested in his life than his poetry and many of these still derive their knowledge of Browning from *The Barretts of Wimpole Street*, which depicted him as the dashing, romantic lover whose runaway marriage to Elizabeth Barrett brought them unqualified happiness.

More recent biographies have shown this to be a false account of their relationship, for although their love remained constant throughout their marriage, Browning, after his wife's death, said he felt as if they had both been walking across a torrent on a straw. The play showed nothing of this and hardly mentions his poetry except for the comment about its supposedly impenetrable difficulty; something that amused the audience but was hardly likely to increase his readership. Even worse, the picture of Browning it presented suggested that his poetry was the expression of the muscular Christianity found in many of the English public schools of his day. This view of Browning was not new for even Gerard Manley Hopkins, who might have known better, said that Browning was like 'a man bouncing up from the table with his mouth full of bread and cheese and saying he meant to stand no blasted nonsense'.

An even more damaging accusation was made by W. B. Yeats, who said that Browning's poetry was boring. In a letter to Florence Farr, he told the story of how a woman 'brought a prosperous love-affair to an end by reading Browning to the poor man in the middle of the night'. Few poets, not even Yeats, would pass such a test, but Browning would have sympathised with the man for he, too, agreed that life was more important than art. Equally amusing but more penetrating, was Oscar Wilde's observation that 'Meredith is a prose Browning, and so is Browning', for this recognised that Browning's subject-matter was similar to that of the Victorian novel. Although Browning wrote superb lyrics, much of his poetry is dramatic or narrative, and closer to Victorian fiction than to the narrative poetry of, say, Tennyson's *Idylls*. The comparison with

Meredith is also suggestive, for Meredith's novels and Browning's poetry often present us with characters facing critical decisions. The writer who comes to mind even more readily than Meredith is George Eliot. Central to Browning's dramatic poems and her novels is the importance of moral choice, of duty obeyed or overcome by self-interest, the importance of love as the mainspring of human behaviour, and above all, the inexorability of the events that follow the choices we make. Both writers, although they have great descriptive powers, rely more on psychological analysis and an acute understanding of human behaviour to tell their stories.

It is strange then that George Eliot's present popularity is not matched by a similar admiration for Browning; stranger still that he is rarely credited with the virtual invention of the dramatic monologue, a form taken up and used with great effect by T. S. Eliot and one that especially commends itself to modern taste. Browning's skilful exploitation of the form allowed him to focus on a character who stands at a critical crossroads in his life, where his whole future will be decided. The events leading up to this point are cleverly conveyed in what the speaker reveals about himself, often without his being aware of this. Browning's dramatic monologues are not simply soliloquies; at times we seem to be listening to one side of a conversation in which we can guess the other side. In some poems this conversation is a dialogue between the speaker and his *alter ego*. A brilliant example of this is 'Two in the Campagna' in which two lovers revisit the countryside outside Rome and the speaker is bringing himself to tell the girl that he no longer loves her. As the poem proceeds we realise he is not speaking to the girl but conducting a debate within himself, asking himself questions, and trying to analyse the ambivalence of his own feelings:

I would that you were all to me,
You that are just so much, no more.
Nor yours nor mine, – nor slave nor free!
Where does the fault lie? What the core
Of the wound, since wound must be?

The poem ends with the speaker's recognition that the relationship has followed a familiar pattern; one which shows him incapable of really giving or receiving love, of committing himself to another, of making a decision.

Some have complained that Browning's dramatic monologues, especially when concerned with fundamental questions of belief, attempt to dodge the issue and to hide behind a persona. Even his wife thought he should abandon this dramatic technique and speak out in his own voice. But quite apart from his poetic gifts, which were best suited to this form, we see on reflection that his beliefs were best expressed dramatically. Browning believed that faith was the same as commitment and his dramatic monologues present us with characters who at a critical moment reveal the nature of their commitment or their inability to make it. This is central in Browning's religion; it governs his approach to life and extends even beyond religious and moral imperatives. His insistence on the need for one to commit oneself, to act even without a full knowledge of the consequences or the moral implications, is put vividly at the end of 'The Statue and the Bust'. Two lovers, in sixteenth-century Florence, failed to run away together, not because of any moral scruples (though the lady was married) but through failure of nerve, convention, and finally sheer apathy. For Browning their inaction was a greater sin than the action they contemplated but failed to achieve:

> The counter our lovers staked was lost
> As surely as if it were lawful coin:
> And the sin I impute to each frustrate ghost
> Is, the unlit lamp and the ungirt loin,
> Though the end in sight was a vice, I say.
> You of the virtue, (we issue join)
> How strive you? *De te, fabula*!

It does not follow from the importance Browning and George Eliot gave to moral decisions and their consequences that their religious views were the same. At one time Browning was seen as a defender of Christianity, but this was followed by the suggestion that his beliefs were derived from German philosophy and the Higher Criticism and far removed from any orthodox faith. The argument implies a change in his beliefs over the years and certainly it would not be true of the time when he wrote *Christmas Eve and Easter Day* which was published in 1850.

The poem falls into three parts. The first recounts a visit on Christmas Eve to Mount Zion chapel, a scene well known to Browning, for as a boy he had attended the nonconformist chapel in Camberwell, where his parents were members. Although he had been bored by the services and repelled by the ugliness of the surroundings, this had given him an intimate knowledge of the Bible. His visit to Mount Zion Chapel in the poem is made on a wet and stormy evening, but he is glad to cut it short and go outside again:

> I very soon had enough of it.
> The hot smell and the human noises,
> And my neighbour's coat, the greasy cuff of it.

Even so, he is fascinated by the odd assortment of people who make up the congregation,

> the fat weary woman,
> Panting and bewildered, down-clapping
> Her umbrella with a mighty report
>   and
> the many tattered
> Little old-faced, peaking, sister-turned-mother
> Of the sickly babe she tried to smother
> Somehow up, with its spotted face.

But his fascination turns to distaste at

> the pig-of-lead like pressure
> Of the preaching-man's immense stupidity,
> As he poured his doctrine forth, full measure,
> To meet his audience's avidity.

He leaves the chapel in doubt not only at what he has heard, but at all attempts to convince the unbeliever:

> Each method abundantly convincing,
> As I say, to those convinced before,
> But scarce to be swallowed without wincing.

He leaves and outside again, as he feels the wind and rain on his face, he reflects on the Romantic belief he had held as a young man that God is manifested in nature and how this had passed into the conviction that human love provides a surer foundation for religion. There comes flooding into his mind the realisation that God must be personal since love belongs to persons and not natural objects, and then as he ponders this, God himself appears to him:

> I saw the back of Him, no more –
> He had left the chapel, then, as I.

With this comes the sense that because God is love he, too, had been in the chapel to fulfil his promise to be 'Where two or three should meet and pray'. Those whom he had despised were after all the friends of God.

The scene changes dramatically as he is translated to the Basilica of St Peter's in Rome, where high Mass is being celebrated. The splendour and beauty of worship carry him away, although his Protestant sensibility is revolted by the 'posturings and petticoatings' of the ritual, and eventually he finds himself left 'outside the door'. Even so, he recognises that here too there is love, 'I see the error; but above / The scope of error, see the love'.

The scene changes again, this time to a lecture-hall in a German university ('It may be Göttingen, – most likely'), and he is cautious now not to let prejudice overcome his charity:

how I suffer to slip
The chance of joining in fellowship
With any that call themselves His friends,
As these folk do.

Nevertheless, the description of the German professor expounding the Higher Criticism is an even more satirical account than that at Mount Zion chapel and St Peter's. The professor's sermon explains in Hegelian terms the notion of truth as a balance between contradictions and the idea of Christianity being more important than its historicity. The speaker asks for the evidence of the 'Myth of Christ',

Demanding from the evidence,
(Since plainly no such life was liveable)
How these phenomena should class?
Whether 'twere best opine Christ was,
Or never was at all, or whether
He was and was not, both together –
It matters little for the name,
So the idea be left the same.

This comic portrait is modelled on Strauss or perhaps, even more likely, on Feuerbach, for as the professor develops his theme the figure of Christ when subjected to this kind of treatment becomes Man, but 'a right true man, however'.

Here the poet feels no divine command to enter into a sympathetic understanding with what he has heard. The nonconformist and the Catholic may have poisoned the pure air of divine truth with their doctrines; 'Truth's atmosphere may grow mephitic / when Papist struggles with dissenter'. But the Higher Critic has left a vacuum, an 'exhausted air-bell', in which it is impossible to breathe and live. God is not an intellectual abstraction known only to the intellect; he is a living person who declares himself to the whole soul of man. The notion advanced by the professor that God is a projection of man's own mind, that God is only man himself, leaves the poet not knowing whether to laugh or cry:

Surely for this I may praise you, my brother!
Will you take the praise in tears or laughter.

Finally the poet finds himself back in the little chapel where his journey began, sitting on the same bench; the vision he has been given of 'the raree-show of Peter's successor' and 'the laboratory of the Professor' remains, even if it came to him as he dozed through the minister's sermon. This is where he belongs and while others may come to God in different ways he is content to accept this as his own. 'I choose here! / The giving out of the hymn reclaims me'. And so he joins with the queer assortment of humanity which surrounds him as they sing

> The last five verses of the third section
> Of the seventeenth hymn in Whitfield's collection,
> To conclude with the doxology.

None of this can possibly be construed as a defence of the Higher Criticism; on the contrary, the satirical portrait of the Göttingen professor can only be seen as hostile. Some argue that while this may be so, Browning's beliefs changed with the years and led to an increasing scepticism. Certainly Browning's views changed, but the charge of scepticism needs severe qualification and to bring in 'Bishop Blougram's Apology' at this point, as some have done, is to misread the poem. Even to see it as an attack on the Roman Catholic church is to misunderstand it. 'Bishop Blougram's Apology' was first published in *Men and Women* in 1855 and Browning freely admitted that he took as his model Cardinal Wiseman, who became the first Archbishop of Westminster and head of the Roman Catholic church in England when the Roman Catholic hierarchy was restored in 1850.

Wiseman was a clever, worldly, and sophisticated ecclesiastic and the poem was seen by some as a satirical portrait, even perhaps as a sardonic commentary on Roman Catholicism itself. But neither of these satisfactorily explains what Browning intended. Sir Charles Gavan Duffy, himself a Roman Catholic, records in his memoirs a conversation he had with the poet, in which Browning said, 'Certainly I intended it for Cardinal Wiseman, but I don't consider it a satire, there is nothing hostile about it', and how Browning denied any antipathy to the Roman church. Wiseman himself reviewed the poem in *The Rambler* in January 1856 and though he thought it could have a harmful effect on some readers, was generous in praising its merits and not at all offended.

In talking to the young rationalist journalist Gigadibs, who has come to interview him, the Bishop uses the cynical argument that he has made the best of both worlds, this one and the next. His faith promises immortality, but even if he is mistaken in this, he still enjoys power, acclaim and wealth in this life. As for Gigadibs, his doubt promises nothing hereafter and gives him little here. Why then should not Gigadibs make the gamble of faith rather than of doubt? We do not know how far the Bishop accepts this argument himself or whether he uses it simply as a debating tactic. Browning tells us that 'Blougram, he believed, say, half he spoke'. But behind any cynicism there is the fact that faith must necessarily be a wager, something attested by Pascal and others of far deeper spirituality than the Bishop, and we meet again Browning's conviction that we must all make the decision of what to believe. Faith is not knowledge and cannot be proved by reason alone, but neither can scepticism be proved; doubt itself is only another kind of faith.

The Bishop does not always argue at a cynical level, for he reaches profound depths and sublime heights; his argument at times shows a nobler belief than his own worldliness would suggest. This, of course, is true of all of us, who have to admit that our beliefs are better than our conduct, but few of us could match the Bishop's eloquence. How can one rest in unbelief?, he asks, as he takes the argument beyond the scope of rational testimony:

Just when we are safest, there's a sunset touch,
A fancy from a flower-bell, some-one's death,
A chorus-ending from Euripides, –
And that's enough for fifty hopes and fears.

It is the paradoxical nature of human experience, with its depths and heights, its mixture of good and evil, the doubt and belief that haunt all of us, with which the Bishop confronts the shallow and naive rationalism of Gigadibs. In lines which caught the imagination of Graham Greene and provided an epigraph for his novels, the Bishop points out the contradictoriness of human experience and behaviour:

Our interest's on the dangerous edge of things.
The honest thief, the tender murderer,
The superstitious atheist, demireps
That love and save their souls in new French books –
We watch while these in equilibrium keep
The giddy line midway.

The Bishop confounds Gigadib's confident scepticism and the end of the poem finds the journalist in a state of doubt about his doubt. He is so shaken by the interview in which he had thought to demolish the Bishop's belief by rational argument that he gives up journalism and decides to emigrate to Australia. At this point Browning drops the form of the dramatic monologue and speaks in his own voice, wishing Gigadibs well in his new country:

there I hope,
By this time he has tested his first plough,
And studied his last chapter of St. John.

Some have found this ending enigmatic, but the obvious suggestion is that Gigadibs should set about finding a faith by reading the end of St John's Gospel, for it is here that the risen Christ appears to his disciples and gives them the command, 'Feed my sheep'. The suggestion is surely that Gigadibs would find a faith not by speculation but in doing the will of God.

The last chapter of St John's Gospel contains an account of the mistaken impression the disciples had gained from something Jesus had said, that John alone among their number would not die, but would still be alive at the second coming of their Lord. This would have caught Browning's attention and in 1864 he published 'A Death in the Desert', which recounts how John, when lying on his death-bed, thinks of future generations who never knew Christ on earth. They may doubt the truth of his record of Christ's life and death and may feel that divine love cannot be proved by the testimony of their own hearts; they may argue that they see in the figure of Christ only what they find best in themselves.

This, of course, is what the Higher Criticism argued. Strauss had regarded Christianity as a construct of the mythopoeic imagination and Feuerbach saw Jesus as no longer an historical figure but the highest in human nature which man had abstracted from himself. Then in 1863 appeared Renan's *Vie de Jésus* which gave an even less sympathetic account of the origins of Christianity. Strauss had questioned whether John the evangelist was the same person as the apostle John (a question still debated today), but Renan while accepting their identity makes the serious accusation that the Fourth Gospel is based on deceit. His approach is less that of the German followers of Hegel and more that of Voltaire. He charges Jesus and his disciples, and especially John, with fraud over the miracles, pointing out, for instance, that the story of the raising of Lazarus is found only in John's Gospel and in none of the others. He maintains that John is a liar and accuses him of self-aggrandisement, of depicting himself as Christ's favourite disciple and more important than St Peter, and of inventing episodes not found in the other Gospels to support this picture. John's greatest lie, he argues, is pretending to be present at the Cross when Jesus gives his mother into his charge. This is not recorded by the other evangelists who only mention the presence of women there. In support of his allegations Renan turns to St Mark's Gospel which tells us that the disciples fled when Jesus was arrested and in particular how a young man in a linen cloak threw this off and ran away naked when the soldiers tried to arrest him. Scholars today believe that this young man was John Mark, the evangelist himself, but when Browning wrote his poem it was assumed that he was St John the author of the first gospel and so Renan thought he had confirmation of his thesis.

The Rev. Llewellyn Davies stated at a meeting of the London Browning Society in 1887 that Browning wrote 'A Death in the Desert' many years before Renan's book appeared.[27] There is no evidence to support this and in a letter to Isa Blagden in 1863 Browning tells her that he has already read *Vie de Jésus*, and it has generally been assumed that Browning had in mind not only Strauss and possibly Bruno Bauer (who had questioned the historicity of John's gospel in the 1840s) but Renan as well. Indeed, the poem was seen as a counter argument to Renan. A more recent essay, however, claims that 'A Death in the Desert', far from being an attack on Renan shows Browning's agreement with his interpretation of St John's Gospel.

This essay forms a chapter in Elinor Shaffer's *Kubla Khan and the Fall of Jerusalem* in which she argues that German Biblical criticism gave literature a new mythological schema and moved it towards becoming a new secular religion. A good deal of her book is devoted to Coleridge whose 'late perception', she writes, 'that Christian European civilization rests upon a lie is never far from Browning, and both poets learned this from the higher criticism, and learned too how to transform it into something like a virtue, indeed, into a philosophical method.'[28]

The crux of Dr Shaffer's argument concerning 'A Death in the Desert' is that John confesses in the poem that he was not at the Crucifixion, whereas he declares in his Gospel that he was. From this it is a simple step to conclude that Browning accepted the contention that John was a liar and that his religious beliefs coincided with those of Renan. But the lines from the poem she quotes do not support anything of the kind. John says:

Even a torchlight and a noise,
The sudden Roman faces, violent hands
And fear of what the Jews might do! Just that,
And it is written, 'I forsook and fled',
There was my trial and it ended thus.

The torchlight and other features in these lines make it clear that they refer not to the Crucifixion, but to the events in the Garden of

Gethsemane. There is nothing contradictory in John's acknowledgement of cowardice at the arrest of Jesus and the recovery of courage which brought about his presence at the Cross. The phrase 'And it is written' refers, of course, to the account in St Mark's Gospel, but even if Browning believed the young man in the linen cloak to be St John, this does not throw doubt on the evangelist's claim to have been at the Crucifixion.

Nothing else in the poem challenges John's veracity and there is nothing left to support Dr Shaffer's argument; the traditional view of the poem as an answer to Strauss and Renan remains. Archbishop William Temple, a recognised authority on St John's Gospel, was convinced of its veracity and wrote in the Introduction to his *Readings in St John's Gospel*, 'It is then vital to St John's purpose that the events which he records should be actual events', and he even declared Browning's poem to be 'the most penetrating interpretation of St John that exists in the English language'.

What then is Browning's 'interpretation of St John'? John lying on his death-bed is concerned that once he has gone there will be no-one left to give personal testimony to the events he has witnessed, for he is an old man who has outlived all the other disciples. What can be the ground of belief for future generations? They may deny not only the existence of Jesus, but of John as well, and may treat the written records as unreliable or corrupt. They may argue that men see in the figure of Christ only what they aspire to themselves. In other words, man's idea of God may be only anthropomorphic. John's answer is that this is spiritual blindness. To find love in ourselves and yet deny it to ultimate reality is spiritual arrogance. This takes up the argument Browning had deployed in 'Saul', where David rouses the king from deep depression by telling him of a vision he has been given in which he realises that the love of God must be like his own love for the king, but infinitely greater. The highest we can see and do at the natural level is what we find in human nature, so that the *summum bonum* must be like ourselves, but far higher.

Another argument found in 'A Death in the Desert' concerns miracles. John realises that future generations will be puzzled by the Gospel miracles and ask why such miracles no longer happen. This, of course, is a question asked by Browning with the hindsight of modern science and with sceptics like Voltaire and Hume in mind. Browning's St John answers the question by recourse to the Platonic notion that the truth can best be conveyed to simple minds by allegory and myth, which can be left behind by the more sophisticated. Miracles were necessary in earlier times but may be dispensed with in later ages. Browning is here interpreting St John's Gospel in the light of the Biblical studies of his own day, but he goes beyond these to anticipate more recent scholarship. Unlike the synoptic Gospels, St John's develops a theology indebted to Greek thought and the Platonic tradition. C. H. Dodd in *The Founder of Christianity* suggests that it was probably intended for readers at Ephesus or some other Greek city and that 'The 'set pieces' of the Fourth Gospel, composed with great art, are comparable with the Greek philosophical dialogue'. Browning's close reading of the Bible combined with his poetic sensibility delivered him from the sterile debates of his own day about the Biblical texts and led him to appreciate what a modern scholar such as Dodd goes on to say:

> This use of symbolism is fundamentally poetic. It is not a flight into fantasy. It means that the facts are being viewed in depth, not superficially. This must be taken into account when we consider the stories of miracles which have so large a place in some parts of the gospels. In the Fourth Gospel these are treated frankly as 'signs', that is, symbols. Not that John thought they did not happen, but their happening was of less interest to him than their meaning.[29]

But what if those who actually witnessed these 'signs' and saw the results of these miracles remained unconvinced? Browning explores this possibility in 'An Epistle Containing the Strange Medical Experience of Karshish, the Arab Physician', published in 1855, in the form of a letter from Karshish to his teacher Abib. This first-century physician relates how he encountered Lazarus and was confronted with the preposterous story of his being raised from the dead. The story fascinates Karshish, but can he really believe it? He would like to search out 'the Nazarene / Who wrought this cure', but learns that he is dead. The letter breaks off in embarrassment for a moment here, for he can hardly bring himself to write about what comes next, the story of the Resurrection. He feels this would make him look ridiculous to Abib and sacrifice his reputation as a man of science. He dismisses Lazarus and his story, but cannot refrain from adding a postscript which reveals the impact the incident has had on him:

> think Abib; dost thou think?
> So, the All-Great, were the All-Loving too –
> So, through the thunder comes a human voice

Saying, 'O heart I made, a heart beats here!
Face, My hands fashioned, see it in Myself.
Thou hast no power nor may'st conceive of Mine,
But love I gave thee, with Myself to love,
And thou must love Me who have died for thee!'
The madman saith He said so: it is strange.

How then can one jump Lessing's 'wide and ugly ditch' which opens out between the honest enquirer and the 'facts' to which St John and Lazarus bear witness? One can only do it by a leap of faith; there is nothing else that can validate their story. Browning takes up this problem in 'Caliban upon Setebos' which appeared in *Dramatis Personae* in 1864, with the suggestive sub-title, 'or Natural Theology in the Island'. This is one of Browning's most mature works where we see his developed ideas about religion.

Caliban's religion is a projection of his own personality. He pictures Setebos, the deity his mother Sycorax has taught him to fear, as cruelly capricious and indifferent to human pain as he himself is, who pulls off the limbs of animals or (perhaps a sideways look at Calvinism on Browning's part) stones the crabs that pass before him:

Let twenty pass, and stone the twenty-first,
Loving not, hating not, just choosing so.

Caliban's mother tells him that there is a higher power than Setebos known as the Quiet and that Setebos is as much in fear of this power as Caliban is of Setebos and Prospero. This instils in Caliban a religion based entirely on fear and leads him to invent a god not very different from Satan. Caliban's view of the world as seen from his cave is not unlike Tennyson's nightmare of nature 'red in tooth and claw'.

Two implications emerge from Browning's description of Caliban's religion. The first is his belief that an individual develops over his lifetime, just as mankind itself does over the ages. If Caliban's picture of God is limited by his primitive personality, our own limited theology may develop over our lifetime and be superseded by the insight of ages still to come. The religious believer should not regard himself as defending a fortress but as a pilgrim in search of the truth. The truth may be absolute and immutable but our perception of it is not. Browning joins Carlyle, George Eliot, Maurice, Newman, and Arnold, who all in their different ways, take into their theology the idea of development or progress. The second implication of the poem is the realisation that we are prisoners of our own human condition and our apprehension of God will always be a projection of ourselves, unless we accept that religion is not only man's search for God but God's search for man.

True spirituality leads to a dissatisfaction with life as we know it and an acknowledgement of an ideal which lies beyond our ordinary experience. The artist knows this from the nature of his work and Browning captures it brilliantly in 'Andrea del Sarto', the story of the artist whose paintings were technically better than those of Rafael, Michael Angelo, and others, but lacked the 'truer light of God in them'. Andrea recognises even in his failure that 'a man's reach should exceed his grasp, / Or what's a Heaven for?' The ideal informs us of a reality that transcends the present world and is greater than ourselves. It cannot be proved, for logic cannot derive ought from is; it can only be authenticated by a leap of faith. The leap, Browning believed, may be into the dark, but once made it is supported by a power that enables us to land safely. God is not only the end of man's search for truth and integration, but also the initiator and fulfilment of it.

A comparison is sometimes made between Browning and Kierkegaard and, although Browning could not have known any of Kierkegaard's writings, there are undoubtedly similarities between them. Both of them reacted strongly against the Hegelian rationalism which had dominated the approach to religion in German thought; both regarded religion as concerned with what a man does and is, rather than with intellectual abstractions. Both felt that religion is a personal encounter between the believer and God, and Browning would have agreed with Kierkegaard that 'the crowd is untruth'. Both were indifferent to institutionalised Christianity, although Browning did not share Kierkegaard's hostility to the church. Above all, perhaps, what united them was their love of paradox and a realisation of the paradoxical nature of Christianity itself; a religion that was 'foolishness to the Greeks, whose advocates spoke as 'deceivers yet true', and which proclaimed that in order to live we must first die.

Browning's theology owed most to his close reading of the Bible which had started when he was a child. Faith as he found it in the Bible is the commitment to a living God who reveals himself in history and it is confirmed by conduct, not by intellectual speculation. As noted earlier Coleridge at the end of *Biographia Literaria* declared that 'we can only *know* by the act of *becoming*' and supported this by quoting St John, 'Do the will of my Father, and ye shall know whether I am of God'. The parables of Jesus illustrate this by stressing the need for action and choice at critical moments in our lives. The foolish virgins let the moment of choice slip by and missed their chance by being unprepared. A merchant who is offered a valuable pearl has to gamble all his wealth to beat others who are in the market for it. A servant threatened with dismissal has to act quickly and devise a plan to escape this threat. A defendant on his way to face a legal charge is advised to settle out of court and has to make up his mind on whether this is the best course. All these characters are like those we meet so often in Browning's poems; they have to decide and decide quickly. If there is agreement here with Kierkegaard it is because both of them knew their Bible.

Some might suggest that on one important point there is opposition rather than agreement between them. The caricature of the bluff, self-assured optimist which is sometimes mistaken for the real Browning, certainly does not fit in with the concept of *angst* which is central to Kierkegaard's thought. *The Concept of Dread* (1844) was one of Kierkegaard's most famous essays in which he argued with great eloquence that our feeling of dread tells us that we belong not to this world but to eternity. This is not entirely foreign to Browning's poetry, which frequently expresses fear and dread, a sense of man's alienation in a world in which he finds himself a stranger. Many of his characters are failures or misfits, worldly bishops and lax priests, corrupt rulers and venal artists; he was fascinated by abnormal personalities and states of mind, by neurotics and psychotics, and by sexual deviants. He rightly believed that human nature in all its complexity, its depths as well as its heights, was the concern of religion; that the best and the worst are mixed together and common to all of us.

Where Browning really parted company with Kierkegaard was in refusing to accept the radical opposition of faith and reason. In his *Concluding Unscientific Postscript* (1846) Kierkegaard pushes the 'absurdity' of Christianity to its utmost limits and argues that faith requires commitment against all rational argument. For him neither historical nor philosophical enquiry can authenticate the truth of the Gospel. There is no such thing as a natural theology since God is not an idea in the mind; not even the New Testament records can validate the claim that God was in Christ. The real question for Kierkegaard is not whether Christianity can be shown to be true, but 'How can we become Christians?' Coleridge, who is sometimes described as an existentialist, refused to accept this extreme dichotomy. In *Biographia Literaria* he called the reason 'the outer Court of the Temple' and 'Faith . . . the completing KEY-STONE'. Coleridge followed Hooker in believing that faith and reason are congruent and Browning keeps company with them. He believes that the Gospel is the best explanation of man's nature and provides the answer to his needs and that this does not entail a rejection of reason. We need not question that his own St John speaks for him when he declares that the acknowledgement of God in Christ

Accepted by the reason, solves for thee
All questions in the earth and out of it.

V

Yeats and Eliot

Yeats illustrates very graphically the truth of T. E. Hulme's observation that if real religion is denied a man he will either make or find a substitute for it. What Yeats substituted for orthodox Christianity was an amalgam of various traditions and in many ways was also his own creation. Unlike all those discussed so far, Yeats was not brought up in a Christian household; his father was a disciple of Tyndall and Huxley, an upholder not of Victorian faith but of Victorian doubt. From an early age Yeats decided that his vocation was to be a poet and as this conviction grew he became aware that the world of Victorian scepticism was not only uncongenial in itself but had a devitalizing effect on poetry. He probably read Darwin's *Autobiography* and would have understood and sympathised with the sad record of the price Darwin paid for his devotion to science. First, Darwin tells us, he lost his love of music, then his sense of wonder, then his consciousness of God. 'My mind', he wrote, 'seems to have become a machine for grinding general laws out of a large collection of facts.'

More and more Yeats was convinced that contemporary poetry was the impoverished heir of a written tradition which had cut itself off from the folk-memory of earlier ages, with their vibrant images, symbols, and myths, and a history that went back for centuries. If poetry was to live again it must put its roots down and find nourishment in this old and traditional culture. What was true of poetry was also true of religion, for the two were intimately related and both had suffered the same deracination. In *The Trembling of the Veil* he gives an indication of this relationship. 'I was unlike others of my generation', he wrote, 'in one thing only. I am very religious, and deprived by Huxley and Tyndall of the simple-minded religion of my childhood, I had made a new religion, almost an infallible church of poetic tradition.' It was not to any form of Christianity that he turned for a supernatural view of the world, but to a tradition older than Christianity itself. Later in life when he had developed an interest in mysticism, he was attracted by the Roman Catholic mystic and theologian, Baron von Hügel, but the attraction was only transitory:

> I – though heart might find relief
> Did I become a Christian man and choose for my belief
> What seems most welcome in the tomb – play a
> predestined part.
> Homer is my example and his unchristened heart.
> The lion and the honeycomb, what has Scripture said?
> So get you gone, von Hügel, though with blessings on
>   your head.

'Vacillation'

Yeats rejected Christianity because he felt it was concerned more with the consolations of a life to come than the celebration of the joys of this life. The pagan Homer sings of a world of heroes rather than the lives of saints, and even the Old Testament with stories such as Samson's finding a swarm of bees in the carcass of a dead lion, celebrates sweetness and strength. Yeats regarded Christianity as little different from the mystery religions with their myths of death and resurrection, which had recently been brought to public attention by Frazer's *The Golden Bough*. For his own 'predestined part' he preferred the heroic myths of the Homeric epic.

Yeats was one of those Romantics who believed religion and poetry to be the same, that life is best understood by myth, ritual, and symbol, rather than the conceptual explanations of either scepticism or theology. He declared this in the lines:

> We were the last romantics – chose for theme
> Traditional sanctity and loveliness;
> Whatever's written in what poet's name
> The book of the people; whatever most can bless
> The mind of man or elevate a rhyme.

Yeats found his 'sanctity and loveliness' in art and initially in the work of the Pre-Raphaelites and the French Symbolist poets, who disliked English Puritanism and were inspired by an age not yet taken over by the industrial revolution, and this was reinforced by his early training as a painter. He found it too in the legends and folk-stories of rural Ireland, an indigenous tradition which had resisted the attempts of the English to drag Ireland into the mainstream of modern society. His study of Irish folk-lore also fostered an interest in the occult which can be seen in the essay he wrote in 1914 for Lady Gregory's *Visions and Beliefs in the West of Ireland*. In this he related these 'Visions and Beliefs' to an eclectic group which included the Cambridge Platonist, Henry

More, the Swedish theosophist and mystic, Swedenborg, and a long line of neoplatonists stretching back to Plotinus.

This study led Yeats to accept the existence of what Henry More termed the *Anima Mundi*, a world spirit and universal memory from which the poet and visionary can draw images and symbols that have a resonance in everyone's mind; an idea carried on in modern times by the Jungian theory of a Group Unconscious and archetypes. Yeats's interest in the occult developed in various and overlapping stages. The first was marked by his membership of the Theosophical Society, founded by Madam Blavatsky, who claimed to have had revealed to her a universal religion which combined all the world religions, together with the wisdom of the Hermetic and Cabbalistic writings, and the teaching of the Rosicrucians.

This was followed by his membership of the Order of the Golden Dawn, a society which had been founded in 1889, only a year before Yeats joined it. The Order was a secret one and its membership restricted to those who were regarded as serious students of the occult. Its teaching was not all that different from theosophy, but it put greater emphasis on Western influences rather than the Indian ones favoured by Madam Blavatsky, and it engaged its members in sharing their experiences. Not content with these ventures into what some regarded as the wild shores of the occult, Yeats also embarked on spiritualist seances and automatic writing. Surprising as it may seem, it was on their honeymoon that Yeats's wife started to practise automatic writing and startled them both by receiving messages which seemed to come from another world and used the images and symbols they had encountered in their studies in the occult.

Many find these interests of Yeats and his wife eccentric and even disreputable, and their suspicions are reinforced by the charges of fraud which were successfully brought against Madam Blavatsky's claims to have received direct revelations from her Indian masters. T. S. Eliot in *The Use of Poetry and the Use of Criticism* accused Yeats of trying to make poetry out of nonsense:

> He [Yeats] was very much fascinated by self-induced trance states, calculated symbolism, mediums, theosophy, crystal-gazing, folk-lore and hobgoblins. Golden apples, archers, black pigs and such paraphernalia abounded. Often the verse has an hypnotic charm; but you cannot take heaven by magic, especially if you are, like Mr Yeats, a very sane person.

Auden was even more trenchant in his criticism. 'How on earth',

he wrote, 'could a man of Yeats's gifts take such nonsense seriously?
.. How *could* Yeats, with his great aesthetic appreciation of
aristocracy, ancestral houses, ceremonial tradition, take up something
so essentially lower-middle class ... Mediums spells, the
Mysterious Orient – how embarrassing.'[1] The answer to Auden's
question can be found in many of Yeats's writings and is always
the same; it is his belief that all these experiences testify to the
existence of a universal mind and memory, and that our own minds
are parts of this. Access to this universal mind is available through
what can loosely be called the practice of magic, and poetry makes
this supernatural world known to others. Not everything in Yeats's
religion derived from the dubious sources which caused Auden
embarrassment and distaste. Some of it came from a long and at
times a distinguished tradition going back to Plato and descending
through Plotinus, the Christian mystics such as St John of the Cross,
Dame Julian of Norwich, and St Theresa of Avila, and respectable
theosophists like Jacob Boehme and his translator, William Law. In
the East one could find similar traditions handed down by the
Buddhist and Hindu mystics.

Yeats was widely read and familiar with many of the great
figures of these traditions. Later in life he turned to a study of
philosophy to support his religion and Richard Ellman in *The
Identity of Yeats* mentions Hegel, Whitehead, Russell, and G. E.
Moore, whose brother, T. Sturge Moore, was a close friend, as
philosophers whom Yeats had read. One is surprised to find
empiricists like Russell and Moore in this list, but not Hegel whose
logic of thesis, antithesis, and synthesis had been anticipated by
Boehme and now emerged in Yeats's belief in the principle of
contradiction. To these might have been added F. H. Bradley, who
was to influence T. S. Eliot so strongly, and whose combination of
logic and mysticism would undoubtedly have been attractive to
Yeats. Bradley's doctrine of internal relations, which maintains
that truth both realises and loses itself in unity would also have
supported his belief that all statements about the Absolute are partial
and even contradictory.

Opinion is divided as to whether Yeats's religion had any
coherent basis of thought. Graham Hough in his brilliantly lucid
The Mystery Religion of W. B. Yeats argues that Yeats's synthesis
of theosophy, the Golden Dawn, and spiritualism gave him a
complete system of thought, but Richard Ellman is probably nearer
the mark in suggesting that Yeats could hold in his mind discordant
and contradictory elements and use them all in the service of his

poetry. He points out that in 'Reprisals', a poem on the death of Major Robert Gregory, 'The poet, a Buddhist one moment, a stoic the next, and a spiritualist the next, can look at death as well as other images with changing eyes'.[2] We should realise, however, that behind this eclecticism there remained for Yeats an important truth. For him the Absolute which lies behind this phenomenal world is apprehended at different times and in various ways by different people, but the poetic imagination affords the best approach and is the royal road to reality. Poetry, indeed, *is* religion. T. S. Eliot in a sustained criticism of Yeats in *After Strange Gods* recognised the importance of this for Yeats, but is rather patronising about the 'somewhat artificially induced poeticality' of Yeats's verse. 'Mr Yeats's supernatural world', he wrote,

> was the wrong supernatural world. It was not a world of spiritual significance, nor a world of real Good and Evil, of holiness and sin, but a highly sophisticated lower mythology summoned, like a physician, to supply the fading pulse of poetry with some transient stimulant so that the dying patient may utter his last words.

Yeats himself did not see it in this way; he did not regard his mythology as a remedy to arrest the decay of poetry. He thought he was restoring to poetry its traditional role and recovering something that had been lost. Nevertheless, Eliot was right to question this mythology Yeats purported to be recovering, for it was a strange melange of heterogeneous elements; there is a world of difference between Madam Blavatsky on the one hand and Plato and Plotinus on the other. Even more important, Yeats never answered Eliot's question and leaves us in the dark about 'real Good and Evil'.

What Eliot failed to question was Yeats's belief that the poetic imagination is a means of salvation; a belief central to Yeats's religion and one that calls Keats to mind. Yeats shared with Keats a belief in 'negative capability', a state of mind in which he could entertain visions 'without any irritable reaching after fact and reason'.[3] Although glad to have his religious views confirmed by philosophers, he regarded himself as a poet, who held up a vision of the truth not by argument but by symbol and myth. He would have agreed with Keats that 'What the imagination seizes as Beauty must be truth – whether it existed before or not'.

For all his strictures Eliot shared some of Yeats's views about poetry. He agreed with Yeats that the role of the poet was not that of the philosopher, and in a well-known review in *The Dial* for November 1923, he praised Joyce's '*Ulysses*' for 'manipulating a continuous parallel between contemporaneity and antiquity'; and perhaps with Yeats in mind, for establishing 'a method for which the horoscope is auspicious'. 'Psychology', he continued, 'ethnology and *The Golden Bough* have concurred to make possible what was impossible even a few years ago. Instead of narrative method, we may now use the mythical method.' Eliot acknowledged that Yeats as well as Joyce had brought this about. Indeed, Yeats had perceived a 'continuous parallel between contemporaneity and antiquity' more radically than either Eliot or Joyce for this spilled over from poetry to politics.

Although he came of Anglo-Irish Protestant stock, Yeats's interest in the indigenous Irish culture almost inevitably led him to sympathise with Irish nationalism, and this sympathy was fed by his infatuation with Maud Gonne, the tempestuous revolutionary leader. 'Pallas Athene in that straight back and arrogant head', who fascinated him for many years, had swept him towards seeing the struggle for national independence in terms of Irish legend, to perceiving in the nationalist leaders a reincarnation of the epic heroes of the past. This was not easy at first, for Yeats was a patrician by temperament and could see little in the petit-bourgeois leaders of the revolution to compare with the legendary figures of Celtic mythology. His distaste for them led him at one time to quote Goethe, who had declared that 'The Irish always seem to me like a pack of hounds dragging down some noble stag'.[4] But to counter this he had aristocratic friends such as Lady Gregory and the Gore-Booth family, as well as those associated with the Abbey Theatre, who showed in different degrees sympathy with the nationalist cause. Irish history had been distinguished in the recent past by statesmen such as Parnell and further back there was a line of great writers like Swift, Goldsmith, Berkeley, and Burke, who although belonging to the Anglo-Irish ascendancy, had been conscious of the wrongs Ireland had suffered at the hands of the English. All these helped Yeats to support the call for independence.

Some have written about Yeats as if his poetry moved abruptly from the Celtic twilight to the day-light world of contemporary politics, from a realm of dreams and shadows to a world of reality. They join with Maud Gonne in regarding the earlier Yeats as an idle dreamer and welcome the political commitment of the new poetry he began to write. Certainly they are correct to discern a change in his poetry; a new directness and urgency in his language. All this is true, but the change was not a movement away from a mythological to a demythologised account of people and events. His poetry still exploited myth, but myth was more potent now because it was lived out in contemporary politics and persons.

In 1913 Yeats wrote, 'Romantic Ireland's dead and gone, /It's with O'Leary in the grave.' John O'Leary, who died in 1907, was the old Fenian leader who had returned to Ireland after twenty years in exile and who had gathered around him a group of young writers which included Yeats. O'Leary had encouraged this group to take up Irish subjects in their work and Yeats owed much to his inspiration. O'Leary had invoked the theme of patriotism, but this had been submerged in the meanness of Irish politics until Yeats began to recapture the heroic past and to make it a type of the present conflict. In place of a debased, romanticised Ireland, a new one was being born. The events of 1916, when the Irish rebels took over the Post Office in Dublin and opened fire on the British, had given the little men of Ireland a new status. It is true that these events ended in what looked like disaster, for the ringleaders had been caught and executed. But these seemingly insignificant men acquired in death a grandeur they failed to achieve in life. They had become Irish heroes. Yeats had been ready to dismiss them with 'a mocking tale or a jibe/To please a companion/Around the fire at the club,' but they have now been transfigured and become part of Irish legend and destiny:

> Now and in time to be,
> Wherever green is worn,
> Are changed, changed utterly:
> A terrible beauty is born.

Yeats's religion, then, was not simply rooted in the folk literature of the past or in ancient mythologies; it was concerned with the present and was being acted out in contemporary history. Already a collection of poems published in 1914, with the significant title *Responsibilities*, included the poem 'A Coat', in which Yeats writes of stripping down his poetry to the essentials. He describes his early poetry as a coat 'Covered with embroideries/Out of old mythologies', but now confesses that 'there's more enterprise/In walking naked'. He is not suggesting the abandonment of mythology, but rather that he is not content to use it merely as decoration. It will now be given a more serious purpose and will be seen to have a universal significance.

After 1916 the process of stripping down went even further. Hitherto Yeats had believed that the individual could choose for himself either a life of action or one devoted to art and contemplation. He had always regarded himself as an artist rather than a man of action, but as the struggle for Irish independence became more intense and then turned into a bitter civil war, he felt he could influence events and even play an active part in politics. With the war over, Yeats served for a time as a member of the Irish Senate in response to his sense of civic duty, but the experience was not a happy one.

Yeats had wanted the old aristocratic tradition of the Anglo-Irish community to continue and to make its contribution to the new Republic and had hoped that the Protestant and Roman Catholic churches might come together to influence the national life. He viewed with growing dislike the dominance of commercial interests, the narrow vision of the Roman Catholic hierarchy, and the power taken to themselves by men with who had little regard for culture. The old mansions of the Anglo-Irish had been burnt down and pillaged and for Yeats there had gone with them a good deal of the graciousness of civilised life.

An incident which illustrated the meanness of spirit of the new society was the failure of the Dublin municipal authority to provide a home for the bequest of pictures left by Sir Hugh Lane in 1915. For ten years the municipal authority failed to provide a gallery to house the pictures which remained in the National Gallery in London. Lane had added a codicil to his will bequeathing the pictures to Dublin on condition that a suitable home be provided for them within five years of his death. This codicil had not been signed, but even so it seemed that Lane's gift might be lost to Ireland because of the philistinism of the 'political class in Ireland – the lower-middle class from whom the patriotic associations have drawn their leaders for the last ten years'; a class, he continued, who 'have suffered through the cultivation of hatred as the one energy of their movement'.[5] In 'A Prayer for My Daughter', he lamented how Maud Gonne his 'sweetheart from another life', whose husband, John MacBride, had been executed for his part in the Easter rising of 1916, had become, along with so many others, a ranting creature full of hatred:

> Have I not seen the loveliest woman born
> Out of the mouth of Plenty's horn,
> Because of her opinionated mind
> Barter that mind
> Barter that horn and every good
> By quiet natures understood
> For an old bellows full of angry wind?

There were those who accused Yeats of fascist sympathies and, indeed, he was for a short time associated with General O'Duffy's

Blue-shirts. Certainly he had an autocratic temper and his disillusionment with the way Irish politics were going led him to stress the need for discipline and strong authority in government. For many years he had entertained an admiration for Nietzsche whom he had probably first read as early as 1902; on doing so he had written to Lady Gregory describing him as a 'strong enchanter', adding, 'I have not read anything with so much excitement since I got to love Morris's stories'.[6] Nietzsche's notion of the 'superman' with its suggestion that history owes most to its great leaders fitted in well with Yeats's idealisation of the heroic figures of legend and myth.

Along with the notion of the superman went Nietzsche's proclamation of the death of God and his dismissal of Christianity as a pale and ineffective religion. Yeats's attitude to Christianity was less hostile than Nietzsche's and was moderated by his study of Blake and especially by *The Marriage of Heaven and Hell*. Blake's version of Christianity turns what is conventionally regarded as evil into the source of energy and life, and what most people see as good as the product of a devitalised reason. Blake's aphorism, 'The tigers of wrath are wiser than the horses of instruction', finds frequent echoes in Yeats's poetry and was easily accommodated to the philosophy of Nietzsche who remained a strong influence on Yeats. Nietzsche's 'death of God' led to a rejection of history as a divine drama with the Incarnation at its centre and saw it instead as an endless recurrence of decay and rejuvenation. Yeats was quick to adopt and elaborate this into his own view of history as a cyclical pattern operating in 'gyres', each of which lasts about two thousand years. This process, he believed, was governed by the Great Wheel of lunar phases. He placed himself at phase seventeen of this cycle, whereas the world was at phase twenty-two. This left him as one of the 'tragic minority' for whom the times were out of joint and was reflected in the lack of sympathy he felt for Irish politics.

Events in Ireland, however, were only a microcosm of what was happening in the world at large and he felt that one of the great historical cycles he believed in was about to end. The Christian period which had lasted for two thousand years was almost finished and would be replaced with something new. 'The Second Coming', written in January 1919, instead of celebrating the return of Christ, greets the age about to be born with a foreboding bordering on terror. Instead of Christ we are probably to see the Anti-Christ, but the poem ends not with certainty, only with a deeply disturbing question:

> but now I know
> That twenty centuries of stony sleep
> Were vexed to nightmare by a rocking cradle,
> And what rough beast, its hour come round at last,
> Slouches toward Bethlehem to be born?

Some may consider this mere fantasy and accuse Yeats of the naivety displayed by the religious zealots who regularly prophesy the end of the world and read the Bible as though it were Old Moore's Almanac. But his outlook is far more sophisticated than that. 'The Second Coming' invites comparison with Eliot's *The Waste Land*, which was seen as simply a product of the disillusionment and weariness that followed the first World War, but to which Eliot himself gave a universality not recognised by its first readers.

In 'Meditations in Time of Civil War', written in 1921/2, Yeats reflects on those who built the ancestral houses of the Anglo-Irish which had been destroyed in the 'troubles', and recognises that they too had engaged in violence:

> Some violent bitter man, some powerful man
> Called architect and artist in, that they,
> Bitter and violent men, might rear in stone
> The sweetness that all longed for night and day,
> The gentleness none there had ever known.

Violence had begot violence and the dream of independence had been drowned in a tide of hatred:

> We had fed the heart on fantasies,
> The heart's grown brutal from such fare;
> More sustance in our enmities
> Than in our love; O honey bees,
> Come build in the empty house of the stare.

These lines are taken from 'The Stare's Nest by My Window' which is one of the poems in 'Meditations in Time of Civil War' and refers to Thoor Ballylee, the tower home at Gort in County Galway, to which Yeats took his newly-married wife in 1919. The honey bees who are invited to build in the masonry of the old tower anticipate the image of 'the lion and the honeycomb' in 'Vacillation', where the bees coming out of the dead lion symbolise the birth of sweetness out of strength. In 'Vacillation' Yeats had written, 'Between extremities/Man runs his course' and along with Blake he constantly viewed life as a balance of opposites, a marriage of heaven and hell; mingled with this there is a Nietzschean belief that violence may be a necessary prelude to peace. Even so, he was sickened by the violence of the Civil War in Ireland. An incident that moved him personally was the shooting of an innocent woman by the Black and Tans as they drove through Kiltartan, and his feeling of outrage at how 'a drunken soldiery/Can leave the mother, murdered at her door, /To crawl in her own blood'.

Some of those who belonged to the Protestant Ascendancy had supported the nationalist cause and of these the Gore-Booths who lived at Lissadell, near Yeats's boyhood home at Sligo, had been most important to him; along with Lady Gregory they had encouraged him as a poet and set before him an example of the good life. As a young man he had been captivated by the beauty of the Gore-Booth sisters, whom he described as 'Two girls in silk kimonos, both/Beautiful, one a gazelle', in the poem he wrote in 1927, 'In Memory of Eva Gore-Booth and Con Markiewicz'. Eva, the younger sister, was a poet whose talent Yeats had admired and encouraged; Constance, the elder, later married the Polish ambassador in Dublin. Both sisters had been caught up in the nationalist movement and Constance, who played an active part in the Rebellion, was arrested and sentenced to death. She was subsequently pardoned and went with her husband to live on the Continent. But now their earlier beauty – and not just their physical beauty – is gone:

> The older is condemned to death,
> Pardoned, drags out lonely years
> Conspiring among the ignorant.
> I know not what the younger dreams –
> Some vague utopia – and she seems,
> When withered old and skeleton gaunt,
> An image of such politics.

The Ireland that had emerged from all the bloodshed was not the Ireland he had hoped for; it had failed to unite the virtues of the old Gaelic culture and the values of Lissadell, both of which had disappeared in the new commercially-minded Republic. The war itself with the blood which had been spilt, 'all the folly of a fight/ With a common wrong or right', as Yeats describes it, was not worth the fighting. Yeats condemns himself as well as the two girls for not recognising the real enemy:

> The innocent and the beautiful
> Have no enemy but time;
> Arise and bid me strike a match
> And strike another till time catch.

Yeats uses the decay of physical beauty as an image of something more profound. The struggle in which they had all been engaged had destroyed the things it had set out to achieve. Their experience illustrates a larger truth and can be universalised, for he sees Ireland as a microcosm of the human situation. The truth for all of us is that behind the contingencies of history, the armed struggles, the shabby compromises of politics, there are absolute values which, although we may not be able to realise them fully, we ignore at our peril. He now sees Irish politics as a folly (a gazebo) from which he surveys the history of his own times; and he ends his poem with a cry for penitence and purgation:

> Should the conflagration climb,
> Run till all the sages know.
> We the great gazebo built,
> They convicted us of guilt;
> Bid me strike a match and blow.

In 1927, the year in which this poem was written, Yeats had also written 'Sailing to Byzantium', which appeared in *The Tower* (1928), and in 1928 'Byzantium', which was published in *The Winding Stair* (1933). These two poems have attracted a great deal of critical discussion; they are amongst the most important he wrote and mark a turning point in his beliefs. Byzantium was a powerful symbol for Yeats; it brought together several meanings, but central to these was the reconciliation of opposites. Historically the city in its prime had produced a magnificent flowering of artistic achievement. It had brought together East and West, Christianity and Islam, the modern world and classical antiquity. At the emblematical level it represented for Yeats the union of Dionysus and Apollo, war and peace, body and soul, time and eternity. It gave Yeats a vision of the celestial City, his own version of the New Jerusalem, and for this reason he described it as 'the holy city of Byzantium'. This was the home of the sages who had convicted Yeats and his friends of guilt at the end of the verses 'In Memory of Eva Gore-Booth and Con Markiewicz':

> O Sages standing in God's holy fire
> As in the gold mosaic of a wall,
> Come from the holy fire, perne in a gyre,
> And be the singing-masters of my soul.
>
> Once out of nature I shall never take
> My bodily form from any natural thing,
> But such a form as Grecian goldsmiths make
> Of hammered gold and gold enamelling

To keep a drowsy Emperor awake;
Or set upon a golden bough to sing
To lords and ladies of Byzantium
Of what is past, or passing, or to come.

Sailing to Byzantium

The images here are rich in their associations. The fire, used by Buddhism as a symbol of purgation and by Western religion as an image of both purgation and inspiration, goes back to Dante, to Plotinus, and beyond them to Pentecost and the call of Isaiah, whose lips were touched with fire by the seraph. 'Perne' was the dialect word in the West of Ireland for the bobbin used in the spinning of thread. It suggests here the shuttle of time which links the sages to the past as well as the future. The 'golden bough' recalls Marvell's 'The Garden' where the poet speaks of how his soul will cast 'the Bodies Vest aside': 'My Soul into the Boughs does glide:/There like a Bird it sits and sings.' It also brings to mind Frazer's study of the mystery religions which was drawn on by Eliot, Lawrence, and other writers at the time. In Frazer the golden bough was found in the sacred wood where it formed part of the tree on which the priest hangs the image of the god.

Yeats uses the fertility rites of the dying god elsewhere in his poetry. The image of the golden bough appears in Section II of 'Vacillation', where the poet takes over the priestly role, and where in Section VIII he dismisses von Hugel and with him Christianity, which for Yeats is no more than another version of the resurrection myth. As the poet becomes the priest so Yeats substitutes for the Christian doctrine of grace a belief in the imagination as a means of salvation. He develops this in the second of his Byzantium poems where the souls of the dead pass to another world and are purified by the kind of process the artist employs in perfecting his own work.

This perfection is symbolised by the city of Byzantium, but the poet (and here Yeats speaks for himself) seems reluctant to enter the city if this means leaving behind sensory delight and devoting himself to a life of contemplation; the contemplation of the Absolute is for the mystic not the poet. Contrary to Plato's teaching that the soul at death flies upward to union with the Absolute, or the belief of Plotinus that our end is to return to the One by contemplation, or the mysticism of suffering practised by St John of the Cross, Yeats believed that the soul is endlessly reincarnated. He rejected the teaching of Buddhism which declared that man can achieve release from this endless cycle by absorption in the unmovable.

Instead he believed that this world is all we have, that there is nothing but the phenomenal; appearance is reality. He expresses his conviction that this life is all there is and our earthly existence is heaven or not at all in 'The Tower', written in 1926:

I mock Plotinus' thought
And cry in Plato's teeth,
Death and life were not
Till man made up the whole,
Made lock, stock and barrel
Out of his bitter soul.

Richard Ellman observes that Yeats thought he was supported in this by Berkeley's philosophy and believed it was only in old age, when he had become Bishop of Cloyne, that Berkeley propounded the theory that everything exists in the mind of God; something Yeats rejected out of hand.[7]

As Yeats approached old age himself he looked back on his life and in the 'Dialogue between Self and Soul' took stock of the journey he had made. He recalls his love for Maud Gonne, his involvement in Irish politics, and his poetry; he considers the happiness he has found in spite of the ills he has suffered, and feels guilt for his follies and the wrongs he has done. In his study of Yeats, T. R. Henn mentions the importance Yeats gave to his reading of Schopenhauer and quotes from a letter Yeats wrote to Sturge Moore, 'Schopenhauer can do no wrong in my eyes, I no more quarrel with his errors than with a cataract'.[8] But Henn takes this no further and fails to recognise the implications of this for Yeats's poetry and especially for the 'Dialogue between Self and Soul'. At the centre of Schopenhauer's major work, *Die Welt als Wille und Vorstellung* (*The World as Will and Idea*), was his insistence that the self is subject to the will, a life-force which transcends the individual, and that the only escape from this subjection lies in art, in the freedom of aesthetic contemplation. This lies at the centre of Yeats's poem.

In Yeats's 'Dialogue' the soul summons the self to ascend 'the winding ancient stair' to 'That quarter where all thought is done', but the poet looks at the old Japanese sword on his knees and the 'flowering, silken, old embroidery' in which it is bound and is caught up by its beauty. The soul questions why a man 'Long past his prime' should 'remember things that are/ Emblematical of love and war' and promises the poet deliverance from this earthly and physical existence, from 'the crime of death and birth', 'If but imagination scorn the earth/And intellect its wandering'. The summit of this ascent will be a place where the 'intellect no longer knows/Is from the Ought, or Knower from the Known',

> That is to say, ascends to Heaven;
> Only the dead can be forgiven;
> But when I think of that my tongue's a stone.

The poet is unpersuaded. He prefers the beauty of the senses rather than to be 'stricken deaf and dumb and blind'. He is prepared to be pitched into 'the frog-spawn of a blind man's ditch' that is life, and even suffer once again the pain of unrequited love:

> The folly that man does
> Or must suffer, if he woos
> A proud woman not kindred of his soul.

He rejects the suggestion that 'Only the dead can be forgiven'. The part he played in the struggle for Irish independence and the realisation that this might have caused needless death, lies heavily on his conscience, but he is ready to accept this. He looks back and forgives himself, for there is no-one else who can do so; guilt and blame, sin and alienation, forgiveness and absolution, redemption and salvation, exist only in the mind. In lines comparable with those at the end of *The Prelude*, where Wordsworth also reviews his life, Yeats affirms his own mind as the source of all blessing:

> I am content to follow to its source,
> Every event in action or in thought;
> Measure the lot, forgive myself the lot.
> When such as I cast out remorse
> So great a sweetness flows into the breast
> We must laugh and we must sing,
> We are blest by everything,
> Everything we look upon is blest.

As Yeats grew older and death drew nearer it was not always so easy to accept this religion of self-realisation and self-affirmation. He came increasingly to distrust Schopenhauer's idea that the soul can find release in aesthetic contemplation and felt more the other side of his philosophy, which taught that the self is subject to a universal force that operates with a Darwinian disregard for the individual. He remarked in old age that he was driven chiefly by lust and rage, but more important was the fear that his creative imagination was failing him. In one of his last poems, 'The Circus Animals' Desertion', he engages in a demythologising process that leaves him alone, like Lear's 'poor naked forked creature', with all the panoply of office gone. Yeats was a poet and not a king, and the trappings stripped away are the mythical figures, the images and emblems of poetry. He sees them as a circus with himself as ringmaster:

> Maybe at last, being but a broken man,
> I must be satisfied with my heart, although
> Winter and summer till old age began
> My circus animals were all on show,
> Those stilted boys, that burnished chariot,
> Lion and woman and the Lord knows what.

He calls to mind his earlier poems, those that told the stories of the sea-rider Oisin, the Countess Cathleen, and of Cuchulain, who fought with the sea, and whose statue stood in the Post Office in Dublin, where the Irish had fought the English in 1916. In another of the last poems, 'The Man and the Echo', he finds it difficult to forgive himself as he had once done. He lies 'awake night after night' and is troubled by the question, 'Did that play of mine send out/Certain men the English shot?' His poetry had invested the mythical figures of Irish legend with a new importance, but in 'The Circus Animals' Desertion', as he comes to the end of his life, he wonders whether it has been worthwhile:

> Those masterful images became complete
> Grew in pure mind, but out of what began?
> A mound of refuse or the sweepings of a street,
> Old kettles, old bottles, and a broken can,
> Old iron, old bones, old rags, that raving slut
> Who keeps the till. Now that my ladder's gone,
> I must lie down where all the ladders start,
> In the foul rag-and-bone shop of the heart.

Yeats had once thought of the imagination as a ladder which would enable him to ascend to heaven. But what happens when the ladder is kicked away? When the imagination instead of being a means of salvation is revealed as the slut who dispenses the coinage of poetic usage, the currency of the rag-and-bone shop of the mind? What if Schopenhauer was wrong and the imagination, instead of being free, is at the mercy of our instincts and unconscious minds?

At the end of Eliot's *Little Gidding*, after an air-raid on London, the poet meets a 'familiar compound ghost', and their meeting, according to Eliot, was written with Yeats in mind. In a letter to his friend John Hayward, Eliot explained the revisions he made in the first drafts of his poem and one of the reasons for the changes he made at this point was, he said, because 'the visionary figure . . . will no doubt be identified by some readers with Yeats'. 'I do not wish to take the responsibility', he continued, 'of putting Yeats or anybody else into Hell.'[9] Eliot had originally conceived the meeting as comparable to Dante's encounter with his old master, Brunetto Latini, whose presence in Hell comes as a shock to him. Eliot's decision to drop this from his final version coupled with the letter to Hayward, confirms, without doubt, the identification of the ghostly figure with Yeats.

Eliot's admiration for Yeats's poetry was qualified at first by his dislike of Irish legend and the occult, but when Yeats left the Celtic influence behind and developed a stronger and simpler style, Eliot was quick to acknowledge him as the leading poet of the age. Even then, although Yeats's mastery of his material was clear for all to see, it was increasingly the material itself that Eliot questioned. At first the two had much in common. *The Waste Land* no less than 'The Second Coming' foresaw the disintegration of Western society and the poetry of both exploited the parallel they saw between antiquity and the contemporary situation.

Eliot as a young man had followed Yeats in viewing religion through the spectacles of Frazer's *The Golden Bough*, but once *The Waste Land* had been left behind their opinions diverged. Eliot became a Christian and regarded his poetry as a religious vocation which reached its apotheothis in *Four Quartets* and especially in *Little Gidding*. The imagery of *Little Gidding* is similar to that found in Yeats's poetry, but its meaning is very different, for Eliot uses it in the service of God. The purgatorial fire, 'Where you must move in measure like a dancer', extends far beyond Buddhist asceticism to become the instrument of Christian grace. Through purgation it promises freedom and fulfilment, for God's judgement and his mercy are one. History for Yeats was an unending cycle, whereas for Eliot 'History may be servitude, / History may be freedom'. While Yeats in old age felt himself a slave of the passions, Eliot embraced a service which promised perfect freedom.

The ghost of Yeats reminds Eliot of their common beliefs, 'My thoughts and theory which you have forgotten', and their shared concern 'To purify the dialect of the tribe', but concludes with irony to warn him of the 'gifts' that await old age. The first is the decay of the senses and the pleasure they once afforded; the second, the 'impotence of rage/At human folly'. Last of all and most intimidating:

> the awareness
> Of things ill done and done to others' harm
> Which once you took for exercise of virtue.

Yeats had once thought he could forgive himself for the wrongs he had done, but in old age found this impossible. He had put his faith in the imagination as a means of redemption and regarded his poetry as a way of apprehending the vision of beauty symbolised in Byzantium. His ghostly visitation in *Little Gidding* is made with friendly intent and ends 'with a kind of valediction'. As his own old age approaches, Eliot knows that he can fall into errors similar to those that betrayed Yeats: an attachment to sensory pleasures, an indifference to the concerns of others, and above all, pride in his own poetic achievement. One can understand why Eliot was anxious not to establish too close an identity between the ghost and Yeats, for to do so would leave him open to the charge of judging others, but there is no doubt that he regarded Yeats's poetry as seriously flawed by its failure to believe in a personal God who offers pardon, freedom, and peace.

Eliot died in 1965, the centenary year of Yeats's birth. Since his death a great deal of biographical information that was not available or could not be used before, has thrown new light on his life and work. Chief among the studies that have brought his life and work together have been the two by Lyndall Gordon.[10] These have destroyed or sharply qualified Eliot's own carefully elaborated theory of the impersonality of art. We can now see that while his work speaks for a whole generation and even for all time, it is rooted in his own deeply personal experience and that our appreciation of it is increased by an understanding of that experience.

The picture that emerges from Lyndall Gordon's pages is of a neurotic personality, afraid of travel, afraid of the telephone, and apprehensive when alone with a woman. Jungian interpretations of his work had already been made, especially by Elizabeth Drew in her *T. S. Eliot: The Design of his Poetry* (1950), but the information now available will undoubtedly lead to Freudian accounts of his character and poetry. Lyndall Gordon emphasises the New England Puritanism of Eliot's upbringing, something, she contends, that resisted all his attempts to become the quintessential Englishman. Coupled with the influence of a dominant and pious mother, his background gave him a stern super-ego, an unforgiving attitude to his own conduct, and an easily aroused sense of guilt.

One obvious feature of his personality was his attitude to women. When they acted as mother-figures or guardian angels, he found their company congenial, but anything approaching sexual intimacy left him feeling threatened and even disgusted. This is evident in the poetry he wrote before his first marriage where sexuality is sometimes linked to images of violence and even murder. It probably contributed to the breakdown of his hasty marriage, a calamity which brought feelings of guilt and the need to punish himself. The guilt was compounded when he left America for Europe against his father's wishes and by his father's death soon afterwards. From this time onwards his life was lived in a strict routine of self-discipline, a reluctance to accept forgiveness for himself, and a difficulty in relating to people, especially the two women, Emily Hale and Mary Trevelyan, whose love for him over the years was never rewarded with the marriage they had expected. It was only in his last years that he found healing and a safe haven in his happy marriage to his second wife, Valerie.

This account of Eliot's life makes it difficult to avoid Freud's contention that religion is an obsessional neurosis; an attempt to placate the demands of a ruthless super-ego by a ritualistic observance of rules of conduct and to look for protection in ideas and the avoidance of personal relationships. One can discern this not only in Eliot's life but in his work. *The Family Reunion* is the most obvious example and can be seen as largely autobiographical, but the same pattern reveals itself in less direct ways; it can be seen in the imagery he uses, such as the rose-garden, which occurs in several of his poems. In *Burnt Norton* which commemorates the visit he made with Emily Hale to the Harrowby estate near Chipping Campden, he wrote of their love as 'the door we never opened/Into the rose-garden'. In *The Family Reunion*, which has many echoes of *Burnt Norton*, the door into the rose-garden is made more explicitly the symbol of sexual love when Aunt Agatha tells Harry of her affair with his father and her regret that she had never achieved marriage and children:

I only looked through the little door
When the sun was shining on the rose-garden:
And heard in the distance tiny voices

In 'A Dedication to my Wife', written in 1956, a year after his second marriage, he wrote of the happiness he and his wife had found now they had entered and possessed the rose-garden:

No peevish winter wind shall chill
No sullen tropic sun shall wither
The roses in the rose-garden which is ours and ours only.

Such a simple reductionism as this ignores, of course, the real value of Eliot's poetry. Undoubtedly Eliot suffered from some kind of obsessionalism, but there are many similarly afflicted and few if any of them poets of genius. Eliot certainly felt himself threatened with madness and suffered breakdowns of varying degrees of severity throughout his life. At the time when he was writing *The Waste Land* he was consulting a psychiatrist and if the treatment he received had been more successful he might possibly have been happier. But a 'cure' might have led to the loss of his creative powers, for these were certainly fed from the springs of his suffering.

Now that we can view it in perspective, we can understand why Eliot should have regarded his poetic output as one work, for there is a unity which brings together the poetry of his youth and that of his old age and which gives added meaning to the motto he took from Mary, Queen of Scots, 'In my end is my beginning'. This with its corollary, 'In my beginning is my end', is on the tablet which marks his burial place in the church at East Coker. The unity they suggest is that of the journey which took Eliot a lifetime to make and which is mirrored in Dante's *Divine Comedy*; a journey from the *Inferno*, through the *Purgatorio*, until at last he glimpsed the *Paradiso*. His religion, like any system of thought or belief, may have had neurotic elements, but it gave him the strength and what the believer would call the grace, to face the demons that tormented him, and in the end the freedom from the fear of committing himself to another to achieve a happy marriage.

Like Wordsworth and Coleridge, Eliot started as a revolutionary in poetry, but ended as a traditionalist, which means that they all formed the taste by which their poetry could be appreciated. Eliot established a poetic style which dominated his own generation and brought too many imitators. Like Wordsworth and Coleridge, he saw his work as more a revival than a revolution. The metaphysical poetry of the seventeenth century and especially that of Donne and Herbert, together with the Elizabethan dramatists, provided his models. Their work exhibited what he described in a phrase he later came to regret, a 'unified sensibility', in which emotion and intellect were held together; 'A thought to Donne', he wrote, 'was a feeling'. Further back than these was Dante, who remained a dominant influence throughout his life, and behind him Thomas Aquinas, who gave order to the religious and intellectual life of medieval Christendom.

These all combined to encourage an anti-Romantic attitude in Eliot's thought. He shared T. E. Hulme's view that Romanticism is 'spilt religion', a movement that substituted for religion an indulgence of the emotions. The Puritan tradition of New England in which he had been brought up owed little to the Puritanism of the seventeenth century except in the harshness of its moral principles. The Unitarian theology of his family owed far more to Emerson and the liberal Protestantism of America which believed in human perfectibility and progress. His own sense of guilt led him to abandon this faith of his fathers and led him to regard it as a heresy which hardly deserved the name of Christian. But his upbringing left him with a deep reserve about disclosing his personal feelings which reinforced his dislike of poetry that expressed emotion, whether spontaneously or recollected in tranquillity. This was especially so of religious poetry, 'the probable direction [of which] in the immediate future', he wrote in an unpublished lecture, 'is towards something more impersonal than that of [the nineteenth century]. . . It will be much more interested in the dogma and the doctrine; in religious thought, rather than purely personal religious feeling'. In this, he continued, 'it will tend to have more kinship with that of the seventeenth century'.[11]

What Eliot meant by 'religious thought' is a complex question. While the poet may use the dogmas and doctrines of theology in his poetry he is not, for Eliot, a theological thinker himself; still less is he a philosopher or thinker in the strict sense at all. In his *Shakespeare and the Stoicism of Seneca* (1927) Eliot distinguishes sharply between the poet and the philosopher. 'Champions of Shakespeare as a great philosopher', he wrote,

> have a great deal to say about Shakespeare's power of thought, but they fail to show that he thought to any purpose . . . did Shakespeare think anything at all? He was occupied with turning human actions into poetry . . . . All great poetry gives the illusion of a view of life.

Eliot does not countenance Coleridge's notion of a reciprocity between symbol and concept, whereby conceptual thinking feeds the mind of the artist, and works of the imagination stimulate the conceptual thinker. For him there is a sharp divide between thinking and feeling, which is strange for one who lamented the so-called dissociation of sensibility. 'The poet who 'thinks' ', he tells us, 'is merely the poet who can express the emotional equivalent of thought. But he is not necessarily interested in the thought itself.' Even Dante, who might be considered as the great example of the philosophical poet, is denied any such claim. In the same essay he writes:

> In truth Shakespeare nor Dante did any real thinking – that was not their job; and the relative value of the thought current at

their time, the material enforced upon each to use as the vehicle of his feeling, is of no importance.

Eliot's scepticism concerning the limits of thought went further than this and extended to metaphysics; it can be traced back to his philosophical studies, the course of which has been well charted by several writers. As a young man in France he had attended some of Bergson's classes and for a time was greatly influenced by him, but on returning to Harvard he took up the study of Indian philosophy and was then attracted by the writings of F. H. Bradley, the leading exponent of Idealism in Britain. Bertrand Russell was lecturing in Harvard at the time, but Eliot found his logical empiricism unattractive. For him philosophy had to provide an answer to man's deepest needs and Russell's classes in mathematical logic signally failed to do this. In Bradley he found what the was always looking for: a combination of scepticism and a belief in a world that was ordered and coherent even if beyond our full comprehension. Bradley provided the subject of his doctoral dissertation at Harvard which found its way into print many years later in 1964.

In the opening chapter of his *Appearance and Reality* Bradley had declared, 'Metaphysics is the finding of bad reasons for what we believe on instinct, but to find these reasons is no less an instinct'. Bradley would have been better advised, perhaps, to write 'good reasons' instead of 'bad reasons', and such an alternative was provided for Eliot in the seminars of Josiah Royce, an Idealist philosopher at Harvard. In *The Religious Aspect of Philosophy* (1885) Royce had argued that 'philosophy must have a religious aspect. Religion invites the scrutiny of philosophy, and philosophy may not neglect the problems of religion. Kant's fundamental problems: *What do I know?* and *What ought I to do?* are of religious interest no less than of philosophical interest'. Royce's *The Problem of Christianity* was published in 1913, just before Eliot attended his post-graduate seminar on Comparative Methodology. In *The Religious Aspect of Philosophy* Royce had come to appreciate the force of Bradley's contention that 'thought' and 'knowledge' are inadequate terms to describe fully the experience for which identity with reality could be claimed. He believed that 'will' and 'feeling' were needed to supplement 'thought', which was merely an abstraction from a total and larger experience. His lectures ranged over the Upanishads and the Vedanta, and Christian mysticism, both Catholic and Protestant, but alongside this interest in mysticism went an emphasis on the importance of morality leading to action. The Absolute called for more than contemplation; it demanded service and loyalty to the cause of humanity. Only in this service could one achieve freedom.

Royce gave a special place to Christianity which he regarded as 'so far at least, man's most impressive view of salvation, and his principal glimpse of the homeland of the spirit'. Even so, many believers would regard his version of Christianity as idiosyncratic, since the loyalty it called for was not to God, nor Jesus, but the community; the 'Beloved Community', as he described it, with which the church at its best can be identified. Jesus is a symbol, a concrete expression of this community. Schweitzer's *The Quest of the Historical Jesus* had appeared in 1911 and Royce may possibly have been influenced by it, but his scepticism went further than Schweitzer's. For him Christ was a figure who emerged from the theological interpretations put upon the events of his life, not only by the early church, but by succeeding generations. Indeed, the Incarnation was only fully realised in the life and beliefs of the church; the church and not Jesus was the centre of Christianity. Christianity was a religion about Jesus, not the religion of Jesus. It manifested itself in the life, practices, and dogmas of the church and in a continuous reassessment of revelation.

This way of thinking came about partly as a reaction against American liberal Protestantism and it had its counterpart in the Roman Catholic modernist movement which had developed in France. Chief of the Roman Catholics was Alfred Loisy, a French Biblical scholar and priest, whose *L'Evangile et l'Eglise* (1902) had been written in answer to *What is Christianity?* by Harnack, a leading liberal Protestant. Royce's views bear a striking resemblance to Loisy's, but it is unlikely that there was any direct influence of one on the other. Both were the product of that combination of the new Biblical criticism and Hegelian Idealism which permeated theology at the time.

There is no doubt that Eliot was profoundly influenced not only by Bradley but also by Royce. Long before he attended Royce's seminars he had abandoned the religion in which he had been brought up. The Unitarianism of the Eliots had little sense of sin and put ignorance in its place; it entertained an easy-going optimism about human nature and progress and with this went an emphasis on individual salvation and a reliance upon the guidance of an inner light rather than dogma. Apart from the belief in an inner light which allied itself to his interest in mysticism, Eliot found this kind of religion uncongenial. It is possible that he learnt something of Roman Catholic modernism during the year he spent in Paris before returning to Harvard to study philosophy. If so, any sympathy he may have had for the Roman church would have been checked by Loisy's excommunication in 1908 and the condemnation of Father Tyrrell in Britain. When he was baptised into the Christian faith in 1927 one of the reasons for his choice of the Anglican church may have been his recollection of the treatment by the Vatican of its modernist priests and such distinguished lay people as von Hugel.

Although Eliot looked to a traditional and authoritarian form of religion, he maintained a deep-seated intellectual scepticism. The Church of England accommodated both of these in a way that Rome would never have countenanced. In a conversation he once had with Hugh Sykes Davies about Marxists, he said, 'They seem so certain of what they believe. My own beliefs are held with a scepticism which I never even hope to be quite rid of.'[12] Davies perceptively remarked that this made him appreciate Eliot's 'natural affinity with the Anglican Establishment of the seventeenth century, for the religious verse of Donne and Herbert turns almost as much on doubt as on faith, and even more on the constant interplay between the two'.

The seventeenth century also saw, as Eliot recognised, the recovery of an interest in the mysticism of the fourteenth century, found in works such as *The Cloud of Unknowing* and the *Revelations of Divine Love* by Dame Julian of Norwich.

When Eliot was received into the Church of England he did not cease to be a follower of Bradley in philosophy and there was no incongruity in this, for Bradley's philosophy could be used, like most doctrines critical of metaphysics, in the service of religious faith or scepticism. In particular, Bradley's was a philosophy that lent itself to mysticism, since he believed that the Absolute is not only appearances but what holds together and contains all appearances. Every appearance, even if only partial or misleading, is subsumed in and a constituent of reality.

His reading of Bradley followed by Royce's seminars, encouraged an interest in mysticism which had already been started for Eliot by his mother's poems about saints and martyrs. As early as 1911 he had also been reading Evelyn Underhill's *Mysticism* and Lyndall Gordon suggests that the turning point in his religious life 'came not when he was baptised in 1927 but in 1914 when he first interested himself in the motives, the ordeals, and the achievements of saints'.[13] Whether this is so or not, he made at this earlier time a detailed study of 'the lives of saints and mystics, St Theresa, Dame Julian of Norwich, Mme Guyon, Walter Hilton,

St John of the Cross, Jacob Boehme, and St Bernard'.[14] According to Eloise Knapp Hayes, the notes Eliot made at Harvard included 'forty-one cards largely on the subject of mysticism and the psychology of religious experience, indicating that he had read some forty-five books and many more articles on these subjects'.[15] Undoubtedly the most important of these for its influence on Eliot was Evelyn Underhill's *Mysticism*. For Bradley the Absolute was not to be identified with God, if in fact God existed, and in *Appearance and Reality* he had written about religious experience:

> Religion naturally implies a relation between Man and God. Now a relation always. . . is self-contradictory. It implies always two terms which are finite and which claim independence. On the other hand a relation is unmeaning, unless both itself and the relateds are the adjectives of a whole. And to find a solution of this discrepancy would be to pass entirely beyond the relational point of view. This general conclusion may at once be verified in the sphere of religion.[16]

Underhill believed that Christian doctrine had resolved this problem. For her God is the Absolute who resolves all contradictions and Christ is the bridge between God and Man, the supreme example of a concrete Universal. This would not have satisfied Bradley, but even so, he could speak of philosophy 'as a satisfaction of what may be called the mystical side of our nature'[17] and he was reluctant to follow Hegel in regarding philosophy as superior to religion. In his *Essays* (written after *Appearance and Reality*) he went so far as to say that 'If a man is assured on the part of philosophy that his religious belief is false, he is warranted at least formally in replying that this is so much the worse for philosophy'.[18]

It was Royce, however, rather than Bradley who allowed Eliot to accept mysticism as intellectually respectable. Royce described the mystics as 'the only thoroughgoing empiricists in the history of philosophy'[19] because they claimed to know reality without the intermediary of ideas. He himself gave religion and mysticism a central place in his own Idealist philosophy and probably answered any doubts in Eliot's mind about the intellectual foundations of mysticism. It was Underhill, however, who led him in the direction of Christian mysticism. She believed that Christianity gave mysticism an added depth because it emphasised the personal. While other religions regarded the Absolute as unknown or impersonal,

Christianity taught that the Absolute was a personal God who had manifested himself in Christ. At what precise stage in his spiritual journey Eliot accepted this we do not know, but a point on which he quickly agreed with Evelyn Underhill was the relationship between mysticism and the imagination. Underhill explains the visions the mystics recounted as rarely direct and factually true experiences. They are works of art formed by the imagination from the raw material of these experiences. This material has remained in the mind perhaps for some time and been give an imaginative coherence that brings out their meaning.

This helps us to understand Eliot's later poetry, but it also throws light on the poems he wrote on leaving Harvard and settling in England. A group of these was never published and one can understand why he suppressed them, for they reveal a sado-masochistic element which has a disturbing effect on the reader. 'The Love Song of Saint Sebastian'(1914) and 'The Death of Saint Narcissus'(1914/15) both show this and they were probably shaped in part by impulses which came into his mind when he first attempted mystical contemplation and had put aside conscious control of his thoughts. Their association of violence and sanctity may have been the expression of a revolt against his mother, who had also written poems about the saints, and extended beyond this to reveal a rebellion against his family which led him to leave America. It is not difficult to see here the origins of the hostility and guilt which were to provide the material his imagination would later shape into *The Family Reunion*.

Two of the poems published in 1920, 'The Hippopotamus' and 'Mr Eliot's Sunday Morning Service' are attacks upon the church which do not read at first as if written by a believer in Royce's 'Beloved Community'. But it is possible to put a different interpretation on them. The epigraph to 'The Hippopotamus', 'And when this epistle is read among you, cause that it be read also in the church of the Laodiceans', refers to those whose religion is 'neither hot nor cold', and the poem can be read as a satire at the expense of the church as it is, not as it was meant to be. Similarly 'Mr Eliot's Sunday Morning Service' can be read as a criticism of what Eliot felt to be the dessicated worship of the New England churches of his boyhood. Neither of the poems is of any great merit; they display a certain wit but no depth of thought or feeling. They should not be regarded as evidence one way or the other about Eliot's religious convictions. If anything they show us a man who views institutionalised Christianity with a sceptical eye, but they leave us uncertain about his religious convictions. 'Gerontion', the most considerable poem in the 1920 collection, is very different and looks forward to *The Waste Land*. When he wrote it Eliot had been married for four years, but the marriage had failed to give him the emotional awakening he longed for. The Great War, in which he had seen his friends killed, had ended, leaving behind exhaustion and a sense of waste. Like Gerontion, he had not been a combatant, 'I was neither at the hot gates/Nor fought in the warm rain', but he now sits 'waiting for rain'. Although young, he feels old and seeks a spiritual renewal.

The speaker of this dramatic monologue is a prototype of Tiresias, the old man in *The Waste Land* who 'sat by Thebes below the wall/And walked among the lowest of the dead'. Tiresias, the soothsayer, had his sight removed when a young man for watching the goddess Athene bathing. As a compensation for this loss he is given the gift of prophecy, but with the ironic twist that no-one will believe his prophecies. Tennyson had also written a dramatic monologue about Tiresias in which he changed some of the details of the original story in Euripides and Aeschylus. These changes suggested that the pagans yearned 'For larger glimpses of that more than man' and foresaw the coming of Christianity in Menoeceus who sacrificed his life to save Thebes. Eliot would certainly have known Tennyson's poem and his Gerontion also looks backwards and forwards through the 'contrived corridors' of history where people, like those who met Christ, cry out, 'We would see a sign!' When it comes, the sign appears as a baby, 'The word within a word, unable to speak a word, /Swaddled with darkness'. This was the birth not only of a child but of a new age which brings a terrifying and yet beautiful power: 'In the juvescence of the year/Came Christ the tiger'.

Gerontion can be seen as the mouthpiece of Eliot himself, for Eliot had left his family and country behind, had suffered the loss of friends and experienced the weariness of war, had abandoned the promise of an academic career but had not found himself as a poet. He looks for a new start and asks whether it is possible to find the refreshment of spirit the mystics had promised. He could have made his own the words of Tennyson's Tiresias:

> Then, in my wanderings all the lands that lie
> Subjected to the Heliconian ridge
> Have heard this footstep fall, although my wont
> Was more to scale the highest of the heights

With some strange hope to see the nearer God.

The mystics insisted that only after penitence was the divine vision granted. Eliot's most radical disagreement with the theology of the Unitarians was in their refusal to take sin seriously, for he now felt that standing between him and the inner peace and freedom he longed for were his sins of omission and commission. 'After such knowledge, what forgiveness?', asks Gerontion. The knowledge that even our virtues may be 'forced upon us by our impudent crimes' brings the realisation that 'we have no power of ourselves to help ourselves'. This is followed by Gerontion's declaration, 'These tears are shaken from the wrath-bearing tree'.

The lines that follow begin, 'The tiger springs in the new year. Us he devours', which confirms that the tears are Christ's and the tiger, who is Christ himself, comes in judgement but also mercy to the penitent. And so the poem makes a tentative move towards faith and Gerontion is led to believe that we are more than our physical bodies; the death of the body, 'the rented house', is not the end. 'Think at last/We have not reached conclusion, when I/Stiffen in a rented house'.

When Eliot was writing 'Gerontion' he knew that his marriage was failing. He had fallen in love with a lively, highly-strung girl with the temperament of an actress, and had hoped that she would liberate his repressed and Puritanical personality, but already this hope had faded. She found him stiff and undemonstrative and he had begun to regard her as vulgar and exhibitionist. Eliot sank even deeper into the feelings of guilt and depression expressed by Gerontion:

I have lost my passion: why should I need to keep it
Since what is kept must be adulterated?
I have lost my sight, smell, hearing, taste and touch:
How should I use them for your closer contact?

This question addressed to God leads to the heart of the mystical experience. The dryness of spirit, the loss of vitality and the sensory deprivation Eliot suffered, are recognisable features of the spiritual life and were treated at length by some of the mystical writers. While at Harvard Eliot had read *The Dark Night of the Soul* by St John of the Cross and knew that such a state may be the prelude to a spiritual rebirth. 'Gerontion', then, is not a poem of despair; it makes no affirmation of faith, still less commitment to a creed, but suggests rather a time of expectant waiting. The poems written before this give one a sense of contrivance, of a too self-conscious desire on Eliot's part to be a poet. It is hardly surprising then that the 1920 volume was followed by a period when he found it difficult to write, but 'Gerontion' at least looked to a relief of his sufferings.

The silence was broken by the publication in 1922 of his first masterpiece, *The Waste Land*. Before he wrote it Eliot went home every evening from the City bank where he was employed, took out a sheet of paper, sharpened his pencil and sat down ready to write. But the words never came. It was a very unhappy period in his life and eventually led to a breakdown. Eliot was notoriously reticent about *The Waste Land* and there is no doubt that in spite of his repeated remarks about the impersonal nature of art, it was closely related to his own misery. The poem was written while he was on sick-leave from the bank, partly at Margate and partly at Lausanne, where he had gone to consult a Swiss psychiatrist. His wife was herself emotionally deranged and was later confined to a mental hospital. To add to his distress his father, whose wishes he had disregarded by leaving the U. S. A., had died in 1920. Strangely enough, when the breakdown came he found himself writing almost obsessionally, no doubt as part of a therapeutic process.

When the original and lost manuscript of *The Waste Land* was published in 1971, his widow introduced it in a radio programme in which she informed us that the passage in Eliot's essay on Pascal in 1928 really referred to the composition of his own poem:

> it is a commonplace [he wrote] that some forms of illness are extremely favourable, not only to religious illumination, but to artistic composition.

After this association of religious illumination and the imagination which, as we have seen, he would have encountered in Evelyn Underhill's *Mysticism*, he continued:

> A piece of writing meditated, apparently without progress for months or years, may suddenly take shape . . . and in this state long passages may be produced which require little or no retouch . . . he to whom this happens assuredly has the sense of being a vehicle rather than a maker . . . You may call it communication with the Divine, or you may call it a temporary crystallization of the mind.

This did not mean that the poem was the product of some kind of automatic writing. It was given to the public only after drastic revision with the help of Ezra Pound. The public received it with some initial bewilderment as a poem which expressed the weariness and sense of futility of the post-war generation. Part of the puzzlement that greeted it was because it was known that the published version was a much shorter version of the original work. It was thought that if this fuller draft could be recovered it would throw new light on the poem. This hope was realised when the original version, which had been in the possession of John Quinn, a New York bibliophile, was found and edited by Eliot's widow, with the annotations Pound had made.

In one sense this event was a disappointment, for the longer version of the poem was not a lost masterpiece, nor did it throw much light on the published version. Nevertheless, it provided knowledge of a negative kind. In the first place it showed that Pound was right to suggest cuts. The original was too diffuse and any idea that the cancelled passages would give it greater unity was dispelled altogether. Some of the passages, such as the description of a drunken riot in Boston and a record of the heroic deaths of sailors off the New England coast, were clearly more autobiographical than those that remained, but in fact they told us little more about Eliot or the poem, except to confirm that it was rooted in his own experience.

When it appeared, *The Waste Land* was greeted as an *avant-garde* work, not only as poetry but for what was thought to be its left-wing politics. Bewilderment grew when five years later its author joined the Church of England and declared himself a Monarchist and Classicist. Few readers suspected that the poem originated in the very personal Hell Eliot had suffered. But they would have found a clue to this in the Notes Eliot appended to the poem for here he informed the reader that 'Tiresias, although a mere spectator and not indeed a 'character', is yet the most important personage in the poem, uniting all the rest'. They might have guessed from this that Tiresias was Eliot himself and that the poem had a very personal significance for its author. Another clue could have been found later when the epigraph Eliot chose for the original version became known. This was taken from Conrad's *Heart of Darkness*, where Kurtz at the end of the novel looks into the wickedness of his own soul. Although this epigraph was dropped, it was, Eliot told Pound, 'much the most appropriate I can find and somewhat elucidative'. Perhaps it was too revealing, for reading it, one can only think that this is Eliot speaking for himself:

> Did he live his life again in every detail of desire, temptation, and surrender during that supreme moment of complete knowledge? He cried in a whisper at some image, at some vision – he cried out twice, a cry that was no more than a breath – 'The horror! The horror!'

Here Eliot looks into what Yeats called 'the foul rag-and-bone shop' of his soul. The experience he had passed through was no doubt what he gave dramatic form to in *The Family Reunion*; the story of sin, guilt, and the need for expiation. It explains why he was critical of Yeats's early mythology which was hardly concerned with good and evil. The theme of *The Waste Land* was far more radical than the cultural disintegration contemporary critics found in the poem; this was certainly present, but was only a symptom of a sickness that went deeper than cultural concerns. This was confirmed by Eliot in *Thoughts After Lambeth* in 1932 in which he said:

When I wrote a poem called *The Waste Land* some of the more approving critics said I had expressed 'the disillusion of a generation', which is nonsense. I may have expressed for them their own illusion of being disillusioned, but that did not form part of my intention.

What, then, was his intention? Eliot never gave a clear answer to this but dodged the question when he argued that what may be a private experience for the poet may have a public meaning for his readers. Many years later, in 1951, he wrote:

A poet may believe that he is expressing only his private experience, his lines may be for him only a means of talking about himself without giving himself away; yet for his readers what he has written may come to be the expression both of their own secret feelings and of the exaltation or despair of a generation. [20]

We may take it then that in *The Waste Land* Eliot is 'talking about himself without giving himself away'. In his life-time he was no doubt right to protect his privacy, but at this distance it is no longer impertinent but very rewarding, to try to recover the poem as he originally conceived it.

The first thing that strikes the reader of *The Waste Land* is the number of voices that speak in the poem. The original title Pound and Eliot chose for it – no doubt jokingly – was taken from Dickens's *Our Mutual Friend* (where it was used in connection with reading newsprint) and was 'He do the Police in different Voices'. This suggests mimicry, of one person assuming different personae as a dramatic device and one of the most significant features of *The Waste Land* is that all the voices in their different ways and historical contexts, are saying the same thing: they all dwell in death's own kingdom and speak of death-in-life. There is one exception; the babble of voices dies away in the last Part and there is only one voice, followed by silence.

At one level the poem can be seen as an account of the disintegration of the personality, its various parts all speaking against each other, but all witnessing to breakdown, impotence, and sterility. This dissociation of personality is a well-known feature of mental breakdown, as if the patient had split into different people and was unsure of his identity. The last Part can be seen as the recovery of identity, of a re-integration in which the personality can once more 'give, sympathise, control' ('Datta. Dayadhvam. Damyata.') in a newly achieved harmony. At this level the poem is about breakdown and recovery.

But it is more than this. The central figure in the last Part, which came so spontaneously, and which Eliot told Bertrand Russell was 'the only part that justifies the whole', is the Hanged Man. In the Notes to the poem Eliot tells the reader that 'The Hanged Man, a member of the traditional [Tarot] pack [of cards], fits my purpose in two ways: because he is associated in my mind with the Hanged God of Frazer, and because I associate him with the hooded figure in the passage of the disciples of Emmaus in Part V'. Part V is the last Part of the poem and here it is clear from the text itself, as well as the Notes that Eliot has Christ in mind. The poem ends on a note of benediction after Eliot refers to what has come before as 'These fragments I have shored against my ruins' and Hieronymo's madness. (Hieronymo in Kyd's *Spanish Tragedy* bit out his tongue in his madness; perhaps a reference that indicates Eliot's doubts about disclosing his own thoughts and feelings in the poem.) The final words are 'Datta, Dayadhvam, Damyata', followed by the Hindu 'Shantih' which he translates in the Notes as 'The Peace which passes understanding'.

This collocation of the Tarot cards used in fortune-telling, Frazer's *Golden Bough*, the New Testament, and Hinduism, is joined by references to the Buddha's Fire Sermon, St Augustine's *Confessions*, the Grail Legend, and Dante's *Divine Comedy*, and we are faced with the question of what religious beliefs, if any, Eliot had at the time when he wrote *The Waste Land*. Behind all these references there seem to be two principles at work in Eliot's mind. One is the belief he held at the time that in religion truth and meaning become one; it is pointless to attempt to verify historical facts, for what is important is the meaning the believer invests in them. The other is the importance he gave to mystical experience as an approach to the Absolute and along with this Bradley's coherence theory of truth which taught that truth is not correspondence with the facts, but belongs to a single complete system of thought of which individual experiences are only a part. Eliot quotes from Bradley's *Appearance and Reality* in the Notes to Part V of his poem, a passage which ends with the sentence, 'In brief, regarded as an existence which appears in a soul, the whole world for each is peculiar and private to that soul'. It follows from this that all religious statements can only be partly true.

We see in *The Waste Land* an acknowledgment of truth in all religions and a perception of recurring patterns of belief throughout history. In the review of *Ulysses* in *The Dial*, the year before *The Waste Land* appeared, and from which we have already quoted, Eliot in praising Joyce revealed something of the method he adopted in writing his poem. In using myth, in 'manipulating a continuous parallel between contemporaneity and antiquity', and in drawing on 'ethnology, and *The Golden Bough*', Eliot thought he was adopting an alternative to the narrative style and 'making the world possible for art, toward . . . order and form'.[21] This can be read as a statement of Jung's theory of archetypes, which emerge from a group unconscious in images and rituals with a universal significance. It also suggests a common basis to all religions and Eliot seems at this time to have viewed all religions as manifestations, even if incomplete, of the Absolute.

The three great religions which come together in *The Waste Land*, Christianity, Buddhism, and Hinduism, have much in common. They are all aware of man's alienation and need of redemption, his fear and anxiety, and the suffering he endures from forces inside and outside himself. All recognise death as the last enemy and look forward to liberation from these burdens, and all accept that man is sinful and requires forgiveness. They all believe in a Divinity who is merciful and who offers man forgiveness and reconciliation. But the ways in which deliverance comes is different in each of them. Buddhism teaches that the cause of suffering is a selfish attachment to life from which we can escape only by relinquishing our present state and moving on from rebirth to rebirth. The final release from this cycle of reincarnation is salvation by absorption in the Absolute and the only way to achieve this is the Negative Way of asceticism; an emptying of one's mind of all images and desires. Hinduism embraces a wide variety of ideas and is tolerant of other religions, but central to its beliefs is the practice of mystical asceticism, and like Buddhism it sees the final release from man's suffering in a unity with the Absolute at the end of a cycle of births and rebirths.

There was a great deal in both these religions which attracted

Eliot and which fitted in with the views he had developed from Bradley's theory of knowledge and Evelyn Underhill's mysticism, but in the Christian mystics such as St John of the Cross and St Theresa of Avila he had encountered a mysticism of suffering. In this Christian tradition there was not only an emptying of the mind, not only the Negative Way, but a discipline in which the mystic meditated on the suffering of Christ on the Cross. The belief in a suffering God is Biblical and, above all, Christian. It is accompanied in Christianity by the doctrine that through his death on the Cross Christ gives us new life and fulfilment. Bradley in *Appearance and Reality* had written of the disappearance of the individual in the Absolute:

> The individual can never himself become a harmonious system.
> In the complete gift and dissipation of his personality *he as
> such* must vanish; and with that the good as such is transcended
> and submerged . . . Most emphatically no self-assertion or self-
> sacrifice nor any goodness or morality has as such any reality
> in the absolute.[21]

a view that Buddhism, but not Christianity,.could accomodate

Another great influence on *The Waste Land*, and indeed on Eliot throughout his life, was Dante, considered by Evelyn Underhill to be a mystical writer. We know that when he was writing *The Waste Land* Eliot carried a copy of the *Divine Comedy* in his pocket and the poem contains many references to and echoes of Dante. In his 'Dante' (1929) Eliot wrote of the vision of mystics as not 'a device to enable the uninspired to write verses, but really a mental habit, which when raised to the point of genius can make a good poet as well as a great mystic or saint'.[22] Mysticism should not mean the annihilation of the individual but his fulfilment, and for the poet too it allows him to see his work as a religious vocation. Eliot regarded Dante as his exemplar and detected similarities in their lives, such as exile from their home countries and unhappy marriages. *The Waste Land* can be seen as showing the soul's progress from the 'Inferno' to the 'Purgatorio'. The emphasis given in the Notes to Frazer's *Golden Bough* and Jessie Weston's *From Ritual to Romance* obscured this for the first readers of the poem and turned attention away from the spiritual to the anthropological and cultural; it concentrated the reader's mind not on the progress of the soul but on the decay and death of civilisation.

This last is present in the poem, of course; the falling towers of Jerusalem, Athens, Alexandria, Vienna, and London, all mark the vanity of human wishes and the precarious nature of our own and earlier civilisations. What happens to mankind at large is mirrored in the progress of the human soul and the crisis in Eliot's own spiritual journey is a reflection of that in human history. As we have seen in previous chapters from the time of St Augustine's *Confessions*, and even earlier in St Paul's Epistles, Christian tradition has viewed the Biblical story of the Fall and man's redemption as a pattern which reveals itself in the life of the believer, and Dante relates the rebirth of the individual to the rebirth of society. As Adam and Eve were driven from Eden and as their descendants were taken into captivity and wandered in the wilderness until rescued by a second Adam, who himself suffered the wilderness experience, so the believer reduplicates this pattern in his own life.

The Waste Land employs the language of Buddhism and Hinduism, the myths of the fisher-king and the corn-god which speak of resurrection and renewal, but behind the poem there is the Biblical schema which belongs to *The Divine Comedy* and of special importance is the story of the Tower of Babel. The book of Genesis tells the story of how our ancestors after they had been driven from Paradise set out to recapture Heaven by building a great tower. This folly met with disaster, for all the endeavours and aspirations of civilisation, which were represented by the tower, could nor reach Heaven. Indeed, God cursed the enterprise and scattered the people who, like those in *The Waste Land*, found themselves speaking in different voices. It was only after this episode in the Biblical story that Abraham was sent by God to lead his people on the long journey to salvation. When this came it was not by human endeavour, nor by civilisation and culture, but as a gift of God. Man cannot construct a tower which will reach Heaven, nor a ladder which will enable him to climb out of the 'foul rag-and-bone shop' of his heart. The ladder, if it comes, will descend from Heaven, not be contrived by those on earth.

This much Eliot had come to believe when he wrote *The Waste Land*, but full religious conviction did not come until later. The poem expresses the fears, the doubts, the self-disgust, and the helplessness of those who look for salvation, but who lack belief. It would be wrong to suggest that the poem offers any real hope; even when he reached the spiritual maturity of *East Coker* he still writes,

> I said to my soul, be still, and wait without hope
> For hope would be hope for the wrong thing.

The years that followed *The Waste Land* found Eliot waiting for a resolution of the problems that confronted him in his marriage and his writing. Both were at a low ebb and reacted on each other. His wife's mental and physical health deteriorated badly and he himself was in poor shape, and although his work at the bank brought them sufficient money, it left him little time or energy for writing. This period of great unhappiness was punctuated by Eliot's becoming a director of Faber's in 1925, his baptism into the Church of England in 1927, and finally separation from his wife in 1933. The fragmentary *Sweeney Agonistes*, part of which he wrote in 1926 and the rest in 1927, expresses the murderous thoughts of Sweeney towards the woman he wants to be rid of and the guilt he feels, a subject taken up again in *The Family Reunion* which has two epigraphs at its beginning. The first is from Aeschylus' *Choephoroi* where Orestes says of the Furies, 'You don't see them, you don't – but I see them:/They are hunting me down, I must move on.' The second is from St John of the Cross:

> Hence the soul cannot be possessed of the divine
> union, until it has divested itself of the love
> of created beings.

These suggest the despair and guilt Eliot felt and his determination to preserve his sanity and perhaps his soul, by divesting himself of earthly attachments, including any love he might still have for his wife. At first he and his wife lived separate lives while still sharing the same house or flat, but then on the advice of his confessor, Father Underhill, and friends, they formally separated. The decision to leave his wife may appear heartless, but to have stayed with her would not have helped either of them; even so, it left him with a burden of guilt made heavier when she was later confined to a mental hospital.

During this period he became interested in Thomas Aquinas, who had provided Dante with the philosophical structure of the *Divine Comedy*, and was impressed with Jacques Maritain's neo-Thomism; but as we have seen, he decided that it was 'just Dante's luck' to have had such a philosophical system behind him. The suspicion of metaphysics he had acquired from Bradley remained with him and his conversion to Christianity never led him to think that a philosophy of religion was possible. His Christian belief always remained a matter of faith which existed alongside a rational scepticism. The influence of Bradley persisted in his readiness to accept all religions, including Christianity, as only partial revelations of a larger and all-embracing truth. When Lawrence Durrell told him that he was more like a Buddhist and not a Christian at all, he replied equivocally with the question, 'Perhaps they haven't found me out yet?'.[23] This ecumenical attitude did not extend to other forms of Christianity and when proposals for a united Church of South India in the 1940s brought together in one church Anglicans, Methodists, and Presbyterians, he wrote a pamphlet with the hostile title, *Reunion by Destruction*. Even the Church of England beyond the Anglo-Catholic branch to which he belonged aroused less than enthusiasm on his part. He retained a sympathy for Buddhism and Hinduism, but this did not extend to Islam or Judaism, although they had their own traditions of mysticism.

In the 1930s Eliot became a leading member of the ecclesiastical as well as the literary establishment. He played an active part now and during the war years in the discussions by the Christian intelligentsia concerning the role of the church in modern life and in the society that would emerge after the war. He was a member of the planning committee for the 1937 Oxford Conference on Church, Community, and State and belonged to various groups and ad-hoc bodies that followed from this. These included the Moot, presided over by Dr J. H. Oldham, one of the conveners of the Oxford Conference, the *Christian News Letter* and the World Council of Churches, and these brought him into contact with Christian thinkers outside the ranks of Anglo-Catholicism.

Already in 1927 he had written 'The Journey of the Magi', the first of the 'Ariel' poems, which signalled his conversion to Christianity. These poems were followed by the 'Ash-Wednesday' group and then in 1935 came the first production of *Murder in the Cathedral*, which became an immediate and lasting success. In the same year *Burnt Norton* was published and this became the first of the *Four Quartets*, Eliot's second masterpiece and one of the great achievements of English religious poetry. In 1936 and when he had completed *Burnt Norton*, Eliot began work on *The Family Reunion*, which elaborated some of the themes and feelings already touched on in *Sweeney Agonistes*. It was written after the visit of Eliot's old love, Emily Hale, to England.

During this visit Eliot took Emily to Burnt Norton where he experienced bitter regret, hatred, and guilt, as he contrasted the happiness he might have had with the misery he now endured. These feelings are expressed in *The Family Reunion* but originated in 'Burnt Norton'. It is not simply the bitter-sweet memories that are recalled as Eliot lives again his youthful love for Emily Hale, but the realisation that the past can never be recovered, whereas guilt for the past remains. And so *Burnt Norton* opens on the sombre note of

> Time present and time past
> Are both perhaps present in time future
> And time future contained in time past.
> If all time is eternally present
> All time is unredeemable.

The supposition contained in the last two of these lines was to become a leitmotif of all the *Four Quartets*.

In the closing lines of *Burnt Norton*, 'Ridiculous the waste sad time/Stretching before and after', Eliot returns to his childhood in St Louis and 'the hidden laughter/Of children in the foliage'; regret for the past haunts him as he looks back on the happiness he had once known. He and his companion look at the 'drained pool' at Burnt Norton, an image for Eliot of his aridity of spirit, and suddenly 'the pool was filled with water out of sunlight, /And the lotos rose, quietly, quietly'. The lotos in Hinduism is the emblem of the supreme god Brahma and symbolises peace and fecundity, but it vanishes as quickly as it had appeared and takes with it Eliot's momentary hope of a new life.

With this hope gone, Eliot is left to bear his suffering alone and he does this by attempting to escape from time by the mystical way:

> Descend lower, descend only
> Into the world of perpetual solitude.

Only thus can we achieve freedom from sensory desire, 'while the world moves/In appetency, on its metalled ways/Of time past and time future.' He dares to hope that his poetry may be a religious vocation and that mystical contemplation and art may become united in the service of God, but realises that language cannot express the inexpressible:

> words strain,
> Crack and sometimes break, under the burden,
> Under the tension, slip, slide, perish ,
> Decay with imprecision.

Even the incarnate Word of God is subject to these pressures: 'The Word in the desert/Is most attacked by voices of temptation'. Nevertheless, the Word of God triumphs to speak of love which, unlike language, remains absolute and unchanging:

> Love is itself unmoving,
> Only the cause and end of movement.

The theme of love as the cause and end of life is taken up in the opening words of *East Coker*, 'In my beginning is my end'. This is an inversion of Mary Queen of Scots' motto, 'En ma fin est mon commencement', which is put in its original form in the closing words of the poem, 'In my end is my beginning'. *Burnt Norton* reflected on the relation between man's temporal life and eternity, but now Eliot turns from his own life to the Somerset village of East Coker, the home of his ancestors. What he has said in *Burnt Norton* about the individual he now applies to the village: 'You say I am repeating/Something I have said before. I shall say it again'. He is conscious of the successive generations who link him to his ancestors; he owes his existence to them, for 'Home is where we start from'. He looks for salvation not only for himself, not only for his forebears, but for the whole of mankind; for a deliverance from 'Adam's curse'. This will be brought about by the 'wounded surgeon' who probes our sickness with his scalpel, the suffering Christ who shows us that suffering can bring spiritual health. This is the message of Good Friday.

East Coker was concerned with Eliot's Somerset ancestors; *The Dry Salvages* takes Eliot back to his early years in St Louis on the Mississippi. Eliot remembered the river from his childhood, but the title itself is taken from the group of rocks he had known in his Harvard days when sailing off Cape Ann, Massachusetts. The river and the sea are brought together in the poem as images of time and eternity. For Eliot the river also recalls his American forebears who had moved from Boston to the new frontier. Like the sailors in the poem, who go to sea not knowing whether they will return safely, his ancestors were also pioneers; they too faced forward with faith in the future.

Although the poem is set in America, it was written in war-time England when the British were required to kill as part of their Christian duty. Perhaps in deference to those who could not agree with this, he refers not to a Christian source but to Krishna, the incarnation of the Hindu god Vishnu, who tells Arjuna that we must accept the slaughter of the battle-field, both for the sake of the enemy and ourselves, and that he should 'face forward' in faith.

Although it is only the third in the sequence of poems *The Dry Salvages* completes the previous two and Eliot came to write *Little Gidding* as an afterthought. In *Burnt Norton* he had faced a personal crisis and the realisation that there was no escape from the suffering and guilt that followed his unfortunate marriage. *East Coker* reminds us that this experience is not his alone, but the condition of all humanity, including Eliot's own family, who bear a part in the communal ill of which we are all heirs. In *Burnt Norton* he 'had the experience but missed the meaning', but now the meaning has become clearer,

the past experience revived in the meaning

> Is not the experience of one life only
> But of many generations.

This does nothing to assuage his own grief; indeed the guilt and suffering of *Burnt Norton* return with renewed force as he is made aware that time is not a healer, for our memories are permanently with us: 'People change, and smile: but the agony abides. /Time the destroyer is time the preserver'. The only hope of escape from this slavery to time is through the apprehension of the eternal in 'the moment in and out of time'. The saint devotes his life to this, but for most it comes in 'the unattended/Moment', although it can be cultivated by 'prayer, observance, discipline, thought and action'. Above all, for all of us,

> the gift half understood, is Incarnation.

> Here the impossible union
> Of spheres of existence is actual.

Eliot had come to this central affirmation of the Christian faith and found in it the answer to his needs, and it gave what he felt was the fitting conclusion to his three poems. But *Little Gidding* provides a far more satisfactory end to *Four Quartets* for it sums up what has preceded it and takes Eliot a stage further on his spiritual journey. *Little Gidding* takes the reader from the Incarnation to Pentecost, which reverses the events of the Tower of Babel. There God had withdrawn himself from his people and left them unable to communicate with each other, now he returns and people of all tongues speak to one another again. *The Waste Land* opened with,

> April is the cruellest month, breeding
> Lilacs out of the dead land,

Little Gidding opens with, 'Midwinter spring is its own season', and the promise of an awakening of the spirit by 'pentecostal fire/ In the dark time of the year'. The season is 'the spring time/But not in time's covenant'.

Unlike the other poems in the sequence *Little Gidding* has no particular autobiographical significance, but recalls the visit Eliot made some years before he wrote the poem, to the place where Nicholas Ferrar founded his religious community in the seventeenth century. This was where Charles I sought refuge after the defeat at Naseby, and the poem speaks of the defeated Royalists,

> a king at nightfall,
> Of three men, and more, on the scaffold

and of the Roundheads and their Latin Secretary, Milton, 'one who died blind and quiet'. Both sides are now united in death. It was a fitting place in which to set the poem, for Ferrar's community was an Anglican one living in a time of war and Eliot's poem was written in 1940-41, when war was being fought on English soil again for the first time since the seventeenth century.

The war probably played its part in encouraging Eliot to write *Little Gidding*, for at the time many were led to consider the collective guilt which had brought it about and to meditate on the mystery of God's purposes in history. But as with *The Waste Land*, personal concerns are reflected in the larger events taking place; the difference here is that in spite of the war there is a new hope which Eliot has rarely expressed so clearly before. The earlier *Quartets* find him still traversing the desert or, as with Dante, lost in a thick wood, but *Little Gidding* gives us a vision of man's redemption and a glimpse of the City of God, and this at a time when it seemed possible, as it did when St Augustine wrote his *Civitas Dei*, that civilisation might collapse.

This change was almost certainly influenced by Eliot's reading of Charles Williams's study of Dante and his *The Descent of the Dove*. Williams was a poet, playwright, and writer of theological thrillers, who is largely forgotten now, but who had many admirers in war-time England and the years that immediately followed it. Eliot admired Williams's writings, and *The Descent of the Dove* which first appeared in 1939, was taken over and re-issued by Faber in 1950. It is a short history of the Christian Church viewed as the continuing work of the Holy Spirit from Pentecost onwards. Williams follows St Augustine in believing that man was born into sin and that we all share in this corruption, but that we are rescued by the grace of God, for as St Paul declared, 'As in Adam all die, even so in Christ shall all be made alive.'

Because of this and throughout history men's sinful acts are made the means of his ultimate salvation. The supreme example of this is the Crucifixion, for the worst crime man could commit paradoxically brings about his redemption, and, as Eliot says in *Little Gidding*, 'That is why we call this Friday good'. This paradox led Dame Julian of Norwich to say in a quotation Eliot introduces into his poem, that 'Sin is behovely', and that at the end 'All shall be well'.

In the meantime we have to live in the temporal world, but although in this world we are not entirely of it, and as Williams declares, 'the title of the grand activity of the Church' should be 'The conversion of time by the Holy Ghost'. We can redeem the times because God has redeemed time itself; if we live on the eternal side of things we obtain a freedom from the tyranny of events. This is what Eliot meant when he wrote, 'History may be servitude, / History may be freedom'. The Incarnation exhibits the coming together of time and eternity and in Christ we see what Williams calls the co-inherence of the two.

The double nature of our existence is seen in the two means by which we apprehend God: The Negative and the Affirmative Ways. The Negative Way eschews all images and empties the mind of all thoughts centred on temporal concerns; it embraces asceticism and the mysticism of suffering. This was the Way adopted by St Augustine, but among his followers it led to a neglect of the Affirmative Way, the celebration of God's goodness in the natural order, in the achievements of civilisation, the arts, justice, and love, including sexual love between men and women. Williams insists that there should be a co-inherence between the two Ways, since one without the other leads to a distortion of reality; co-inherence forms a pattern which runs throughout the history of Christendom.

For a long time Eliot had followed the Negative Way, the path of renunciation and the mysticism of suffering; the descent of the Dove had meant for him personally 'the flame of incandescent terror'. But now he seems to have come to a new realisation that for too long he had refused to accept God's forgiveness and grace. For many years he had believed that the past was irredeemable, but if Christ has redeemed time itself, all time, past, present, and future are in God's hands and the past can be forgiven. The life of the individual as well as the nation can be servitude, but it can also be freedom.

Eliot's interest in mysticism had given him an other-worldly disregard of the temporal, but the war and his participation in Christian discussions about the society likely to emerge from the conflict, led him to give greater importance to God's purpose in human history. This was undoubtedly helped by his reading of Williams's *The Descent of the Dove*. It also came to him through a recognition that the liberal American Protestantism he disliked so much had met its most radical criticism not in the revival of medieval scholasticism by Catholic theologians, but in the writings of the American theologian Reinhold Niebuhr. Eliot had come to know Niebuhr through the Oxford Conference on Church, Community and State and *The Christian Newsletter*, and stayed with him and his wife, Ursula, who was an Anglican theologian, when he visited America. Niebuhr was in Britain in 1939 when he delivered his

Gifford Lectures on *The Nature and Destiny of Man* in which he dismissed the shallow account of human nature and the optimistic promises of social progress by some forms of Christianity.

Niebuhr also rejected the possibility of accommodating the Christian notion of selfhood to the Idealist philosophies of Royce and Bradley, which he correctly identified with mysticism. He argued that mysticism presented an unsatisfactory view of human nature and history, and illustrated his argument by quoting the third book of the *Enneads*, where Plotinus declares that the eternity of the 'Intellectual World' negates rather than fulfils history. Similarly Hinduism and Buddhism in most of their forms seek to redeem man from history rather than in history. Even Christian mysticism, maintained Niebuhr, made '*gnosis* rather than *agape* the final form'.[24] In reading *Little Gidding* one is aware of a change from the earlier Quartets and it is likely that Niebuhr played a part in this. The reader feels that the burden of perfectionism has been lifted from Eliot's shoulders and that he is now ready to accept grace as an unconditional gift of God which does not have to be earned; that instead of searching for a vision of God he is conscious of God's initiative in love.

The unity of *Four Quartets* is circular with a structure similar to the music of Bartok's or Beethoven's Quartets. They are not philosophical poems, for he had no system of thought to create anything like the *Divine Comedy*, even though he was influenced by Dante. In many ways the sequence is not unlike Wordsworth's 'Prelude', for they too trace the growth of his mind as he makes his spiritual journey. There are passages in the poems reminiscent of the 'the spots of time' passage in *The Prelude* where Wordsworth mystically apprehends a unity which transcends our ordinary experience, and Eliot fits very well Wordsworth's description of 'those higher minds' who live

By sensible impressions not enthralled,
But by their quickening pulse made more prompt
To hold fit converse with the spiritual world,
And with the generations of mankind
Spread over time, past, present, and to come,
Age after age, till Time shall be no more.

Throughout *Four Quartets* there is an emphasis on their circularity in sentences such as, 'The end is where we start from', 'In my beginning is my end', and 'Home is where one starts from'. These refer not only to the structure of the poems but to the story they relate. The poems start with the garden at Burnt Norton with its suggestion of Eden in the phrase, 'Through the first gate, /Into our first world', and they end with the 'children in the apple tree' of *Little Gidding*, that is, with redeemed mankind to whom Paradise has been restored. The poems tell the story of Man's Fall, his wanderings through history, and his redemption. This pattern gives shape not only to history but to Eliot's own life; it is the pattern of the Mystical Way which Eliot made his own.

Little Gidding makes a distinction between detachment from and indifference to history. The poems begin with the statement that

If all time is eternally present
All time is unredeemable.

They end with a vision of restored mankind, but this has taken place in history; time has been redeemed and we now live in a state of what C. H. Dodd called 'realised eschatology', the end-time in which we can re-enter our lost Eden.

There may seem to be a great deal of repetition in *Four Quartets* but Eliot is speaking of exploration ('each venture is a new beginning') and discovery; images are repeated but each time with a deepened or changed meaning. London, for instance, may be 'the unreal city'; it may be Hell for Eliot uses the London Underground to recall Dante's Inferno. But through God's providence it can become the Celestial City. This is not just the vision of a new political order, though it may have political implications, nor is it a 'Paradise within', though it can also be that. It is the City of God of which we can become citizens now.

Yeats had thought to reach it by the ladder of his proud imagination, but Eliot believes we can only arrive there by the humility of the divine grace which comes down from heaven to rescue us. Poetry is not a means of redemption; it may be, in Eliot's own fine phrase, 'a raid on the inarticulate', but it does not give us certainty, still less salvation. The poetic imagination may become a glass of vision in which we catch glimpses of eternity, and poetry is part of man's cultural achievement, symbolised by Eliot in the rose, the emblem of all that is good in the natural order. But that order reaches fulfilment only when it is caught up in and united with the love of God:

And all shall be well and
All manner of thing shall be well
When the tongues of flame are in-folded
Into the crowned knot of fire
And the fire and the rose are one.

VI
Auden and Larkin

There are many poets whom one might choose to illustrate the religious temper of the second half of the twentieth century. Edwin Muir, John Betjeman, Charles Williams, Elizabeth Jennings, Charles Sisson, R. S. Thomas, David Gascoyne and others come immediately to mind. All are distinguished poets who deserve attention, but if one is to restrict the choice to two, then Auden and Philip Larkin select themselves. Auden, for all his individual talents, is a representative figure whose work charts the changes in the religious currents running through the period; moving from agnostic and liberal humanism, through Marxism, to an individual and Protestant faith, but one within the Anglican church. Larkin, in a different way, is no less representative. In reaction to what he regarded as an alien element in English poetry in the work of Yeats, an Irishman, Eliot, an American, and Auden, a naturalised American, he looked to the native tradition he found above all in Hardy, and took over from him the scepticism and pessimism which undermined the optimistic humanism of the first part of this century.

Auden grew up in a comfortable middle-class home, the son of a father who was a medical doctor and, like his wife, the child of an Anglican clergyman. While Auden's father took a rather detached view of religion, his mother was a woman of firm Christian principles of an Anglo-Catholic kind, who took her children to morning and evening services on Sundays and at an early age the young Auden became an altar server. In later life he looked back on this without resentment and, indeed, counted it an advantage to his spiritual development. His mother was the dominant partner in the marriage and Auden remembered her as the main emotional influence in his childhood and his father as a weak but benevolent figure. He was the youngest of three boys and separated from the elder two by a gap of some years, and naturally as the youngest was subject to his mother's authority and affection.

At the outbreak of the 1914-18 war, when Auden was seven, his father joined the RAMC and the family did not see him for the next four years. This, coupled with his mother's personality, played a large part, or so he thought, in his subsequent homosexuality. His mother's dominance may have contributed to his rejection of the faith in which she had brought him up, but this seems unlikely, for throughout his life he retained affection for her and respect for her religious views.

His rejection of Christianity while a pupil at Gresham's school sprang more from a feeling that his religion had little intellectual basis and was largely disguised sexuality. At Oxford, like many of his contemporaries, he found left-wing politics more interesting than religion and his sexual promiscuity fitted well into an intellectual climate formed by notions of self-expression, experiment, and liberal views of human personality which discounted any idea of original sin.

The two great formative figures of the period were Marx and Freud, but the liberalism which characterised British thought took the hard edges off both of these and made them more acceptable to Auden and his contemporaries. It even made possible the reconciliation of their respective theories, although they were basically incompatible. Auden was never a convinced Marxist and never joined the Communist Party. He found D. H. Lawrence, Gerald Heard, and Aldous Huxley, with their theories of self-expression, pacifism, and attacks on emotional repression, more congenial than those who explained human nature in terms of class-warfare and economic history. He was probably influenced in this by his father whose profession as a doctor led Auden from an early age to take an interest in healing; throughout his life he saw himself as a healer rather than a revolutionary. Revolution for him was something that happened to the individual rather than society. A good illustration of his early beliefs can be found in a poem which appeared in his *Collected Poems*, 1945, but which he dropped from later collections. It is in the form of a prayer to a benevolent but otherwise ill-defined deity, who is ready to forgive us all our sins, except the turning of the personality against itself in self-destruction, in the Freudian death-wish:

Sir, no man's enemy, forgiving all
But will his negative inversion, be prodigal:
Send to us power and light, a sovereign touch
Curing the intolerable neural itch,

Publish each healer that in city lives
Or country houses at the end of drives;
Harrow the house of the dead; look shining at

New styles of architecture, a change of heart.

One of the reasons he gave later for suppressing the poem was its dishonesty for, he said, he had never liked modern architecture. In spite of this disowner, it reveals the dual role he chose for himself of healer and teacher. He was a gifted expositor with a natural gift for teaching and on leaving Oxford after the disappointment of a third-class degree, he settled into the job of schoolmaster, not reluctantly as Evelyn Waugh and others of his contemporaries had done, but with interest and enthusiam. Before this, though, he spent a year in Berlin where he indulged his homosexual practices and where he met John Layard, a disciple of Homer Lane and an exponent of the view that all illnesses had a psycho-somatic component and that full health depended on the satisfaction of our physical appetites, especially the sexual ones. Auden already knew and admired Lawrence's *Fantasia of the Unconscious* and welcomed these ideas; and although he was to modify them, they coloured his later thinking.

During 1928-29, the year Auden spent in Berlin, the Weimar Republic was still in place, even though there was political unrest and dissatisfaction with the government. Hitler had not yet taken over and the Nazis and Communists were locked in a bitter struggle to overthrow the government and seize power for themselves. Auden witnessed some of the street-fighting and violence of this struggle and became politically aware in a real sense for the first time. While at Oxford he had supported the workers in the General Strike of 1926 by driving a car in London, but like most of his fellow-undergraduates, he never took the strike seriously. While most of them acted as strike-breakers, he supported the strikers, but not with any political conviction or even understanding. If he had any serious motivation it was the simple desire to help the under-privileged against the powerful.

On his return from Germany he had far greater political awareness, but still without any great ideological commitment. In 1936 in his 'Letter to Lord Byron', part of his contributions to *Letters from Iceland*, written jointly with Louis MacNeice, he prophesied that he would end up as 'A selfish pink old Liberal'. Apart from the self-denigratory term 'selfish', this proved true. Auden's basic political impulse was the radical desire to serve justice and to relieve the oppressed. This was so even in 1937 when he went to Spain during the civil war and enlisted as an ambulance driver on the Republican side. As he explained to his friends, his decision had less to do with the Spanish struggle than the wish to enlarge his experience by finding out what war was like at first hand. In many ways his experience was similar to George Orwell's, another radical motivated less by doctrinaire opinions than an honest attempt to find out what was going on. Both men ended with a deep suspicion of communism as well as fascism. Auden discovered that both sides treated their political enemies with great cruelty when captured and carried out executions with little regard for justice or humanity. He returned to England disillusioned and with any expectation of more civilised behaviour on the part of the Republicans completely gone.

Even more surprising both to himself and to those who had formed a picture of Auden based on their own political sympathies, was the effect of the Spanish civil war on his religious beliefs. He was shocked by the fiercely anti-Catholic behaviour of the Republicans as they destroyed church buildings and persecuted the clergy. Writing in a collection of essays entitled *Modern Canterbury Pilgrims* (1956), he recorded his reaction at the time. 'I found', he wrote, 'as I walked through the city [Barcelona] that all the churches were closed and there was not a priest to be seen. To my astonishment, this discovery left me profoundly shocked and disturbed.' In examining the reasons for this he realised that religion was more important to him than he had been ready to admit. 'I could not escape acknowledging', he continued, 'that however I had consciously ignored and rejected the Church for sixteen years, the existence of churches and what went on in them had all the time been very important to me. If that was the case what then?' [1]

Auden was back in England in May, feeling frustration at not having his services used and filled with revulsion at the senseless violence and futility of the civil war in Spain. This led to a deep suspicion of politics on his part and a feeling that beneath the political struggles of the time lay a malaise that called for a spiritual remedy. It encouraged him for a time to embrace pacifism, but although at first this re-awakened his religious interest, it remained a matter of sensibility and hardly involved theological thinking. Nevertheless, his awareness of human wickedness that came out of the civil war was to keep him clear of the easy-going liberalism that glossed over the reality of evil and in this he was to follow T. E. Hulme and T. S. Eliot and others who had rebelled against romanticism.

This did not happen at once, however, and on his return from Spain he read and was much taken with Christopher Caudwell's *Illusion and Reality: A Study of the Sources of Poetry.* Caudwell was the nom-de-plume of Christopher St John Sprigg, the Marxist poet and critic, who had just been killed serving with the

International Brigade in Spain. Caudwell's book had a certain vogue as one of the few studies of Marxist aesthetics; it explained the history of poetry as the result of economic forces, and its assumptions all derived from an economic determinism tempered by a liberal element which saw history advancing towards a millenarian and earthly paradise. Auden was too honest to pretend that the Spanish war was anything other than the cruel and undemocratic conflict he had seen for himself, but some of Caudwell's views found their way into the poem 'Spain' he wrote at this time, which was published as a pamphlet by Faber's, and the profits of which went to medical aid in Spain. Although Orwell praised the poem for being 'one of the few decent things' that had come out of Spain, he objected to the cynical notion that the end justified the means, which was contained in the line, 'The conscious acceptance of guilt in the necessary murder', where Auden subscribed to the Marxist doctrine of 'the freedom of necessity'. He tried to justify the line in answer to Orwell's objection by suggesting that it made a case for the idea of a just war, but later he changed 'necessary' to 'fact of' murder.

As the war clouds gathered over Europe Auden experienced a feeling of depression which was increased by his memories of what had happened in Spain and his realisation that the war there had not been a clear-cut struggle between tyranny and democracy, still less between good and evil. This, he felt, would be true of the larger conflict that now threatened. He had not made any move towards Christian commitment at this time, but he became more and more convinced that events demanded an explanation that went beyond politics and were the concern of religion. This conviction was increased by his meeting with Charles Williams in 1937.

Charles Williams worked at the London office of the Oxford University Press, but the meeting took place in Oxford where Auden made the suggestion that he should edit an *Oxford Book of Light Verse*; a suggestion recommended by Williams and subsequently approved by the Press. The two men discussed mainly poetry and not religion, but the meeting had a profound effect on Auden. He found, as many others did, that Williams carried with him an aura of sanctity that elicited a spiritual awareness they had not known they possessed and which left them feeling better for their meeting.

Since his death in 1945 Williams's work has largely been neglected, but during the war when he lived in Oxford and lectured in the English Faculty, he had a large circle of admirers and friends, including C. S. Lewis, who wrote a study of Williams's poetry entitled *Arthurian Torso*. But it was his theological work, *The Descent of the Dove*, which was to influence Auden when it appeared in 1939. This was still a couple of years ahead and before then Auden visited China with Isherwood to cover the Sino-Japanese war. It was on their return from witnessing yet another war that both men decided to emigrate to the USA.

Their departure in January 1939, shortly before Britain declared war against Germany, caused an outcry which lasted for many years and brought accusations of cowardice and a lack of patriotism. By this time both of them, and Auden especially, were well-known as writers and public figures. Auden had written two volumes of poetry, *Look Stranger!* and *Another Time*; four plays, all but the first written in collaboration with Isherwood, *The Dance of Death*, *The Dog Beneath the Skin*, *The Ascent of F6* and *On the Frontier*; and two travel books, *Letters from Iceland* with Louis MacNeice, and *Journey to a War* with Isherwood. The libretto for *Midnight Mail* which Auden wrote for the GPO film had been an immediate and enormous success. The literary public realised that here were two considerable talents and one an original poetic voice that expressed the sensibility of the period as no-one else did. Their departure for America left this public feeling deep disappointment, while it left others with a sense of outrage and betrayal.

Many have seen Auden's departure for America as marking a break between his earlier and his later poetry and many have regarded his early poetry as superior to anything he later achieved. Certainly, as Barbara Everett in her excellent *Auden* (1964), demonstrated, there was an astonishing variety, versatility, and freshness in the poetry Auden wrote as a young man. Some of it is uneven, but this is balanced by the spontaneity and ease of movement, which many felt he lost when he went to America and wrote in what they considered a more prosaic style. There is a parallel here with what was said about T. S. Eliot, for many similarly thought *The Waste Land* the high-water mark of his achievement which was followed by what they considered the prosaic style of *Four Quartets*.

The parallel goes beyond a matter of style, for both show the same pattern in their lives; Auden as much as Eliot underwent a Waste Land experience and emerged to find religious faith. Throughout all the variety of Auden's early poetry there is a persistent refrain: the sense of alienation in a world in which he felt a stranger. Instead of the pilgrimage through the bare landscapes of the Grail legend which Eliot's spirit had to traverse in *The Waste Land*, Auden's poetry chooses the detritus of the discarded mines and iron-works of an out-dated industrial revolution to symbolise his spiritual quest. One often hears in his early poetry an echo of A. E. Housman's couplet, 'I, a stranger and afraid/In a world I never made.' and it is significant that the title he gave to the first volume of his collected poems in 1936 was *Look Stranger!*

It would be wrong to deny the change in Auden's poetry, but it would also be a mistake to see this as a sudden and sharp one. Auden's poetry, like Eliot's, moved forward, assimilating and modifying his earlier practices rather than discarding them completely. Some have seen it as a movement from a Marxist and Freudian outlook to an acceptance of Christian belief, but this again is too simple though not entirely wrong. When he went to America Auden was looking for a place where he could settle and feel at home in a way he never found possible in Britain or Europe. It was not the war itself that drove him away, but the sense of a failed and sick civilisation of which the war was only a symptom; the feeling that America did not carry the cultural burdens that frustrated the freedom his spirit desired. There is a strange irony that as Eliot looked to England as the heir of a rich historical tradition, so Auden saw America as free of the corruptions of such a tradition.

Some accused Auden of deserting the communist cause and the battle against fascism taking place in Europe, of leaving the action for a life of poetry and thought. In the verse play *On the Frontier*, published in 1938, in which Auden and Isherwood collaborated, the 'Frontier' is not the American frontier where the original settlers made a new world, but the frontier between a communist and a capitalist state, but it also represents – and this is a favourite image of Auden's – the place where decisions have to be made, and his departure for America was one of these. It was not an abandonment of communism, for there had never been any real commitment on his part, and ever since his experience in Spain his doubt about any communist solution to the problems of modern society had been confirmed. The decision to leave for America did not signal then a sudden break with Marxism; it was much more a disillusionment with European society and its problems and a desire for mental and spiritual elbow-room.

The decision grew out of his conviction that his vocation was to be a poet, but equally the realisation that his poetry was unlikely to bring about any political or social change. In 1939, the year in which war was declared, there occurred the deaths of two men whom Auden admired and to whom he owed much. These were Yeats and Freud, and the memorial verses Auden wrote in paying tribute to them reveal his own beliefs at the time. Of Yeats he wrote, 'Mad Ireland hurt you into poetry. /Now Ireland has her madness and her weather still, /For poetry makes nothing happen'. The suggestion that poetry could influence politics as little as it could the weather was repeated in the prose obituary he wrote for Yeats, 'Counsel for the Defence', in which he argued that 'If not a poem had been written, . . . the history of mankind would be materially unchanged.' This was an opinion that was to remain with him from now on. The job of the poet is not political reform, but 'In the prison of his days/Teach the free man how to praise'.

The influence of Freud, who died in the month that war broke out, had been more pervasive: 'to us he is no more a person/Now but a whole climate of opinion.' His teaching, seen by some as subversive of the established order, showed a compassion for the oppressed individual and the sinner: 'Of course they called on God, but he went his way/Down among the lost people like Dante.'

Auden's left-wing opinions had always been qualified by the belief that beneath the corruptions and betrayals of society lay a sickness that needed curing before parties and their programmes could become effective. His Marxism such as it was had been increasingly diluted by his Freudian ideas and at one time by the hope that his poetry might even be an agent in the healing process. His experience in Spain had led to a disillusionment with politics and he was now left with the spectacle of a sickness that had brought men to a war that threatened civilisation.

It was in this state of mind that he wrote the poem '1st September 1939', in which he looks back on the events that had led to the inevitability of war now that Germany had invaded Poland:

I sit in one of the dives
On Fifty-second Street
Uncertain and afraid
As the clever hopes expire
Of a low dishonest decade.

He traces these events beyond his own time; back to the break-up of medievalism and the emergence of the nation-state after the Reformation:

Accurate scholarship can
Unearth the whole offence
From Luther until now
That has driven a culture mad
Find what occurred at Linz.

Linz was the birthplace of Hitler but Auden sees National Socialism

as the result not only of Hitler's personal neurosis which had created
'A psychopathic god', but of a general madness brought about by

> What all schoolchildren learn,
> Those to whom evil is done
> Do evil in return.

The notion of collective guilt for the Treaty of Versailles ran deep
in the consciences of those in the Western democracies and
encouraged the spirit of appeasement among liberal-minded people
in the 1930s. The feeling that there was little to choose between
different shades of grey led to a refusal to make moral judgments
and silence in the face of what called for condemnation. Auden
came to realise this and he later suppressed the poem. In his Foreword
to B. C. Bloomfield's *W. H. Auden: A Bibliography* (1964), he
explained his reasons for this:

> Rereading a poem of mine, '1st September, 1939', after it had
> been published, I came to the line 'We must love one another or
> die' and said to myself: 'That's a damned lie! We must die
> anyway.' So, in the next edition, I altered it to 'We must love
> one another and die'. This didn't seem to do either, so I cut the
> stanza. Still no good. The whole poem, I realised was infected
> with an incurable dishonesty – and must be scrapped.

This was a pity, for not all of the poem deserved to be abandoned
and some of the sentiments expressed there he carried forward
into his later work; in particular, a theme already encountered in
his poetry, the conflict between the collective and the individual
good. What stands in the way of universal love is original sin; we
may all want love but self-interest always comes between the desire
and its realisation. Auden uses a quotation from *The Diary of Vaslav
Nijinsky* to make his point:

> For the error bred in the bone
> Of each woman and each man
> Craves what it cannot have,
> Not universal love
> But to be loved alone.[2]

This brings Auden close to the Christian teaching that the human
will is corrupted from the start and not by social institutions,
economic forces, or upbringing, but by an intrinsic self-centredness
which is known as sin. This poem marks a conscious turning to
Christian belief, but already when they were collaborating in writing
On the Frontier Isherwood complained about Auden's religious
inclinations. 'I have to keep a sharp eye on him' he said, ' – or
down flop the characters on their knees; another constant danger is

that of choral interruptions by angel voices.'[3] At the time Auden was still an agnostic in the liberal manner of E. M. Forster to whom he and Isherwood dedicated *Journey to a War*, their travel book on China. This included a sonnet sequence by Auden, 'In Time of War', which sketches the history of mankind and its culmination in the madness of world war. Although the later version[4] ends with a tribute to Forster and an appeal to sweet reasonableness, the imagery is taken from the Bible and hints at a primal innocence now lost by man's sin:

Some lost a world they never understood,
Some saw too clearly all that man was born for. (XVI)

The awareness of sin as real gathered conviction in Auden's mind as Europe moved into war and became a central theme in *New Year Letter*[5] which he wrote to greet the New Year, 1940, and which he dedicated to his friend Elizabeth Mayer, at whose house he had spent Christmas. The epigraph is a quotation from Montaigne which recognises the duality of human nature, of how we see and approve the good but are unable to achieve it: 'We are, I know not how, double in ourselves, /So that what we believe we disbelieve, and/ Cannot rid ourselves of what we condemn'. The work shows evidence of immensely wide reading, but running through it there is an obvious indebtedness to Charles Williams's *The Descent of the Dove* which had been published in 1939.

As we saw in the last chapter Williams treats the history of the Christian church as a series of antitheses between apprehending the reality of God by the Negative Way and the Affirmative Way. The Negative Way eschews sensory images and embraces asceticism as the approach to God, whereas the Affirmative Way celebrates the presence of God in the natural order and the achievements of civilisation: in justice, the arts, the family, and sexual love. Williams believed that both were necessary and that Christian history works through a dialectic between these two, but that the Affirmative Way had been neglected in a one-sided emphasis on asceticism. For Williams the Eucharist brings both together by raising up the material world in the service of God and by bringing down the spiritual world in material form. In this it replicates the Incarnation.

Auden was tremendously impressed by Williams's book which came at a turning point in his religious thinking. By the time he wrote *New Year Letter* Auden had become disillusioned with any political solutions to contemporary problems and was convinced that the only remedy to cure the sickness that afflicted mankind was a spiritual one. As he celebrated the New Year in Elizabeth Mayer's home he found in the company of his friends, and the warm affection that surrounded them, the love he longed for; something of the joy felt by the dispossessed when summoned to the wedding-feast in the story recounted by Jesus:

I felt the unexpected power
That drove our ragged egos in
From the dead-ends of greed and sin
To sit down at the wedding feast,

Our privileged community
That real republic which must be
The State all politicians claim,
Even the worst, to be their aim. (Pt. III, 845-859)

This ideal can be achieved only fitfully on this side of eternity, but Auden's poem looks for an approach to it in a reconciliation of the two Ways; bringing together asceticism and the pleasures of the senses in an attempt to apprehend the eternal in the temporal.

The most keenly felt of the dualisms thus revealed was, for Auden, the antinomy (in the literal sense of the word) expressed plangently in St Paul's cry, 'For the good that I would I do not; but the evil which I would not, that I do'. The conflict between the spirit and the flesh was brought home to him in a personal manner by his homosexual practices, which he never regarded as anything but wrong, but which he endeavoured to channel into a union that for him, but not for his companion Chester Kallman, was a model of fidelity akin to marriage. St Augustine followed St Paul in believing that only God's grace could deliver him from sin; he acknowledged that the moral law demanded chastity but found himself unable to comply with it and so he prayed in his *Confessions*, 'O da quod iubes, Domine', 'Give what you command, Lord'. This prayer is quoted by Charles Williams in *The Descent of the Dove* and again by Auden at the end of his poem where it is incorporated in a petition that asks God to

Instruct us in the civil art
Of making from the muddled heart
A desert and a city where
The thoughts that have to labour there
May find locality and peace,
And pent-up feelings their release.
Send strength sufficient for our day,
And point our knowledge on its way,
O da quod iubes, Domine. (Pt. III, 1676-1684)

The Notes which acknowledge Auden's indebtedness to Charles Williams's book, run to more pages than the poem itself and provide a brilliant commentary, mixing wit and wisdom, apothegms, epigrams, and allusions to a wide range of authors and books, including the Bible, Freud and Marx, and Blake, Rilke and Kierkegaard. The last-named especially made a strong impact on his thought and led him to write an Introduction to his own selection from Kierkegaard's writings. Although he did not adopt Kierkegaard's extreme anti-intellectualism and quoted with approval in his Notes Anselm's *Credo ut intellegam*, he accepted that there was no rational proof of religious belief. Kierkegaard's *Stages on Life's Way* (1845), sets out what Auden felt had been his own spiritual progress. The first stage, the aesthetic, embodies the romantic enthusiasm of youth, illustrated most vividly for Kierkegaard in Mozart's *Don Juan*, but it leads only to despair, since it fails to satisfy man's desire for spiritual freedom. The frustration which follows from it combines fascination and fear, or to use the term Kierkegaard made popular with a later generation, it leads to Angst, which he analysed at some length in his most influential books, *The Concept of Dread* (1844), and *Sickness Unto Death* (1849).

Kierkegaard never dismissed the aesthetic altogether, but considered it a stage in the healthy development of the personality, which should then lead on to the ethical. This, though taking pleasure in the senses, is aware of something that transcends them. But the personality cannot rest at the ethical level, for the demands of the moral imperative are impossible to meet. As St Paul knew, the harder one tries the greater the frustration and one can only escape from this by an act of faith, which demands absolute obedience, but in return gives one freedom. Kierkegaard illustrates this in *Fear and Trembling* (1843) by the story of Abraham and Isaac. Faith of the kind shown by Abraham is an example of Kierkegaard's leap in the dark which lands the believer safe in the arms of God. It takes one beyond reason and beyond conscience and entails that Christianity is foolishness to the Greeks and a scandal to the Jews. Faith can only be experienced subjectively and to the outsider is absurd; it involves a gamble which cannot be justified except by the believer himself.

The dual nature of man, part belonging to a world of material causation, part to a world of spiritual freedom, informs 'For the Time Being', subtitled 'A Christmas Oratorio', which Auden wrote in 1941. While it narrates the story of the Nativity it is also about the contemporary situation and especially the outbreak of war. The Biblical characters are depicted in modern terms; Herod appears as a liberal humanist and on his first appearance Joseph speaks in a modern idiom: 'My shoes were shined, my pants were cleaned and pressed, /And I was hurrying to meet/My own true Love'.

For Auden the radical flaw in human nature brought about by the Fall is the split between the temporal and the eternal which has destroyed the unity man was meant to enjoy. In the Notes to *New Year Letter* he quotes with approval Blake's *Marriage of Heaven and Hell* and adopts Charles Williams's belief that evil is the agent of God in history and used by God to bring about man's salvation. The Crucifixion is the supreme example of this; man's worst crime paradoxically brings about his salvation and the marriage between the eternal and the temporal recovers what was lost at the Fall. This is reflected in the ambiguity of the title which juxtaposes the unchanging nature of being and the flux of the temporal. The message of the Oratorio is summed up in the Narrator's reminder to Mary and Joseph that religious faith consists in living one's ordinary life with an awareness of the eternal:

> The Exceptional is always usual
> And the Usual exceptional.
> To choose what is difficult all one's days
> As if it were easy, that is faith, Joseph, praise.

When he wrote *For the Time Being* Auden had met and become a friend of Reinhold and Ursula Niebuhr. As we saw in the last chapter, Niebuhr as well as Charles Williams played an important part in shaping Eliot's thought and we encounter both again when we read Auden's work. When he read Niebuhr's *An Interpretation of Christian Ethics* (1936), Auden found in it confirmation of what he had come to believe himself about liberal humanism. Niebuhr accused the modern Church of naivety in its simplistic account of Christian ethics. It embraced, he wrote, 'the naive optimism of the Age of Reason, rather than the more paradoxical combination of pessimism and optimism of prophetical religion'.[6] He developed his views in his Gifford Lectures in 1939-40, and when the first of the two volumes appeared in 1941, Auden praised it in a review he wrote as 'the most lucid and balanced statement of orthodox Protestantism that we are likely to see for a long time'.[7]

Niebuhr had been influenced by Kierkegaard and especially by Kierkegaard's account of the paradoxical situation, poised between freedom and necessity, in which man finds himself. This is seen in the various dualisms into which life falls; in history, for instance, it leads to the dualism which he describes at the end of the first volume of his Gifford Lectures:

> Both Renaissance and Reformation explored complexities of human nature beyond the limits understood in the 'mediaeval synthesis'. But the discoveries of each stood in contradiction to each other. Some of the confusions of modern culture about human nature arise from this contradiction. Others are derived from the fact that the Renaissance triumphed over the Reformation so completely that the insights of the latter were preserved only in a few backwaters and eddies of modern culture.[8]

Auden was ready to accept this idea, but was uncertain how to articulate it in poetry. He had seen the devaluation of Eliot's later poetry by those who considered the *Four Quartets* a falling off from the originality of *The Waste Land. For the Time Being* had tried to put the story of the Nativity into a modern idiom rather in the manner of Eliot's verse drama, but he realised that it was not entirely successful; its characters lacked life and it dealt with abstractions rather than the genuinely dramatic. In places in the oratorio Auden leaves verse behind, but in one of these, the 'Meditation of Simeon', the prose reads like philosophical speculation and is far removed from the beauty of the Biblical original. Herod is a brilliantly drawn picture of a liberal and sophisticated personality, but carries little conviction in the context in which the story places him. One admires Auden's cleverness but is never wholly moved.

The solution to this problem which he adopted in his next major work was the outcome of Auden's gathering conviction that it was impossible to write Christian poetry in a secular age. He had dedicated *For the Time Being* to the memory of his mother who had died in 1941 and by this time he had resumed his habit of attending the Episcopalian church and taking the sacrament at Holy Communion. It was natural for him, perhaps, to choose the form he did for his tribute, but it did not lead him to choose a specifically Christian form for his next major work, *The Sea and the Mirror*, which was subtitled, *A Commentary on Shakespeare's 'The Tempest'*. Although not explicitly Christian it takes up questions of paramount importance to the Christian poet: What is the relation of art to reality? Is the fine-fabling of the poet merely make-believe or is it a means of apprehending the truth? Is the artistic imagination in Wordsworth's phrase, 'Reason in her most exalted mood', or is it simply an escape from the real world?

The critics were not uniformly impressed with *The Sea and the Mirror*, but Auden himself considered it one of his most important works. He felt this especially of the last section, 'Caliban to the Audience', which consists of a long prose reflection on the nature of art. Some readers have been puzzled because it is an obvious pastiche of Henry James's style and find it strange when this is put in the mouth of Caliban. Auden explained this by saying that because Caliban is inarticulate he had to borrow from Ariel the most sophisticated style available and this happened to be James's. Presumably this was intended to emphasise the artificiality of art and its distance from the brute world of Caliban.

When he wrote the poem Auden was teaching a course on Romanticism at Swarthmore and no doubt would have had in mind the letters of Keats and especially perhaps the letter of 22 November 1817, addressed to his friend Benjamin Bailey, in which Keats declared, 'The Imagination may be compared to Adam's dream – he awoke and found it truth'.[9] It is doubtful, however, whether Keats continued to believe this, or if he did whether he meant by it what the ordinary reader does. Keats praised Shakespeare for his gift of presenting life truthfully, ready to rest in doubt and uncertainty; Adam's dream is true only in the sense that the poet shows us life as he sees it at the time when he writes, whether it is comic or tragic. The end of Keats's 'Ode to a Nightingale' where the song of the nightingale is an emblem of poetry, ends not with affirmation but a question, 'Do I wake or sleep?'. The declaration in the 'Ode on a Grecian Urn', 'Beauty is truth, truth beauty', is made not by the poet but the urn, which claims something with no validity beyond its own representation of the truth. At this time, near the end of his short life, Keats was reading Shakespeare and making an extensive study especially of *King Lear*. The play, for Keats, exhibited the quality of 'Negative Capability' and suggested that the capacity of being in 'uncertainties, Mysteries, doubts, without any irritable reaching after fact and reason', could be a matter of life as much as art.

The last of Keats's great Odes, 'To Autumn', echoes Edgar's *sententia* at the end of the play:

Men must endure
Their going hence, even as their coming hither:
Ripeness is all.[10]

The Preface to *The Sea and the Mirror*, subtitled 'The Stage Manager to the Critics', also echoes Edgar's speech and suggests that the attempt of art to penetrate the mystery of human experience is at the heart of Auden's poem:

> the Bard
> Was sober when he wrote
> That this world of fact we love
> Is unsubstantial stuff:
> All the rest is silence
> On the other side of the wall;
> And the silence ripeness,
> And the ripeness all.

The only reference to nightingales in the poem is in the song of the Master and the Boatswain where they serve not as the emblems of poetry, but are the cant term for prostitutes:

> The nightingales are sobbing in
> The orchards of our mothers,
> And hearts that we broke long ago
> Have long been breaking others.

This carries the Freudian suggestion of the search for a substitute maternal love which offers the same kind of compensation that art does for others. The Preface carries on this suggestion by viewing poetry (as Yeats did in 'The Circus Animals' Desertion') as a wish-fulfilment dream which satisfies the unarticulated desires of its readers like performers in the circus who entrance their audience.

Shakespeare's Hamlet describes drama as a holding up a mirror to nature, but art is not like real life; it does not reflect an exact image of the turbulent sea which is life itself. Art can represent life at the level of Caliban, which leads to tragedy, or it can represent it at the spiritual level of Ariel which offers us a vision of the ideal world of comedy, but it fails to reconcile the contradictions which are part of man's nature. In his address to the audience Caliban describes an indifferent universe which leads to despair; Ariel offers the prospect of an ideal Platonic universe which is equally indifferent to human desires and this also leads to despair. Only when we have come to realise the limitations of art can we believe (not know) that religious faith gives us a glimpse of the perfect work created by the divine will which reconciles the contradictions of life and art: the union of the Negative and the Affirmative Ways. The 'Postscript', a beautiful song in which Ariel expresses his love for Caliban, with an echo provided by the Prompter, foreshadows this union which will heal man's fallen nature by the heavenly love behind the universe:

> we are blessed by that Wholly Other Life
> from which we are separated by an essential
> emphatic gulf of which our contrived fissures of
> mirror and proscenium arch . . . are feebly

figurative signs . . . it is just here, among the
ruins and the bones, that we may rejoice in
the perfected Work which is not ours.

Auden worked on *The Age of Anxiety* throughout the war years, but it was not until 1947 that it was published in the USA and not until 1948 in Britain. The war forms a background to the work and throughout its length the radio announcements act as a chorus to the action, but the war is only a crystallisation of the universal human predicament which the four characters of the drama illustrate and explore. The title suggests the influence of Kierkegaard and this is manifest throughout. For Kierkegaard *Angst*, or dread, reminds us that we belong to eternity and that human existence does not make any sense in terms of this life alone: a notion developed by Niebuhr to explain the failures and discontents of modern society. All the characters are looking for a fulfilment they cannot find in this life and are increasingly aware of something they have lost or never acquired.

The four characters are Quant, an elderly widower who works in a shipping office; Malin, a medical officer in the Canadian Air Force; Rosetta, a Jewish buyer in a department store who has spent her childhood in England; and Emble, a young student who is serving in the American navy. Ingenious attempts have been made to explain their names in terms of the dissociated elements of the human psyche, and however convincing or not these may be, they are clearly more than ordinary people who have just stepped in from the street. The sub-title of the work is *A Baroque Eclogue* and there is a fairy-story quality about the poem which takes it at places into the realms of fantasy; one section when all four characters fall into a dream has been seen by some critics as a joint exploration of the Jungian group unconscious in a search for unity and integration. The term 'baroque' gives an indication of the highly artificial style of the poem and the metaphysical wit it brings to the religious content. It is an experimental work which continues Auden's attempt to find a suitable medium for religious verse drama and invites comparison with Eliot's work in combining psychological analysis and religious explanations of human behaviour.

The four characters meet by chance in a New York bar on All Souls' Night, a setting reminiscent of the scene in a London pub in *The Waste Land*, and it also recalls Auden's '1st. September 1939' which captures the desperate attempt of lonely people to recover the lost security of home:

Faces along the bar

> Cling to their average day:
> The lights must never go out,
> The music must always play.
> All the conventions conspire
> To make this fort assume
> The furniture of home;
> Lest we should see where we are,
> Lost in a haunted wood,
> Children afraid of the night
> Who have never been happy or good.

This condition can never be alleviated until mankind recovers the Paradise lost at the Fall. This is revealed by the characters in *The Age of Anxiety*, each of whom lives in an almost solipsistic world, speaking mainly in soliloquies. They are joined together only by the narrator until they wake from their shared dream. In this they retrace the history of the race and the individual, but even this experience fails to give them the unity they all crave. When the bar closes Rosetta invites them all to her apartment for a good-night drink and a romance begins between her and Emble.

The two older men take their leave, but when Rosetta returns from seeing them to the lift, she finds Emble fast asleep. What looked like the promise of a love that could deliver her from her loneliness has, not for the first time, eluded her. Even so, she gains some self-knowledge from what has happened and accepts that until now she has lived largely in a world of make-believe and a fictionalised account of her childhood in England. After saying good-night to each other and promising to meet again, the two older men 'have immediately forgotten each others' existence'. Malin does not retreat entirely into his old isolation; he recognises their real situation and their failure to act on this recognition. He sees the need for a change of heart to bring people out of the hell of their own self- containment; but realises that men find it difficult to make the change:

> We would rather be ruined than changed,
> We would rather die in our dread
> Than climb the cross of the moment
> And let our illusions die.

God offers us mercy and our suffering may provide the dynamic of change, for 'It is where we are wounded that is where He speaks'; but man refuses the offer; and so Malin returns to his duties, 'its adoption, as usual, postponed'.

The four major works we have considered brought Auden to the end of the war years and from then on there was a different tone in his writing. No doubt this was partly because of the relief that came with the end of fighting and the defeat of tyranny, partly by his increasing maturity, but also by his finding a summer residence at Ischia, the Italian island where he rented a house each summer from 1948 onwards. Here he could relax in the Mediterranean climate and look back on the classical culture of the region and it was here he found inspiration in the poetry of Horace. Instead of thinking about the 'crisis' theology of Kierkegaard and Barth, he turned to consider the practice of the Christian virtues in the routine of daily life and the demands of family and job. He found a contentment in Ischia he had not experienced before and when he came finally to leave it he expressed his gratitude in 'Goodbye to the Mezzogiorno':

> Out of a gothic North, the pallid children
> Of a potato, beer-or-whisky
> Guilt culture, we behave like our fathers and come
> Southward into a sunburnt otherwhere
>
> Of vineyards, baroque, *la bella figura*,
> To these feminine townships where men
> Are males, and siblings untrained in a ruthless
> Verbal in-fighting as it is taught
>
> In Protestant rectories upon drizzling
> Sunday afternoons.

The poem ends with a sense of the unearned happiness that had come to him as a kind of benediction:

> though one cannot always
> Remember exactly why one has been happy
> There is no forgetting that one was.

Auden distinguishes between the pathological guilt which distorts Christian belief and the awareness of sin as a condition of all human existence. In 'Memorial for the City' (1949), which he wrote in memory of Charles Williams who had died in the Spring of 1945, he describes the difference between the world of classical culture and the 'Post-Vergilian City', a term used by Williams for the Christian civilisation which followed it. The one existed in a state of innocence, unaware of sin, whereas the other is conscious of sin as part of human nature. This consciousness brings with it, however, a realisation that 'We know without knowing there is reason for what we bear, /That our hurt is not a desertion'.

The poem gives a brilliantly succinct summary of the history of Christianity which follows Williams's account and adopts his explanation of sin as man's disobedience, which God uses for his own purposes; in the words of Dame Julian of Norwich, 'Sin is Behovely'. Sin is the means by which God brings about our salvation, for without the 'fortunate Fall', the *felix culpa*, there would have been no Incarnation. The poem borrows the epigraph from Dame Julian which Williams had also used, 'In the self-same point that our soul is made sensual, in the self-same point is the City of God ordained to him from without beginning'; the City of God, or the Kingdom, is not remote, it belongs to the here and now.

These themes are continued in the collection of poems entitled *About the House*, published in 1966, which marked Auden's move to Austria where he settled into a small rural community. Some of these poems celebrate the domestic pleasures of living in his own home and take us on a guided tour of the house. He gives thanks for his contentment in the happiness of the Affirmative Way in which sensory pleasures are complemented by the satisfaction of the spirit. Eros is complemented by Agape, the company of friends has an almost sacramental quality and their shared food becomes akin to the Eucharist. He acknowledges in his happiness his sins of commission and omission, but hopes that these too may have been used by God for good. He knows that his deliverance from the shallow secularism of his youth was brought about by the evil done by Hitler and Mussolini and their followers and, while this seems a high price to pay for his own enlightenment, he believes his own rescue is only a small part of a larger process that could bring Western civilisation to a new awareness of God.

These poems are removed from the austerity of Kierkegaard; and the same is true of a collection of poems he had written between 1947 and 1954, which were published in 1955 in *The Shield of Achilles* and again in 1966 in the *Collected Shorter Poems*. These make up the series *Horae Canonicae*, which are based on the devotional Offices of the church, but go beyond any attempt to reproduce in modern form these traditional hours of worship. Instead they reflect upon the central mystery of the Christian religion, the Cross and Resurrection, and attempt to bring out for modern man the significance of the events of the original Good Friday.

One of the finest of the series, 'Nones', gave its title to a collection of poems published separately in New York in 1951 and dedicated to Reinhold and Ursula Niebuhr, the latter of whom had advised him about the historical texts of the Offices and their original use. It was probably the Niebuhrs, and especially Ursula, who reinforced the influence of Charles Williams in softening the austerity of Kierkegaard's theology for Auden.

Kierkegaard had emphasised crisis and judgment, and the belief that man's only escape from the living death of unredeemed existence was by the leap of faith. There was little of the divine initiative which tempered judgment with mercy and rescued mankind by God's sacrifice of himself on the Cross in the person of Christ; Kierkegaard seemed more concerned with man's search for God than God's search for man. These poems of Auden show a marked difference of emphasis.

All the Offices have at their centre the Eucharist, which commemorates the Crucifixion. In 'Nones' which is said or sung at 3 p.m., the Good Friday killing has been done and this is followed by a realisation of its horror and our responsibility for it. 'Vespers' at 6 p.m. is concerned with man's endeavour to return again by God's grace to the lost innocence of Eden by building the New Jerusalem; like Blake's 'Jerusalem' this will bring about a new innocence lying on the far side of experience. It will resolve all the contradictions of human existence and through the death and resurrection of Christ bring about a reversal of the Fall.

In 'Compline' at 9 p.m. the poet falls asleep and, as if he had died, finds his prayer for forgiveness answered in peace of mind and spirit. He has fallen asleep in the hope of awakening to a new dispensation in which the truth will be fully revealed:

(And I shall know exactly what happened
Today between noon and three)
That we, too, may come to the picnic
With nothing to hide, join the dance
As it moves in perichoresis,
Turns about the abiding tree.

The poem ends in a passage reminiscent of Eliot's *Little Gidding* in which the mystery of the Incarnation by which Christ, the second Adam, transforms the Tree of Knowledge into the Cross, is made clear to us as we experience our own resurrection into new life.

Auden works in this later poetry towards a bare cerebral style, devoid of artifice and with a rigorous concentration on the truth, but this leads to a density of meaning and reference which makes it difficult for many readers. (This is illustrated in the use of the term 'perichoresis' in the lines above, a theological term referring to the participation of each of the three Persons of the Trinity in the being of the others.) It has reinforced the tendency to regard the later poetry as inferior to the earlier and increased the prejudice which depicts Auden as a renegade revolutionary, a modern Wordsworth who turns his back on the Left and rejoins the Church of England. This not only underestimates the value of the later poetry, but misunderstands the earlier which always had a spiritual dimension. All this has conspired to produce a popular neglect of Auden as a religious poet. Good poetry brings about the taste which can value it properly and one hopes this will happen with Auden, for he and Eliot must rank together as the two best Christian poets of the century.

To write about Philip Larkin since the publication of his *Collected Poems*, his *Letters,* and his *Life*, presents difficulties not met with before. The previous popular image, which was itself erroneous, was of a reclusive bachelor, frightened of women, who shut himself up in his University library in Hull and celebrated the shabby provincial life of post-war England in poetry that reflected his own depressive personality; a poet who viewed society from the outside with a jaundiced eye, a kind of down-beat Betjeman without Betjeman's humour. This was, of course, all wrong, but it has been succeeded by an even more erroneous image of a foul-mouthed racist with a taste for pornography, and a womaniser, whose works have been banned from some public libraries as politically incorrect. Indeed, his literary executors instead of protecting his reputation have destroyed it by publishing poems he never wished to see in print, a selection of letters many of which were private in character and should not have been published, and a Life that gives the grotesquely distorted image of a showground mirror. One can imagine what reputation Eliot and Auden would now have if their lives and work had received this sort of treatment.

When he became Librarian of Hull University in 1955 Philip Larkin was no hermit. He enjoyed the social life of the university, its Senior Common Room dances, Senate dinners, and the friendships he made with colleagues; he shared with some of these an interest in jazz; he was an entertaining conversationalist and increasingly in demand at dinner parties and social occasions, all of which he enjoyed. He generally lunched in the Staff Refectory and was one of a group of regular drinkers who gathered together in the bar before lunching, a habit that led in later years to excessive drinking and even shortened his life. With increasing age and serious deafness his circle of friends became smaller, consisting mainly of those he had known over the years. Younger colleagues then complained that they never met him and felt he was an isolated figure who rarely left his library, but this was not true of the library staff themselves who found him ready to participate in their social events and concerned for their welfare. He was never taken with the

London literary set and this perhaps led to the charge of his being a hermit, but he was interested in the affairs of the Poetry Society and the Society of Authors and liked to visit London from time to time and always made a point of watching the Lord's test match.

Certainly there was no truth in the notion that he lacked a sense of humour. He was a very funny man who enjoyed listening to or telling a joke, and was a gifted mimic who could assume the voices and mannerisms of colleagues he found boring or ridiculous. In an interview he gave to the *Observer* in which Miriam Gross had said that his poetry was all about unhappiness, he retorted, 'Actually, I like to think of myself as quite funny, and I hope this comes through in my writing. But it's unhappiness that provokes a poem. Being happy doesn't provoke a poem'.[11] This is very revealing, for Larkin found life tragic but used the comic as a defence against its sadness. This was also true of John Betjeman and they had a great admiration for each other. It was always a pleasure to see them together when Betjeman visited Hull for they delighted in each other's company and Larkin liked to 'feed' Betjeman with material almost like the 'straight' man in a music-hall duo. In his perceptive essay on Betjeman, 'It Could Only Happen in England'[11], Larkin recognised this quality he found and enjoyed in Betjeman. 'There lurks within him', he writes, 'someone who weeps at Victorian ballads ('My heart finds rest, my heart finds rest in thee') and roars out Edwardian comic songs ('There's something about a varsity man that distinguishes him from a cad')'.

The mixture of laughter and sadness we find in Larkin as well as in Betjeman, reminds us that there is an element of truth in all legends and the popular image of a melancholy figure sitting alone in his library in Hull is not entirely wrong, for increasing years gave a more sombre quality to his life and work. To his friends it became evident that as his pleasure in company declined, the humour was increasingly becoming a way of coping with loneliness and later still that drink was a means of countering the anxiety that had always beset him but was now turning into fearfulness.

Andrew Motion's biography of Larkin suggests that his personality was greatly influenced by his father, an authoritarian figure who was City Treasurer of Coventry, and who had Nazi sympathies, and by the bad-tempered atmosphere of the family home, from which Larkin was glad to escape physically, but from which he never escaped emotionally. This may need some qualification, but it is true that he turned his back not only on his own childhood but childhood in general. One of his most frequently quoted poems, 'They fuck you up, your mum and dad', sounds an authentic personal note, and its final lines, 'Get out as early as you can, /And don't have any kids yourself', accurately reflect his refusal to adopt a romantic attitude to childhood.

This dislike of children was not an affectation. In the *Observer* interview already quoted, he said of his own childhood, 'Once you started meeting grown-ups life was much pleasanter. Children are very horrible aren't they? Selfish, noisy, cruel, vulgar little brutes'. This dislike even extended to skipping the chapters of biographies devoted to childhood.

It is encountered again in a review article he wrote on *The Lore and Language of Schoolchildren* (1959) which began: 'It was that verse about becoming again as a little child that caused the first sharp waning of my Christian sympathies. If the Kingdom of Heaven could be entered only by those fulfilling such a condition I knew I should be unhappy there.'[12]

Nevertheless, he was always kind to children, seeing them as the 'little victims' of Gray's famous Ode rather than ogres. The disenchantment with childhood we meet in so many of his poems is really centred on his own childhood. Nowhere is this more clearly revealed than in 'I Remember, I Remember', with its almost savage reversal of Hood's romantic poem. The inability to recognise his own birthplace when he sees it from the train and the blanked out memory that can recall nothing of his childhood suggests, especially in the final line, 'Nothing like something, happens anywhere', a forgetfulness of neurotic character.

His frequent protestations either that he could remember nothing of his childhood or that it was of no importance lead one to suspect a need to block it out of his consciousness and would find any forced attempt to recall it a painful experience. 'Dockery and Son', written in 1963, records a visit Larkin made to Oxford some twenty years after he had gone down. The poem compares his own single state with that of his college contemporary, Dockery, who now has a son at the college, and asks why the guiding principles which govern their lives are so different:

> Where do these
> Innate assumptions come from? Not from what
> We think truest, or most want to do:
> Those warp tight-shut, like doors. They're more a style
> Our lives bring with them . . .

Earlier in the poem he has visited his old rooms but finds them locked. 'I try the door of where I used to live:/Locked.' The past remains an unknown and foreign country. Perhaps it is well that we cannot always open the door to the past for it might show us what is distasteful, shameful, and even frightening. Larkin was familiar with Emily Dickinson's poetry and may have had in mind here the image of the door in one of her poems which recounts a similar experience:

I years had been from home
And now before the Door
I dare not enter, lest a Face
I never saw before

Stare stolid into mine
And ask my business there –

Some years later Larkin wrote a review article for the *New Statesman and Nation* (reprinted in his *Required Writing*) which brought together the poems of Emily Dickinson and Walter de la Mare. Not surprisingly he considered Emily Dickinson the greater poet, but both, as he suggested in his title 'Big Victims', were the products of an emotional development arrested in childhood; Dickinson 'the more obvious, the more striking, perhaps one might even say the more clinical of the two'. But the article reveals something of Larkin himself when he observes that 'the Freudian legacy assures us that our childhoods are with us for life: we are what they made us; we cannot lose their gains, or be compensated for their losses'. Since the decline of Romanticism, he writes, 'children themselves have been devalued: we know them for the little beasts they are', but Wordsworth as well as Freud knew that the child is father of the man and could have explained how Larkin's early years threw a shadow across his life.

The edition of Larkin's *Letters* contain none addressed to his mother, although he wrote to her several times a week throughout her long life and in her last years visited her most week-ends until her death at the age of 96. Motion's biography while stressing the influence of his father, says little about his mother, but it is more than likely that her influence was as strong. It is the conflicting loyalties to parents of very different temperaments which typically lay the foundations of future neurotic anxieties and this was true of Larkin. His father was a rationalist and atheist, always ready to pour scorn on religion, while his mother was a gentle and devout woman with Anglican sympathies which she repressed because of her husband.

In a letter to his friend James Sutton (in an unpublished collection in the Brynmor Jones Library at the University of Hull) he wrote 'thirty years struggle [between them] is being continued in me' (12

April 1943). Larkin grew up with emotional leanings towards religion but with a sceptical cast of mind which could not justify them. In this he was very like Hardy, the poet whom he admired above all ; a writer whose heart responded to an English way of life already disappearing and to the traditional worship of the Church of England, but whose head ruled this out as no more than antiquated beliefs and rituals which could not stand up to rational scrutiny.

Like Hardy's, Larkin's scepticism was never savage or bitter. It was a matter of regret to him that he had to reject what attracted him emotionally and as a young man even considered ordination in the Church of England. In later life he gladly accepted an invitation to advise the editors on the style of the New English Bible, even if his advice was largely ignored. He was the only one I ever knew who had read the Bible from beginning to end, for when he was engaged on this task he read a passage every morning while shaving. One of his best-known poems, 'Church-Going', published in 1954 in *The Less Deceived*, came about from the visits he made to country churches at this time. He did not share Betjeman's interest in church architecture but liked to soak in the atmosphere and reflect on his own feelings and beliefs: 'It pleases me to stand in silence here'.

A country church was a place where past generations made their presence felt. It was a place where

someone will forever be surprising
A hunger in himself to be more serious.

Over twenty years later and towards the end of his life he describes in 'Aubade', one of the saddest of his poems, waking in the early hours of the morning to experience the fear of death which had always haunted him, but which now became ever more insistent. For him there is no remedy to cure this fear:

Religion used to try,
That vast moth-eaten musical brocade
Created to pretend we never die,
And specious stuff that says *No rational being*
Can fear a thing it will not feel, not seeing
That this is what we fear – .

But even at the time when he wrote this he was in the habit of occasionally attending Evensong at a neighbouring church, a service that made no doctrinal claims on him as he might have felt the Eucharist would have done, but like Hardy, for the comfort of the traditional liturgy and the faint hope, perhaps, that it might witness to the truth.

In his review article about Emily Dickinson, Larkin writes that her poetic talent was 'crucified between childhood and maturity' and that her preoccupation with unfulfilled love and loneliness was accompanied in her poetry by the other recurrent subject of death; 'not surprising', he adds, 'if we accept the psychologists' assertion that an obsession with death conceals a fear of sex'. This 'crucifixion', he suggests, was the price she had to pay for the flowering of her genius and one could argue that the same was true of Larkin and that he recognised this when he wrote so perceptively about Emily Dickinson. Certainly the fear of death was always with him and, as the *Life* and *Letters* have revealed, his relations with women were tortuous and flawed by a fear of committing himself to a settled and permanent relationship. An adolescent interest in pornography and girlie magazines also suggests a personality arrested between childhood and maturity, but one which endowed him with his poetic gifts.

Some of the poems which had been published depicted women who had suffered violation and many more in the *Collected Poems*, now published for the first time, associate sex with death. A realisation that these revealed his personal obsessions, as well as their lack of poetic merit, probably led him to withhold them from publication. An example of this is 'Under a splendid chestnut tree', written in 1950, which introduces us to 'A corpse-faced undergrad/ Convinced that he was bad', who suffers guilt over his sexual feelings:

His soul was just a sink of filth, he felt.
Hare's eyes, staring across his prayer-locked hands,
Saw, not a washstand-set, but mammary glands;
All boyhood's treasure-trove, a hortus siccus
Of tits and knickers

That he should have been writing this in the 1950s explains why like Emily Dickinson, he was afraid to look back and afraid of going forward.

To put the matter in these terms is to indulge in the reductionism of psycho-biography and one might perhaps make a better attempt at explaining his poetic genius not by dismissing Freud altogether, but by bringing in others to supplement this account. Larkin always insisted on the importance of life as against literature and praised Lawrence for emphasising this. In 'What's Become of Wystan?' he criticised Auden's later poetry for making literature and not life the subject of his poetry. He considered the last twenty years of Auden's poetic output to be largely worthless compared to the first ten years. The English Auden was 'energetic and exciting', the

American Auden 'bookish . . . and too intellectual to be moving'. Larkin praised Betjeman's poetry for its engagement with real life and after a flirtation with writing in the manner of Yeats he himself tried strenuously to free his poetry from literary influences. In this as in other respects he can be compared with Wordsworth who eschewed poetic diction and, in Coleridge's words, sought 'to give the charm of novelty to things of everyday, and to excite a feeling analogous to the supernatural, by awaking the mind's attention from the lethargy of custom'.

The first part of Coleridge's remark fits very well with how Larkin regarded his poetry: he was superb at causing us to look at things we encounter everyday, but with a new awareness of their significance. But the second part of the quotation is equally important and we will return to it later. Before doing so we should notice that although he followed Lawrence, Betjeman, and others in making life the subject of his poetry, he was an almost obsessional letter-writer, making this, one suspects, a substitute for life. He was one of the last great letter-writers, not only for the quality but the quantity of what he wrote; on most days he wrote at least three or four letters, many quite long and all elegantly composed, full of interest and humour, all geared to the views of those he addressed, and all in their ways works of art. For some time I used to think he worked long hours, arriving in the library at about 9am and rarely leaving until 6 or 6.30pm. It was only later that I realised he spent a good deal of each day on private letters and only after his death that I learnt the number of his correspondents. Another strange feature of his letter-writing was that each correspondent was unaware of the others and all, like many of his friends, remained spokes on a wheel of which he was the hub.

In this he lived life vicariously, exhibiting what Kierkegaard called an aesthetic response to life, but this never led to his ignoring the ethical. His conscientiousness went far beyond the demands of duty and showed a compassionate interest in the welfare of his friends. Jean Hartley in *Philip Larkin, the Marvell Press and Me*, recounts how he opened an account in her name at the university bookshop in Hull when she became a mature and impoverished student. If the details were not still confidential, I could testify to his generosity in helping others, even when the recipients of his help were unaware of it. There was a strange paradox in his management of money, for although he died a comparatively wealthy man, he was always worried about money and complained about the bills he had to pay. What looked like a mean streak reflected his insecurity and the need to protect himself against illness and the old-age he never reached.

What amounted to an irrational meanness never stood in the way of helping his friends and acquaintances who were in trouble and his kindness went far beyond a matter of money. He hated hospitals and regarded them as places which were often the ante-room of death, but he never hesitated to visit his sick friends when they were there. In the *Observer* interview already quoted, he remarked, 'Deprivation is for me what daffodils were for Wordsworth', and in saying this he indicated a community of suffering which unites all of us. In 'Ambulances' he describes the group of people who gather round as the sick person is brought out of the house and 'carried in and stowed'. The crowd

> sense the solving emptiness
> That lies just under all we do.
> And for a second get it whole,
> So permanent and blank and true.
> The fastened doors recede. *Poor Soul,*
> They whisper at their own distress . . .

This universality of suffering is recognised as the ambulances make their way and

> come to rest at any kerb:
> All streets in time are visited.

This compassion was never sentimentalised in his poetry and could be accompanied by irony. In 'Faith Healing' the women, 'moustached in flowered frocks', who come to the American evangelist in desperate hope

> as if a kind of dumb
> And idiot child within them still survives
> To re-awake at kindness

have their hopes dashed; their sickness is more than physical:

> In everyone there sleeps
> A sense of life lived according to love.
> To some it means the difference they could make
> By loving others, but across most it sweeps
> As all they might have done had they been loved.
> That nothing cures.

This ironic compassion, so reminiscent of Hardy, was not moderated or abandoned in 'An Arundel Tomb', as many readers have assumed. The visitor to Chichester Cathedral in looking at the tomb sees the earl's hand withdrawn from its glove holding the hand of the countess: sees 'with a sharp tender shock, /His hand withdrawn, holding her hand', and assumes this was a feature of the sculpture ordered by the earl before his death. This struck Larkin as highly unlikely and something not found in any of the memorial sculptures of the time; his scepticism led him to see the clasped hands, not as a token of married love but as a conceit of the sculptor. It was only later, when he had written the poem, that research revealed that the two figures on the Arundel tomb had been brought together from separate places and that Victorian restoration had made the arrangement of the hands. Even without this knowledge, however, Larkin's poem remains highly equivocal. The figures on the tomb seem to be saying what they never really meant: 'Time has disfigured them into/Untruth'. The last lines are hedged about with the same ambiguity and are marked by hope rather than conviction:

> The stone fidelity
> They hardly meant has come to be
> Their final blazon, and to prove
> Our almost-instinct almost true:
> What will survive of us is love.

Often in his poetry the compassion is tinged with grief and the wit with regret. In one of his Journal entries Kierkegaard observed that 'It requires moral courage to grieve; it requires religious courage to rejoice'. While there was laughter in Larkin's life and work it was often a way of keeping his courage up, a means of keeping at bay the depression and fear that threatened him rather than pure rejoicing. In his middle years it took its place alongside the letter-writing, jazz, and above all the 'toad' work:

> give me my in-tray,
> My loaf-haired secretary,
> My shall-I-keep-the-call-in-Sir:
> What else can I answer,
>
> When the lights come on at four
> At the end of another year?
> Give me your arm, old toad;
> Help me down Cemetery Road.

At the end, none of these succeeded and when he turned to drink it made him morose and even more afraid of death.

He found, as Kierkegaard had predicted, that life lived at the aesthetic and moral level leads only to frustration and angst. One might ask why, if this is so, more people do not suffer in this way. The answer, of course, is that many do and especially when they dimly apprehend a spiritual world that remains an aspiration rather than a reality. Larkin never made any affirmation of faith, but he had an awareness of a dimension that lay beyond ordinary experience. He always spoke of his poetic genius as a gift which came from an unknown source outside his own consciousness, as news from a country whose existence he could only conjecture, or music faintly heard played by those he had never met. In his letters he says that a poet has to have a vision and speaks of new-born lambs and new-mown grass as providing him with such a vision, causing him to 'kneel in his heart'. When in his last years he felt that his poetic gift had left him he spoke of it as almost a spiritual deprivation.

In the *Observer* interview he talked of driving down the M1 and having his life put in danger because he was listening on the car radio to 'Time For Verse'. It 'was a lovely summer morning', he recalled, 'and someone suddenly started reading the Immortality Ode, and I couldn't see for tears. And when you're driving down the middle lane at seventy miles an hour . . . it's amazing how effective it was when one was totally unprepared for it!' Wordsworth's intimations of immortality were accompanied by a deeply felt sense of loss; the Ode starts with this sense of a lost Eden:

It is not now as it has been of yore:–
Turn whereso'er I may,
By night or day,
The things which I have seen I now can see no more.

This is echoed in Larkin's poetry as it is in Hardy's and partly explains his admiration for A. E. Housman, another Romantic Tory whose poetry also laments a 'land of lost content'. In 'Betjeman En Bloc', first published in *Listen*, Larkin observes that 'The meeting and conflict of present and past is one of Betjeman's most fruitful situations for poetry, as it was for Hardy', and he might have added that it was also true of his own poetry. It is when the lost innocence of an earlier age is contrasted with our own that his poetry is most moving; and when the lost innocence of human existence, of which this is only a shadow, is touched on we hear the authentic Larkin. Here he reminds us, with Wordsworth, that 'Our birth is but a sleep and a forgetting.' What he added about Betjeman is equally true of himself: 'Human lives, and human lives in time, are his central themes; neither the screens he throws up of absurdity and satire, nor the amount of exploring he does down alleys of minor interests, should prevent the recognition of his poetry's lasting quality as well as its novelty.' For many Larkin is the poet mainly of wit and satire, of *vers de société*, but these are his own alleys of minor interests. His central concern is people and human deprivation; nowhere is this better illustrated than in 'MCMXIV' which speaks

of the loss felt by a whole generation. As the men queue to enlist at
the outbreak of the First World War they are hardly conscious that
they are taking part in something that will change Western society
and which marks the end of an age of innocence. This is where the
past meets and shapes the present:

Those long uneven lines
Standing as patiently
As if they were stretched outside
The Oval or Villa Park . .

Never such innocence,
Never before or since,
As changed itself to past
Without a word – the men
Leaving the gardens tidy,
The thousands of marriages
Lasting a little while longer:
Never such innocence again.

The same concern is focussed on our own generation in 'Going,
Going', which laments the disappearance of the old familiar
landscape; the motor-car, the property developer, and the tourist,
have made England the victim of 'a cast of crooks and tarts'.

The mingling of elegiac regret with the castigation of greed
and carelessness gives the poem a Betjemanesque touch:

And that will be England gone,
The shadows, the meadows, the lanes,
The guildhalls, the carved choirs.
There'll be books; it will linger on
In galleries; but all that remains
For us will be concrete and tyres.

A more personal expression of nostalgic regret is found in 'Love
Songs in Age' and 'Home is so sad'. At its most poignant this longing
for what A. E. Housman called the 'happy highways where we cannot
come again' is evoked by the loss of memory in old age. This is
expressed in the bitter sadness of 'The Old Fools' and more gently
in 'Reference Back', which recounts a visit to his family home where
his widowed mother lives alone. Playing Oliver's *Riverside Blues*
on the gramophone brings back memories common to both of them,
connecting 'your unsatisfactory age/To my unsatisfactory prime.'

Truly though our element is time,
We are not suited to the long perspectives
Open at each instant of our lives.

Generally his intimations of immortality are associated with a sense of loss, but there are a few lyric passages in his poetry which celebrate a happiness which goes beyond this. The coming of Spring always lifted his spirits and his melancholy seemed to vanish when he wrote 'The Trees', in which the last line promised a new beginning, 'afresh, afresh, afresh'. Larkin later dismissed this poem as insincere and it is true that while sensitive to landscape he found rejuvenation mainly in literature and especially in jazz. It was fitting that Westminster Abbey should be filled at his memorial service with the sound of Sidney Bechet's music, since his tribute 'For Sidney Bechet', reads like a triumphant epiphany hardly equalled anywhere else in his poetry:

> On me your voice falls as they say love should,
> Like an enormous yes. My Crescent City
> Is where your speech alone is understood,
>
> And greeted as the natural noise of good,
> Scattering long-haired grief and scored pity.

Larkin, like Hardy, never committed himself to any religious faith, but there is in his poetry a spiritual nostalgia. The deprivation he spoke of as the mainspring of his poetry was not a material, nor even an emotional one; it was the feeling that he had glimpsed a happiness that was now irretrievably lost. His preoccupation with sex was part of this search for a unity that eluded him; an ideal he was never able to realise. He shared the religious sensibility of the late twentieth century and like many in our time was a reluctant agnostic. One should not be surprised that he thought Eliot and Betjeman the two most important and representative poets of the century and this not in spite of their being Christian and Church of England, but because of it. In an Introduction he wrote for the American edition of Betjeman's enlarged *Collected Poems*,[13] he emphasised the Englishness of Betjeman and linked this to Eliot's famous description of the English 'way of life', which included 'Derby Day, Henley Regatta, Cowes, the twelfth of August, a cup final, the dog races, the pin table, the dart board, Wensleydale cheese, boiled cabbage cut in sections, beetroot in vinegar, nineteenth-century gothic churches, and the music of Elgar'.

This reminds us, Larkin writes, above all of Betjeman whose poetry reflected such a catholic range of taste, and he argues that this 'element of cultural inclusiveness' chimed in with 'the fact that both of them by their different ways, were led to Anglicanism and the Church of England'. 'Can it be', he asks, 'that as Eliot dominated the first half of the twentieth century, the second half will derive from Betjeman?' He declares that this is not 'completely unlikely' and that 'although unique', Betjeman 'is not solitary'. He establishes the Englishness of Betjeman's pedigree by tracing it back to 'Hardy, Tennyson, Crabbe, Cowper, the Reverend Robert Stephen Hawker, – all those on whom he descanted so persuasively at Sir Maurice Bowra's dinner table many years ago'. All these, except Hardy, of course, were Christians and Church of England men.

In another essay he dismisses any claim Auden might have had to take Betjeman's place. In a review of *The Shield of Achilles* in *Listen*, entitled 'No More Fever', he maintains that Auden's later work is too intellectual and devoid of feeling. The poetry of ideas has no appeal for him and this reflects his lack of interest in speculative thought, whether in philosophy, theology, or even literary theory. He seems almost unaware that for some people there can be an aesthetic pleasure in argument. He forgets that Eliot said 'a thought to Donne was a feeling, it modified his sensibility', and ignores Eliot's brilliant and moving use of theological ideas in his poetry. He forgets this when he discusses 'Nones' and censures Auden for writing about the Crucifixion as he does: 'when a poet calling himself a Christian, elects to write on such a theme I think we have a right to expect a more significant conclusion than the pious coronal of hopefulness put forward in such terms so conventional as to be meaningless'. This refers to the lines in 'Vespers' quoted earlier, which, whatever might be said of them, are certainly not conventional or meaningless:

> That we, too, may come to the picnic
> With nothing to hide, join the dance
> As it moves in perichoresis,
> Turns about the abiding tree.

Larkin explains what he sees as a fatal decline in Auden's achievement by his decision to leave England for America. He argues that while Auden found security in America his inspiration derived from 'the atmosphere of pre-1939 Europe' which bred, in Auden's own words, 'our fever's menacing shapes'. This overlooks the fact that Auden's angst remained and even increased after he arrived in America and was assuaged only by his religious faith. This gave him hope and led to a new kind of poetry not necessarily inferior to his earlier work. Larkin may be on surer ground when he argues that Eliot and Betjeman had greater appeal for the British, and especially the English, and that their poetry belonged to an English tradition which happened to be Christian. Larkin's poetry has its roots in this tradition even if, like Hardy, he might be termed an agnostic with Christian leanings. More than Eliot and Betjeman and certainly more than Auden, whose poetry is dogmatic and didactic, he embodies the sceptical religious attitudes of the late twentieth century.

Larkin said that *The Waste Land* was merely a piece of 'rhythmical grumbling' and many would regard Eliot's poetry as no more than that. But what was personal for Eliot spoke to a whole generation and the same is likely to be true of Larkin. Indeed, the poetry of both is far from being grumbling; it expresses a discontent with the present which arises from their apprehension of an ideal order beyond the here and now. Larkin more than Eliot or Betjeman has an undogmatic approach to this ideal which matches the mood of our time. If this should deepen into a more serious religious commitment by our contemporaries, he would, if still alive, give it, I suspect, a guarded welcome, even if he played no active part in it himself, for as he wrote in 'Church Going', our Christian faith is where

> all our compulsions meet,
> Are recognised, and robed as destinies.
> And that much never can be obsolete.

NOTES

Notes to Introduction

1. *Fables of Identity: Studies in Poetic Mythology*, (1965).
2. Harold Bloom(ed.), *Deconstruction and Criticism*, (1979).

Notes to I — Wordsworth and Coleridge

1. *The Collected Letters of S. T. Coleridge, 1785-1834*, ed., E. L. Griggs, 6 vols. (Oxford, 1956-71) II, 666-67; hereafter *C.L.*. The reason why Wordsworth alone signed the letter to Wilberforce is probably that he appeared as the sole author on the title page of the second edition, although it contained several of Coleridge's poems, including 'The Ancient Mariner'.
2. Lectures 1795: 'On Politics and Religion', ed. Lewis Patton & Peter Mann (Vol.I of *The Collected Works*, ed. Kathleen Coburn), (1970), 290.
3. *The Letters of William and Dorothy Wordsworth*, ed., E.de Selincourt, *The Later Years, 1821-53*, rev. A. G. Hill, 4 vols. (Oxford, 1978-1988), 111, 1263.
4. *C.L.*, I, 215-16.
5. *C.L.*, I, 137.
6. *C.L.*, I, 267.
7. *C.L.*, I, 78.
8. *C.L.*, I, 397.
9. See Mary Moorman, *William Wordsworth, The Early Years, 1770-1803* (1957), 306.
10. *Wordsworth's Poetical Works*, ed. E. de Selincourt, IV, 463.
11. *Biographia Literaria* by S. T. Coleridge, ed., J. Engell and W. J. Bate, 2 vols., Bollingen, *Collected Coleridge*, VII (Princeton, 1983), I, 201; hereafter *Biog. Lit.*.
12. G. Burnet, *History of his Own Time, 1724-34*, pubd. posthumously, I, 186.
13. *Op. cit.*, I, 217.
14. *C. L.*, I, 407.
15. *The Notebooks of S. T. Coleridge*, ed., K. Coburn, 6 vols. (London, 1957-) (hereafter *C.Notebooks*) I, 467.

Wordsworth

16. H. Darbishire, 'Wordsworth's Prelude', *The Nineteenth Century*, XCIX (May, 1926).
17. *The Letters of William and Dorothy Wordsworth*, ed., E.de Selincourt; *The Early Years, 1787-1805*, rev. C. L. Shaver (Oxford, 1967), 357.
18. Mary Moorman in her *Life of Wordsworth* tells us that William and Dorothy probably took with them on their tour of the Wye valley William Gilpin's guide-book *Tour of the Wye* which refers to the abbey's

being 'a dwelling-place of beggars and the wretchedly poor'. For a discussion of the political commentary by Marxist critics of Wordsworth's failure to develop this point, see M. H. Abrams's 'Doing Things with Texts' in Michael Fischer (ed.), *Essays in Criticism and Critical Theory* (New York and London, 1989).

19. Another influence on *The Excursion* could have been *Octavius* by the second or third century writer Minucius Felix. See A. G. Hill 'New Light on 'The Excursion' ', *Ariel*, vol.5, No.2, April 1974.

20. *The Letters of William and Dorothy Wordsworth*, ed., E. de Selincourt; *The Later Years, 1821-53*, rev. A. G. Hill, 4 vols. (Oxford, 1978-1988), IV, 23-4.

Coleridge

21. *Prose Works*, ed. A. B. Grosart (1876) iii, 469.

22. *Biog. Lit.*, II, 25-26.

23. *Biog. Lit.*, I, 80.

24. *C. L.*, I, 318.

25. *Table Talk*, 31 May 1830.

26. *Biog. Lit.*, I, 80.

27. *Coleridge's Miscellaneous Criticism*, ed. T. M. Raysor, 99.

28. *C. Notebooks*, I, 204.

29. From a conversation with Derwent Coleridge recorded in *Barclay Fox's Journal*, ed. R. L. Brett (1979), 168.

30. *Coleridge's Shakespearean Criticism*, ed. T. M. Raysor, rev. edn. (1960), II, 125.

31. *C. L.*, I, 354.

32. *C. L.*, IV, 791.

33. *C. Notebooks*, III, 3354.

34. *Lessing's Theological Writings*, ed. H. Chadwick (1957), 55.

Notes to II — Carlyle and Arnold

1. Quoted by J. H. Muirhead, *The Platonic Tradition in Anglo-Saxon Philosophy* (1931), 164-5.

2. *Op. cit.*, 80.

3. An essay first published in *The Edinburgh Review* but collected in *Critical and Miscellaneous Essays* (1838).

4. *On Heroes, Hero-Worship, and the Heroic in History*, Lecture 1.

5. *The Collected Letters of Thomas and Jane Welsh Carlyle*, ed. Clyde de L. Ryals and Kenneth J. Fielding (Durham, N.C.), vol., 15, 1987, 129-30.

6. Quoted in Fred Kaplan, *Thomas Carlyle: A Biography* (Cambridge, 1983), 394.

7. *On Heroes, Hero-Worship, and the Heroic in History*, Lecture 1.

8. *Sartor Resartus*, ii, ch., vii, 'The Everlasting No.'

9. *Ibid.*

10. *Ibid.* Baphometic is the adjective pertaining to Baphomet, an idol the

Templars were accused of worshipping and in medieval times referred to Mahomet.Its use here may suggest that Carlyle wished to remove from his 'baptism' any Christian associations.

11. *On Heroes, Hero-Worship, and the Heroic in History*, Lecture 1.

12. *Sartor Resartus*, ii, ch. viii.

13. *Ibid.*, iii, ch. vii.

14. For a detailed discussion of German Idealist philosophy as a version of Romanticism, see M. H. Abrams, *Natural Supernaturalism* (N. Y., 1971). I have made some criticism of this as applied to Wordsworth in Chapter II above.

15. See C. F. Harrold, *Carlyle and German Thought* (1934).

16. *Op.cit.*, ed., C.E.Norton (1887), I, 7.

17. *The Life of F. D. Maurice*, ed. Frederick Maurice (1883), I, 52. A full-length study of Sterling can be found in Anne Tuell, *John Sterling*, (N.Y., 1941). See also C. R. Sanders, *Coleridge and the Broad Church Movement* (1942).

18. *The Collected Letters of Thomas and Jane Welsh Carlyle*, vol. 9, 52.

19. *Ibid.*, vol.10, 18.

20. *The Life of F. D. Maurice*, ed. Frederick Maurice, I, 250-1.

21. *Barclay Fox's Journal*, ed. R. L. Brett (1979), 349. See also Caroline Fox's *Memories of Old Friends*, ed. H. Pym, 1882. These Journals give an interesting account of Sterling from the time when he went to live in Falmouth until his death. Both Barclay and Caroline Fox approved of Hare's *Memoir* and thought Carlyle's *Life* a distortion.

22. *Sartor Resartus*, II, ch. ix.

23. *An Essay in Aid of a Grammar of Assent*, ed. C. F. Harrold (1947), 72.

24. *Op. cit.*, II, ch. ii.

25. *Life of Sterling*, II, ch. iii.

26. *Letters of Matthew Arnold to Arthur Hugh Clough*, ed. H.F. Lowry, (Oxford, 1932), 92.

27. 'Byron', *CPW*, IX, 227.

28. 'Emerson', *Discourses in America*, 1885, *Complete Prose Works of Arnold*, ed. R. H. Super (Ann Arbor, 1960), IV, 351; hereafter *CPW*.

29. See K. Allott, 'Matthew Arnold's Reading-Lists in Three Early Diaries', *Victorian Studies*, II (1957), 254-66. For discussions of Arnold's indebtedness to Carlyle, see the interesting essay by Kathleen Tillotson, 'Matthew Arnold and Carlyle', in Geoffrey and Kathleen Tillotson, *Mid-Victorian Studies* (1965), and also David J. DeLaura, 'Arnold and Carlyle', *PMLA* (1964).

30. *Essays in Criticism*, 1865, *CPW*, III, 110.

31. Letters to A. H. Clough, ed. H. F. Lowry, 42.

32. 'Wordsworth', *CPW*, IX, 48-49.

33. *Op. cit.*, 82-3.

34. 'Pagan and Mediaeval Religious Sentiment', *CPW*, III, 230.

35. 'The Study of Poetry', *CPW*, IX, 163.

36. 'St Paul and Protestantism', *CPW*, VI, 14.

37. 1884 Preface to *God and the Bible*, *CPW*, VII, 378.

38. 'Emerson', *Discourses in America* (1885), *CPW*, IV, 350.

39. *Unpublished Letters*, ed. A. Whitridge (1923), 56, 65-66.
40. *An Essay in Aid of A Grammar of Assent*, ed., C. F. Harrold (1947), 80.
41. See H. F. Davis, 'Was Newman a Disciple of Coleridge?', *Dublin Review*, Oct. 1945; Basil Willey, *Nineteenth Century Studies* (1949), ch. iii; and J. Coulson, *Newman and the Common Tradition* (Oxford, 1970).
42. *Op.cit.*, 83.
43. *Op.cit.*, *CPW*, VI, 404.
44. *Op.cit.*, *CPW*, VI, 460.
45. *Op.cit.*, *CPW*, VII, 368.
46. Hans Kung, *On Being a Christian*, (1977), 416.

Notes to III — George Eliot and Dickens

1. Reva Stump, *Movement and Vision in George Eliot's Novels* (1959), U. C. Knoepflmacher, *Religious Humanism and the Victorian Novel* (1965).
2. *The George Eliot Letters*, ed. G. S. Haight (New Haven, 1954-55), (London, 1954-56), III, 382.
3. *Ibid.*, II, 23-4.
4. J. S. Mill, *Dissertations and Discussions* (1867) I, 394, reprinted in F. R. Leavis, *Mill on Bentham and Coleridge* (1950).
5. 'The Progress of the Intellect', *Westminster Review*, 54, (Jan. 1851), 354.
6. *Ibid.*, 353.
7. *Op. cit.*, 359.
8. *The Life and Letters of Charles Darwin*, ed. F. Darwin, (1887), II, 219 and 147.
9. *Ibid.* 11, 353.
10. *Letters of George Eliot*, ed. G. S. Haight, III, 227.
11. *The Study of Sociology* (1873), 402.
12. *Ibid.*, 328.
13. *Op.cit.*, 1851, 433.
14. *Op.cit.*, 355.
15. 'George Eliot's Life', T*he Nineteenth Century* (March 1885), rptd, in *A Century of George Eliot Criticism*, ed., G. S. Haight (1965).
16. In 'Determinism and Responsibility in the Works of George Eliot', *PMLA*, 77 (1962), rptd. in *A Century of George Eliot Criticism*, George Levine argues that George Eliot derived her views on determinism from J. S. Mill. In his *Autobiography* Mill writes about the influence of Hartley: 'In psychology his fundamental doctrine was the formation of all human character by circumstances . . . and the unlimited possibility of improving . . . mankind by education.' Mill accepted this but Carlyle repudiated it and in his *Life of Goethe* declared, 'It is profoundly false to say that 'character is formed by circumstance', unless the phrase . . . . include the whole complexity of circumstances from Creation downwards . . . the block of granite which was an obstacle on the pathway of the weak, becomes a stepping-stone on the path-way of the strong.' (Bk.I, Ch. iii). This was the view to which George Eliot undoubtedly subscribed.

17. *The Cornhill Magazine*, Feb.1881; rptd. in *A Century of George Eliot Criticism*.
18. 'The Novels of George Eliot', *The Atlantic Monthly*, Oct. 1866; rptd. in *A Century of George Eliot Criticism*, 87.
19. In her Journal account of her visit to Rome in 1860 George Eliot records that 'The visit to the Farnesina was one of the most interesting among our visits to Roman palaces.'
20. *Collected Letters of S. T. Coleridge*, ed. E. L. Griggs, VI, XXXVIII.
21. *Letters of George Meredith* (1912), II, 40.
22. 'George Eliot', *The Times Literary Supplement*, 20 Nov. 1919, 657-58, rptd. in *The Common Reader*.
23. Dennis Walder, *Dickens and Religion* (1981), 115.
24. *The Letters of Charles Dickens*, ed., W. Dexter (1938), III, 352. The letter is quoted in D. Walder, *Dickens and Religion*, 175, and in Michael Wheeler, *Death and the Future Life in Victorian Literature and Theology* (1990), 269.
25. In A. E. Dyson (ed.), *Dickens: Modern Judgments* (1976), 55.
26. For *Little Dorrit* see Dennis Walder (Note 23 above) and for *Our Mutual Friend* see Michael Wheeler (Note 24 above).
27. *Op.cit.* 262.
28. T. Carlyle, *The French Revolution.*
29. *The Letters of Charles Dickens*, ed. W. Dexter, III, 402.

Notes to IV — Tennyson and Browning

1. *Nineteenth Century*, XXXIII (1893), 182.
2. *The Poems of Tennyson*, ed. Christopher Ricks, Longman's *Annotated English Poets* (1969); hereafter *PT*.
3. *Memoir*, I, 109, 297.
4. *PT*, 522.
5. These are the last lines of a Sonnet, 'How thought you that this thing could captivate', which was first printed by Sir Charles Tennyson (*Nineteenth Century*, CIX [1931], 508), who thought it and other similar poems too harsh to relate to Rosa Baring. See *PT*, 652.
6. *PT*, 688.
7. W. D. Templeman, *Booker Memorial Studies* (1950). See *PT*, 688.
8. *Memoir*, I, 396.
9. See R. W. Rader, *Tennyson's 'Maud':The Biographical Genesis*, (Berkeley and Los Angeles, 1963).
10. Quoted by Kathleen Tillotson in 'Tennyson's Serial Poem', *Mid-Victorian Studies* by Geoffrey and Kathleen Tillotson, (1965), an indispensable study of *The Idylls of the King*. Gladstone was reviewing the volume published in 1859 which contained 'Enid', 'Vivien', 'Elaine', and 'Guinevere'.
11. *Essays Ancient and Modern* (1936).
12. *Correspondence of Carlyle and Emerson*, 2 vols. (1883), II, 339-40.
13. J. H. Buckley, *Tennyson:The Growth of a Poet* (Cambridge, Mass. and

London, 1960).

14. *Heroes and Hero-Worship*, Lecture III.

15. *Athenaeum*, 1, 1828, 351. Quoted by W. E. Houghton, *The Victorian Frame of Mind* (New Haven and London, 1957), 152. This and the preceding para. are indebted to this study.

16. Quoted by Harold Nicolson, *Tennyson* (1923), 16-17.

17. J. H. Buckley, *Tennyson: the Growth of a Poet*.

18. Merritt Y. Hughes (ed.), *John Milton, Complete Poems and Major Prose* (New York, 1957), 82.

19. *Essays Ancient and Modern* (1936).

20. *Nineteenth Century*, XXXIII (1893), 182.

21. *Op.cit.*, II, 465.

22. *Ibid.*, II, 418.

23. *Ibid.*, II, 425.

24. *The Letters of Alfred Lord Tennyson*, ed. Cecil Y. Lang and Edgar F. Shannon Jnr., III (1871-1892) (1990), 78. Blood's theories were discussed by William James in *The Varieties of Religious Experience*.

25. *The Life of F. D. Maurice*, by his son F. Maurice (1885), II, 162.

26. *Ibid.*, II, 452.

27. At the meeting of the Browning Society on 25 February 1887 Llewellyn Davies maintained that 'Browning wrote the poem long prior to the publication of Renan's work', *Browning Society's Papers*, 2 vols., 1888; vol.II, pt.iii, 185.

28. E. S. Shaffer, *'Kubla Khan' and the Fall of Jerusalem* (CUP, 1975), 204.

29. *Op.cit.*, (1971), 22 and 31.

30. See, for instance, Philip Drew, *The Poetry of Robert Browning* (1970), which contains one of the best studies of Browning's religion.

Notes to V — Yeats and Eliot

1. In *The Permanence of Yeats*, ed. J. Hall and M. Steinmann (1950), 344.

2. R. Ellman, *The Identity of Yeats* (1954), 232.

3. Letter of 22 Nov 1817, *Letters of John Keats*, ed. M. B. Forman, 4th edn, 67.

4. *Autobiographies* (1955), 483.

5. *Ibid.* 486.

6. *Letters of W. B. Yeats*, ed. Allan Wade (1954), 379.

7. *The Identity of Yeats*, 225-6.

8. *W. B. Yeats and T. Sturge Moore, Their Correspondence 1901-1937*, ed. Ursula Bridges (1953), 117; quoted in T. R. Henn, *The Lonely Tower*, (2nd edn., 1965), 213.

9. Quoted in Helen Gardner, *The Composition of Four Quartets*, 1978, 64-5.

10. *Eliot's Early Years*, 1977, and *Eliot's New Life*, 1988.

11. Quoted by Ronald Bush, *T. S. Eliot: A Study in Character and Style* (1984), from 'Types of English Religious Verse' in the Eliot Collection, King's College, Cambridge.

12. *T.S.Eliot: The Man and his Work*, ed. Allen Tate (1967), 360. The

conversation took place 'in about 1934' in Cambridge.

13. *Eliot's Early Years*, 1.
14. *Op.cit.*, 60.
15. Eloise Knapp Hayes, *T.S.Eliot's Negative Way* (Cambridge, Mass, 1982), 74.
16. *Op.cit.*, 2nd.rpt.Oxford, 394. For a valuable discussion of Eliot's study of Bradley and Underhill, see Donald J. Childs, 'T. S. Eliot and Evelyn Underhill: An Early Mystical Influence', *Durham University Journal*, Dec., (1987), 83-98.
17. *Op.cit.*, 6.
18. *Ibid.*, 14.
19. *The World and the Individual*, I, 81.
20. *The Dial*, Nov 1923.
21. *Op.cit.*, 419-20.
22. *Selected Essays*, 3rd., enlarged edn. (1951), 243.
23. *Atlantic Monthly*, May 1965. Quoted by Peter Ackroyd, T. S. Eliot (1984), 242.
24. Reinhold Niebuhr, *The Nature and Destiny of Man* (1941-43), II, 95.

Notes to VI — Auden and Larkin

1. J.A.Pike, ed., *Modern Canterbury Pilgrims* (1956), 41; quoted by Humphrey Carpenter, *W. H. Auden: a Biography*, the best account of Auden's life.
2. The last two lines are taken from Nijinsky: 'Some politicians are hypocrites like Diaghilev, who does not want universal love, but to be loved alone. I want universal love' (*op.cit.*, 1937, 44)
3. Stephen Spender, ed., *W. H. Auden: A Tribute* (1975), 74.
4. Published as 'Sonnets from China' in the *Collected Poems* and *Collected Shorter Poems*, which omits some of the original sonnets and the 'Commentary'.
5. This was the title given to the English edn. pubd. by Faber & Faber in 1940.The American edn. pubd. in the USA by Random House in 1941 was entitled *The Double Man*. There are some textual differences between the two.
6. *The Nature and Destiny of Man*, I (1941), 180.
7. New Republic, 2 June 1941, 765-6. Quoted by Humphrey Carpenter, *op.cit.*
8. *The Nature and Destiny of Man*, I (1941), 318.
9. *Letters of John Keats*, ed., M. B. Forman, 4th edn., 67.
10. See *Required Writing:Miscellaneous Pieces 1955-1982*.
11. Written as as an introduction to the American edn. of John Betjeman's enlarged *Collected Poems* (Boston, 1971), and reptd. in *Required Writing*, 204-18.
12. *Required Writing*, 111.
13. Reptd. in *Required Writing*; the quotation from Eliot is from *Notes Towards the Definition of Culture* (1948), 31.

BIBLIOGRAPHY

Primary Works

Chapter I — Wordworth and Coleridge

Texts

Wordsworth, W., *The Poetical Works*, ed. E. de Selincourt and H. Darbishire, 5 vols., 1940-49; rev. edn. 1952-58

Wordsworth, W. & Coleridge, S. T., *Lyrical Ballads*, ed. R. L. Brett and A. R. Jones. 2nd. rev. edn., 1991

Wordsworth, W., *The Letters of William and Dorothy Wordsworth*, ed.,E. de Selincourt; *The Early Years, 1787-1805*, rev. C. L. Shaver, 1967; *The Middle Years, 1806-11*, rev. M. Moorman, 1969; *The Middle Years, 1812-20*, rev. M. Moorman and A. G. Hill, 1970; *The Later Years, 1821-53*, rev. A. G. Hill, 1978-88.

Wordsworth, D., *The Journals of Dorothy Wordsworth*, ed. E. de Selincourt, 2 vols., 1941; ed. M. Moorman, 1971

Biographical and Critical Works

Darbishire, H., *The Poet Wordsworth*, 1950

Hartman, G., *Wordsworth's Poetry 1787-1814*, 1964

Legouis, E., *William Wordsworth and Annette Vallon*, 1922

Margoliouth, H. M., *Wordsworth and Coleridge 1795-1834*, 1953

Moorman, M., *William Wordsworth, I The Early Years 1770-1803*, 1957; *II The Later Years 1893-1850*, 1965

Prickett, S., *Wordsworth and Coleridge; The Poetry of Growth*, 1970

Sheats, P., *The Making of Wordsworth's Poetry 1785-1798*, 1973

Texts

Coleridge, S. T., *The Collected Works*, general editor K. Coburn, 1969- ; in progress, will include 16 titles in 22 vols., plus an index vol.

The Complete Poetical Works, ed. E. H. Coleridge, 2 vols., 1912

The Collected Letters, 1785-1834, ed. E. L. Griggs, 6 vols., 1956-1971

The Notebooks, ed. K. Coburn, 1957-; 5 vols. in 10 parts plus an index vol.

Biographia Literaria, ed. J. Engell and W. J. Bate, 2 vols. (*Collected Works of Coleridge*, vol. VII), 1983

'Lectures 1795:On Politics and Religion', ed. Lewis Patton and Peter Mann (*Collected Works of Coleridge*, vol. I), 1970

Coleridge's Shakespearean Criticism, ed. T. M. Raysor; rev. edn., 2 vols. 1960

Coleridge's Miscellaneous Criticism, ed. T. M. Raysor, 1936

Biographical and Critical Works

Beer, J. B., *Coleridge The Visionary*, 1959

Brett, R. L. (ed.), *S. T. Coleridge* (*Writers and Their Background* series), 1971

Campbell, J. D., *Samuel Taylor Coleridge*, 1894

Chambers, E. K., *Coleridge*, 1938

Cornwell, J., *Coleridge, Poet and Revolutionary, 1772-1804*, 1973

Holmes, R., *Coleridge: Early Visions*, 1989

House, H., *Coleridge*, 1953

Lowes, J. L., *The Road to Xanadu*, 1927

Willey, B., *Samuel Taylor Coleridge*, 1972

Chapter II — Carlyle and Arnold

Texts

Carlyle, T., *Collected Works* (Centenary edn.), ed. H. D. Traill, 30 vols., 1896-1901

The Collected Letters of Thomas and Jane Carlyle, ed. Clyde De L. Ryals and Kenneth J. Fielding, Duke University Press, 1970-, still in progress.

Letters of Thomas Carlyle to John Stuart Mill, John Sterling, and Robert Browning, ed. A. Carlyle, 1923

The Love Letters of Thomas Carlyle and Jane Welsh, ed. A. Carlyle, 2 vols., 1909

Critical and Miscellaneous Essays, 1838

Sartor Resartus, 1833-34 (in Fraser's Mag.), 1838

The French Revolution: A History, 3 vols., 1837

On Heroes, Hero-Worship, and the Heroic in History, 4 vols., 1839

Chartism, 1840

Past and Present, 1843

Life of John Sterling, 1851

Reminiscences, ed. J. A. Froude, 2 vols., 1881; ed. C. E. Norton, 2 vols., 1972

Biographical and Critical Works

Fox, B., *Barclay Fox's Journal*, ed. R. L. Brett, 1979

Fox, C., *Memories of Old Friends* (the Journal of Caroline Fox). ed. H. Pym, 1882

Harrold, C. F., *Carlyle and German Thought*, 1934

Maurice, F. D., *The Life of F. D. Maurice*, ed. F. Maurice, 2 vols., 1883

Sanders, C. R., *Coleridge and the Broad Church Movement*, 1942

Tennyson, G. B., *Sartor Called Resartus*, 1965

Tuell, A., *John Sterling*, 1941

Texts

Arnold, M., *The Poems of Matthew Arnold*, ed. K. Allott, 1965
The Complete Prose Works of Matthew Arnold, ed. ed. R. H. Super, XI
    vols., 1960-1990
Letters of Matthew Arnold to Arthur Hugh Clough, ed. H. F. Lowry, 1932
Unpublished Letters of Arnold, ed. A. Whitridge, 1923

Biographical and Critical Works

Allott, K. (ed.), *Matthew Arnold* (*Writers and their Background* series), 1975
'Matthew Arnold's Reading-Lists in Three Early Diaries', *Victorian Studies*,
    II, 1959
Anderson, W. D., *Matthew Arnold and the Classical Tradition*, 1965
Bush, D., *Matthew Arnold*, 1971
Chambers, E. K., *Matthew Arnold: A Study*, 1947
Coulson, J., *Newman and the Common Tradition*, 1970
James, D. J., *Matthew Arnold and the Decline of English Romanticism*, 1961
Lowry, H. F., *Matthew Arnold and the Modern Spirit*, 1941
Newman, J. H., *An Essay in Aid of a Grammar of Assent*, 1870, ed. C. F.
    Harrold, 1947
Super, R. H., *The Time-Spirit of Matthew Arnold*, 1970
Trilling, L., *Matthew Arnold*, 1939

Chapter III — George Eliot and Dickens

Texts

Eliot, George, *Works*, New Cabinet edn., 17 vols., 1913
Works, National Library edn., 10 vols., New York, 1926
The George Eliot Letters, ed. G. S. Haight, 7 vols. 1954-6
The Life of Jesus by David Strauss, trans. anon. by George Eliot, 3 vols., 1846
The Essence of Christianity, by L. Feuerbach, trans. by Marian Evans, 1854
Scenes of Clerical Life, 2 vols., 1858
Adam Bede, 3 vols., 1859
The Mill on the Floss, 3 vols., 1860
Silas Marner, 1861
Romola, 3 vols., 1863
Felix Holt the Radical, 3 vols., 1866
Middlemarch, 4 vols., 1872
Daniel Deronda, 4 vols., 1876
'A College Breakfast Party', *Macmillan's Magazine*, July, 1878

Biographical and Critical Works

Cross, J. W., *The Life of George Eliot*, 3 vols., 1885
Darwin, C., *The Life and Letters of Charles Darwin*, ed. F, Darwin, 1887
Haight, G. S. (ed.), *A Century of George Eliot Criticism*, 1965
George Eliot: A Biography, 1968
Hardy, B., *The Novels of George Eliot*, 1959
Harvey, W. J., *The Art of George Eliot*, 1961
Jenkyns, R., *The Victorians and Ancient Greece*, 1980
Knoepflmacher, U. C., *Religious Humanism and the Victorian Novel*, 1965
Levine, G., 'Determinism and Responsibility in the Works of George Eliot', *PMLA*, 77, 1962
Stump, R., *Movement and Vision in George Eliot's Novels*, 1959

Texts

Dickens, C., *The Clarendon Dickens*, ed. J. Butt and K. Tillotson, 1966- ; in progress
The Pilgrim edition of the Letters of Dickens, ed. M. House and G. Storey, 1965- ; in progress, 7 vols. to date
The Letters of Charles Dickens, ed. W. Dexter, 3 vols., 1938

Biographical and Critical Works

Ackroyd, P., *Dickens*, 1990
Butt, J. and Tillotson, K., *Dickens at Work*, 1957
Chesterton, G. K., *Charles Dickens*, 1906
Collins, P. (ed.), *Charles Dickens: The Critical Heritage*, 1971
Dyson, A. E. (ed.), *Dickens: Modern Judgments* 1976
Fielding, J. K., *Charles Dickens*, 1960
Ford, G. H., *Dickens and his Readers*, 1955
Forster, J, *The Life of Dickens*, 3 vols., 1872-4
Hardy, B., *The Moral Art of Dickens*, 1970
House, H., *The Dickens World*, 1942
Walder, D., *Dickens and Religion*, 1981
Wilson, A., *The World of Charles Dickens*, 1970

Chapter IV — Tennyson and Browning

Texts

Tennyson, A., *The Poems of Tennyson*, ed., C. Ricks, 1969
The Letters of Alfred Lord Tennyson, ed., Cecil Y. Lang and E. F. Shannon Jnr., 3 vols., 1982-1990

Biographical and Critical Works

Bradley, A. C., *A Commentary on Tennyson's 'In Memoriam'*, 1901, rev., 1902, 1930

Buckley, J. H., *Tennyson: the Growth of a Poet*, 1960
Eliot, T. S., 'In Memoriam' in *Essays Ancient and Modern*, 1936
Jump, J. D. (ed.), *Tennyson (The Critical Heritage* series), 1967
Knowles, J., 'Aspects of Tennyson, II: a Personal Reminiscence',
    Nineteenth Century XXXIII, 1893, 164-88
Killham, J. (ed.), *Critical Essays on the Poetry of Tennyson*, 1960
Martin, R. B., *Tennyson: the Unquiet Heart*, 1980
Maurice, F., *The Life of F. D. Maurice*, 2 vols., 1883
Norton, C. E. (ed.), *The Correspondence of Carlyle and Emerson*, 2 vols., 1883
Palmer, D. J. (ed.)*Tennyson (Writers and their Background* series) 1973
Rader, R. W., *Tennyson's 'Maud': the Biografical Genesis*, 1963
Sterling, J., 'Poems' (1842), *Quarterly Review*, LXX, 1842, 385-416
Tennyson, C., *Alfred Tennyson*, 1949
Tennyson, H., *Alfred Lord Tennyson: A Memoir by his Son*, 2 vols., 1897
Tillotson, G. and K., *Mid-Victorian Studies* 1965

Texts

Browning, R., *The Complete Works of Robert Browning*, general editor
    Roma A. King Jr., Athens, Ohio, 13 vols., 1969-89

Biographical and Critical Works

Armstrong, I. (ed.), *Robert Browning (Writers and their Background* series), 1974
Chesterton, G. K., *Robert Browning*, 1903
Drew, P., *The Poetry of Browning: A Critical Introduction*, 1970
Jones, A. R., 'Robert Browning and the Dramatic Monologue', *The Critical Quarterly*, IX, 1967
Langbaum, R., *The Poetry of Experience: The Dramatic Monologue in Modern Literary Tradition*, 1957
Miller, B., *Robert Browning: A Portrait*, 1952
Tracy, C. R. (ed.), *Browning's Mind and Art*, 1968
Ward, M., *Robert Browning and his World*, 2 vols., 1968-9
Whitla, W., *The Central Truth: The Incarnation in Browning's Poetry*, 1963

Chapter V — Yeats and Eliot

Texts

Yeats, W. B., *Collected Poems*, 2 vols., 1949
The various edn. of the *Poems*, ed. P. Allt and R. Alspach, New York, 1957
Responsibilities and Other Poems, 1916
The Tower, 1928
The Winding Stair and Other Poems, 1933
Autobiographies: Reveries over Childhood, and The Trembling of the Veil, 1955
The Letters of W. B. Yeats, ed., A. Wade, 1954
W. B. Yeats and T. Sturge Moore, Their Correspondence 1901-1937, ed.,
    Ursula Bridges, 1953

Biographical and Critical Works

Ellman, R., *Yeats: The Man and the Masks*, 1948; *The Identity of Yeats*, 1954

Gregory, Isabella, A., Lady, *Visions and Beliefs in the West of Ireland* (with two essays and notes by Yeats), 2 vols., 1920

Hall, J. and Steinman, M. (eds.), *The Permanence of Yeats*, 1950

Henn, T. R., *The Lonely Tower*, 1950, 2nd. rev. edn., 1965

Hough, G., *The Last Romantics*, 1959; *The Mystery Religion of W. B. Yeats*, 1984

Jeffares, A. N., *W. B. Yeats: Man and Poet*, 1949

Wilson, F. A. C., *W. B. Yeats and Tradition*, 1958; *Yeats's Iconography*, 1960

Texts

Eliot, T. S., *The Complete Poems and Plays*, 1969

The Sacred Wood, 1920

The Waste Land, New York 1922; London 1923

The Waste Land: A Facsimile and Transcript of the Original Drafts, ed., Valerie Eliot, 1971

Dante, 1929

Ash-Wednesday, 1930

Thoughts After Lambeth, 1931

Selected Essays, 1932

The Use of Poetry and the Use of Criticism, 1933

After Strange Gods, 1934

Murder in the Cathedral, 1935

Essays Ancient and Modern, 1936

The Family Reunion, 1939

The Idea of a Christian Society, 1939

East Coker, 1940

Burnt Norton, 1941

The Dry Salvages, 1941

Little Gidding, 1942

Reunion by Destruction, 1943

Four Quartets, 1944

George Herbert, 1962

Knowledge and Experience in the Philosophy of F. H. Bradley, 1964

Biographical and Critical Works

Bergonzi, B. (ed.), *T. S. Eliot, Four Quartets. A Casebook*, 1969

Bergsten, S., *Time and Eternity. A Study in the Structure and Symbolism of T. S. Eliot's Four Quartets*, 1960

Bradley, F. H., *Appearance and Reality*, 1893, rev. 1897; *Essays on Truth and Reality*, 1914

Bush, R., *T. S. Eliot: A Study in Character and Style*, 1984

Childs, D. J., 'T. S. Eliot and Evelyn Underhill: An Early Mystical Influence', *Durham University Journal*, Dec., 1987

Drew, E., *T. S. Eliot: The Design of his Poetry*, 1950

Gardner, H., *The Art of T. S. Eliot*, 1949; *The Composition of Four Quartets*, 1978

Gordon, L., *Eliot's Early Years*, 1977; *Eliot's New Life*, 1988

Hayes, E. K., *Eliot's Negative Way*, 1982

Kenner, H., *The Invisible Poet: T. S. Eliot*, 1960; (ed.)*T. S. Eliot, A Collection of Critical Essays*,

Smidt, K., *Poetry and Belief in the Work of T. S. Eliot*, 1961

Spender, S., *Eliot*, 1975

Chapter VI — Auden and Larkin

Texts

Auden, W. H., *Collected Poems*, 1945

Collected Shorter Poems 1930-1944, 1950

Collected Shorter Poems 1927-1957, 1966

Collected Longer Poems, 1968

The Dog Beneath the Skin: or Where is Francis?, (with C. Isherwood), 1935

The Ascent of F6 (with C. Isherwood), 1936

Spain, 1937

Letters From Iceland (with L. MacNeice), 1937

'Nightmail', (c. 1938) rptd. in *Collected Shorter Poems 1927-1957*

On the Frontier (with C. Isherwood), 1938

Journey to a War (with C. Isherwood), 1939

For the Time Being, New York, 1944; London, 1945

The Age of Anxiety: a Baroque Eclogue, New York, 1947; London, 1948

The Enchafed Flood: or the Romantic Iconography of the Sea, 1951

Nones, New York, 1951; London, 1952

The Shield of Achilles, New York, 1955; London, 1955

Homage to Clio, 1960

The Dyer's Hand and Other Essays, New York, 1962; London, 1963

City without Walls, 1969

Biographical and Critical Works

Bloom, R. (ed.), *A Tribute to Auden on his Sixtieth Birthday*, 1967

Carpenter, H., *W. H. Auden: a Biography*, 1992

Everett, B., *Auden*, 1964

Hoggart, R., *Auden: an Introductory Essay*, 1951

Larkin, P. A., 'What's Become of Wystan?', *Spectator*, 15 July 1960

Pike, J. A. (ed.), *Modern Canterbury Pilgrims*, 1956

Spender, S., *W. H. Auden: A Tribute*, 1975

Texts

Larkin, P. A., *Collected Poems*, ed. A. Thwaite, 1988
Selected Letters of Philip Larkin 1940-1985, ed. A. Thwaite, 1992
The North Ship, 1945, new ed. with intro. by the author, 1966
Jill, a novel, 1947, new ed. with intro. by the author, 1975
üA Girl in Winter, a novel, 1947
XX Poems, 1951
The Less Deceived, 1955
The Whitsun Weddings, 1964
All What Jazz: A Record Diary, 1961-68, 1970
High Windows, 1974
(ed.), *The Oxford Book of Twentieth-Century Verse*, 1973
Required Writing: Miscellaneous Pieces, 1955-82, 1983

Biographical and Critical Works

Booth, J., *Philip Larkin: Writer*, 1992
Brownjohn, A., *Philip Larkin* (*Writers and their Work* series), 1975
Hartley, G. (ed.), *Philip Larkin 1922-85: A Tribute*, 1988
Motion, A., *Philip Larkin: A Writer's Life*, 1993
Salwak, D. (ed.), *Philip Larkin*, 1989
Timms, D., *Philip Larkin*, 1973
Thwaite, A. (ed.), *Philip Larkin at Sixty*, 1982

Secondary Works

Abrams, M. H., *Natural Supernaturalism*, 1971
Buckley, J. H., *The Victorian Temper: A Study in Literary Culture*, 1952
Chadwick, H. (ed.) *Lessing's Theological Writings*, 1957
Clark, G. Kitson, *The Making of Victorian England*, 1962
Elliott-Binns, L. E., *English Thought 1860-1900: The Theological Aspect*, 1956
Fairchild, H. N., *Religious Trends in English Poetry*, 6 vols., 1968
Frazer, J. G., *The Golden Bough: A Study in Comparative Religion*, 2 vols., 1890
Houghton, W, E., *The Victorian Frame of Mind, 1830-1870*, 1957
von Hügel, Baron, *The Mystical Elements in Religion*, 1908
Knoepflmacher, U. C., *Religious Humanism and the Victorian Novel*, 1965
Kung, H., *On Being a Christian*, 1974; *Great Christian Thinkers*, 1994
Landow, G. P., *Victorian Types, Victorian Shadows: Biblical Typology in Victorian Art and Thought*, 1980
Mill, J. S., *Autobiography*, 1873
Miller, J. Hillis, *The Disappearance of God: Five Nineteenth-Century Writers*, 1963
Muirhead, J. H., *The Platonic Tradition in Anglo-Saxon Philosophy*, 1931
Niebuhr, R., *The Nature and Destiny of Man*, 2 vols., 1941-43
Nietzsche, F., *The Birth of Tragedy*, 1872
Pfleiderer, O., *The Development of Theology in Germany since Kant and*

   its Progress in England since 1825, 1893
Royce, J., *The Religious Aspect of Philosophy*, 1885 ; *The World and the Individual, 1900-01*
Underhill, E., *Mysticism*, 1911, rev. 1912, rev. 1930
Vidler, A., *The Church in an Age of Revolution*, 1961
Wheeler, M., *Death and the Future Life in Victorian Literature and Theology*, 1990
Willey, B., *Nineteenth Century Studies*, 1949; *More Nineteenth Century Studies*, 1956
Williams, C. W. S., *The Descent of the Dove*, 1939
Young, G. M., *Victorian England: Portrait of an Age*, 1953

INDEX

Abrams, M. H., 21, 22, 23, 30
Acton, Lord, 95, 114
Addison, Joseph, 17
Aeschylus, 110
Albert, Prince consort, 117, 132
Alford, Henry, 34
Aquinas, Thomas St., 34, 181, 197;
    Thomism, 144
Aristotle, 48, 100
Arnold, Matthew, 53, 55, 70-83, 93,
    157
Arnold, Dr. Thomas, 79
Auden, W. H., 116, 163, 205-226,
    231, 238
Augustine of Hyppo, St, 31, 83, 192,
    195, 201, 215
Austen, Jane, 26

Bailey, Benjamin, 219
Barbauld, Mrs Anna Laetitia, 38, 39
Barth, Carl, 223
Baring, Rosa, 127, 128
Barthes, Roland, 1, 2
Bartram, William, 41
Bauer, Bruno, 154
Bechet, Sidney, 237
Bentham, Jeremy, 53
Bergson, Henri, 182
Berkeley, George, 10, 17, 18, 23, 24,
    33, 37, 166, 174
Bernini, 105, 107
Betjeman, John, 205, 226, 227, 232,
    235, 237, 238, 239
Blackwood, John, 85
Blagdon, Isa, 154
Blake, William, 29, 116, 169, 216,
    217

Blavatsky, Madame Helena, 163
Blood, Benjamin Paul, 139, 140
Bloomfield, B. C., 213
Boehme, Jacob, 47, 68, 164, 185
Bowles, William L., 38
Bowra, Sir Maurice, 238
Bradley, F. H., 82, 164, 182, 184,
    185, 192, 193, 194, 196, 203
Bray, Charles, 85, 86, 88
Brown, Ford Madox, 65
Browning, Elizabeth Barrett, 133,
    146
Browning, Robert, 70, 146-160
Buckley, J. H., 134
Buddhism, 164, 173, 192, 193, 195,
    196, 197, 203
Bunyan, John, 31
Bürger, Gottfried A., 38, 39, 44
Burke, Edmund, 12, 14, 166
Burnet, Gilbert, 19, 240
Butler, Bishop Samuel, 75
Byron, Lord George, 35, 60, 69, 71,
    72, 74, 75

Calvert, William, 11, 12
Calvinism, 9, 55, 77
Cambridge Platonists, The, 19, 142
Campbell,, J. D., 19
Candwell, Christopher, 208
Carlyle, Thomas, 5, 28, 54-70, 82,
    88, 98, 109, 119, 121, 122, 123,
    128, 135, 144, 157
Carlyle, Jane Welsh, 54, 55, 56
Chambers, Robert, 140
Chaplin, Charlie, 119, 120
Chapman, John, 88
Charles I, King, 7, 35, 200

Chartists, The, 70
Chaucer, Geoffrey, 123
Chesterton, G. K., 116
Clough, Arthur Hugh, 72, 73
Coburn, Kathleen, 240
Coleridge, Berkeley, 10, 18
Coleridge, Derwent, 18, 44, 241
Coleridge, George, 14, 15
Coleridge, Hartley, 10, 18, 37
Coleridge, J. T., 36
Coleridge, Samuel Taylor, 4, 6-54,
    55, 61, 62, 63, 65, 67, 68, 76,
    80, 85, 87, 97, 113, 135, 158,
    180, 181
Coleridge, Sara (née Fricker), 9, 45,
    46
Comte, Auguste, 90, 91, 109
Conrad, Joseph, 73, 190
Cottle, Joseph, 24, 42
Cowper, William, 238
Crabbe, George, 238
Cross, John W, 112
Cudworth, Ralph, 19

Dante Alighieri, 34, 107, 143, 173,
    176, 180, 181, 192, 194, 196,
    200, 203, 204, 212
Darbishire, Helen, 27
Darwin, Charles, 4, 77, 87, 92, 93,
    94, 98, 140, 142, 161, 175
Davies, Hugh Sykes, 184
Davies, Llewellyn, 154
Derrida, Jacques, 3
Deutsch, Emanuel, 113
Dickens, Charles, 3, 62, 70, 86, 115,
    116-124, 131, 191
Dickinson, Emily, 229, 230, 231
Dodd, C.H., 156, 204
Donne, John, 180, 184, 238
Dostoevsky, Fyodor, 119, 120, 121
Drew, Elizabeth, 178
Duffy, Sir Charles Gavan, 151

Durrell, Lawrence, 196

Eagleton, Terry, 4
Eliot, George, 3, 4, 54, 70, 84-115,
    116, 117, 118, 119, 123, 146,
    147, 148, 157
Eliot, T. S., 1, 37, 55, 82, 131, 138,
    146, 163, 164, 165, 170, 176,
    177-204, 205, 208, 210, 211,
    218, 225, 226, 237, 238, 239
Eliot, Valerie, 179, 190
Eliot, Vivien, 188, 189, 196
Ellman, Richard, 164, 174
Emerson, Ralph Waldo, 118, 144, 181
Engels, Friedrich, 69
Evangelical movement, 6, 33, 35,
    53, 85, 86, 117
Everett, Barbara, 210

Fairchild, Hoxie, 26
Ferrar, Nicholas, 200, 201
Feuerbach, Ludwig, 88, 89, 90, 91,
    150, 153
Fichte, Johann, 60, 135
Flower, Benjamin, 14, 15
Forster, E. M., 214
Fox, Barclay, 66, 241
Fox, Caroline, 67
Fox, George, 47
Francis of Assisi, St., 79
Frazer, Sir James George, 162, 173,
    177, 191, 194
Frend, William, 7
Freud, Sigmund, 178, 206, 211, 212,
    216, 220, 229, 231
Frye, Northrop, 1

Gascoyne, David, 205
Gibbon, Edward, 51, 56
Gillman, James, 44, 47
Gilpin, William, 17
Gladstone, William, 131, 132, 136,
    144

Godwin, William, 12, 13, 14, 16, 19, 50, 74, 89

Goethe, Johann W. von, 60, 69, 72, 73, 74, 122

Goldsmith, Oliver, 166

Gonne, Maud, 166, 168, 174

Gordon, Lyndall, 1, 178

Gore-Booth, Eva, 166, 171, 172

Gray, Asa, 94

Gray, Thomas, 76, 228

Greene, Graham, 152

Gregory, Augusta, 162, 166, 169, 171

Griggs, E. L., 240 (Notes)

Grigson, Geoffrey, 41

Gross, Miriam, 227

Guyon, Mme, 184

Haight, Gordon, 85

Hale, Emily, 179, 197

Hallam, Arthur, 125, 126, 135, 137, 138

Hardy, Thomas, 205, 230, 233, 235, 238, 239

Hare, Julius C., 53, 63, 64, 66, 67, 68

Harnack, Theodosius, 183

Hartley, David, 9, 15, 16, 17, 19, 24, 47

Hartley, Jean, 232

Hawker, Robert Stephen, 238

Hayes, Eloise Knapp, 185

Hayward, John, 176, 177

Hazlitt, William, 8, 14, 19

Heard, Gerald, 206

Hegel, G. W. F., 3, 4, 54, 69, 87, 88, 89, 90, 96, 97, 98, 99, 100, 109, 110, 113, 136, 139, 140, 141, 142, 153, 164, 183, 185

Heine, Heinrich, 73

Henn, T. R., 174

Hennell, Charles, 85, 86, 87

Herbert, George, 180, 184

Hilton, Walter, 184

Hinduism, 164, 192, 193, 195, 198, 199, 203

Hitler, Adolf, 207, 212, 224

Hobbes, Thomas, 19

Hood, Thomas, 228

Hooker, Sir Joseph, 160

Hopkins, Gerard Manley, 146

Hough, Graham, 164

House, Humphrey, 117

Housman, A. E., 211, 235, 236

Hügel, Baron von, 161, 173, 184

Hughes, Thomas, 70

Hulme, T. E., 161, 180, 208

Hume, David, 51, 55, 155

Hurwitz, Hyman, 113

Hutchinson, Mary, (Wordsworth), 27, 45

Hutchinson, Sara, 45

Huxley, Aldous, 206

Huxley, T. H., 91, 98, 142, 161

Isherwood, Christopher, 210, 211, 214

James, Henry, 112, 219

Jameson, Anna Brownell, 104, 105

Jennings, Elizabeth, 205

John of the Cross, St., 164, 173, 185, 188, 194, 196

Johnes, Thomas, 41, 42

Jones, Robert, 10, 12

Jowett, Benjamin, 93, 139, 140, 141

Joyce, James, 165, 166

Judaism and Zionism, 110, 111, 112, 113, 114

Julian, of Norwich, Dame, 164, 184, 201, 223, 224

Jung, Carl Gustav, 178, 193

Kallman, Chester, 215

Kant, Immanuel, 4, 47, 49, 50, 60, 61, 63, 65, 73, 76, 97, 140, 182

Keats, John, 165, 219

Keble, John, 36, 78

Kierkegaard, Soren A., 52, 158, 159, 216, 217, 221, 223, 224, 225, 232, 234

Kingsley, Charles, 36, 53, 70

Knowles, James, 125, 136, 138, 139, 144

Kung, Hans, 82

Lamb, Charles, 45, 63

Lane, Homer, 207

Land, William, 35

Lane, Sir Hugh, 168

Larkin, Philip, 226-239

Law, William, 47, 68, 164

Lawrence, D. H., 206, 207

Layard, John, 207

Leavis, F. R., 111, 114

Lessing, Gotthold E., 51, 52, 77, 157

Lewes, George Henry, 35, 90, 93, 94, 96, 97, 101, 114, 115, 116

Lewis, C. S., 32, 209

Lewis, M. G., ('Monk'), 38

Locke, John, 17

Loisy, Alfred, 183, 184

Lowes, J. L., 41

Lubbock, John, 92

Ludlow, John, 70

Lyell, Sir Charles, 92, 140

Mackay, Robert, 88, 91, 95

MacNeice, Louis, 207, 210

Malory, Sir Thomas, 132

Malthus, Thomas Robert, 94

Man, Paul de, 3

Mare, Walter de la , 229

Maritain, Jacques, 196

Markiewicz, Constance, 171, 172

Martineau, Harriet, 70

Marvell, Andrew, 173

Marx, Karl, (Marxism), 1, 3, 4, 5, 69, 89, 145, 184, 205, 206, 209, 211, 212, 216

Mary, Queen of Scots, 180, 198

Maurice, F.D., 36, 53, 55, 63, 64, 65, 67, 70, 123, 135, 142, 143, 157

Mayer, Elizabeth, 214

Meredith, George, 114, 115, 146, 147

Methodism, 20, 53, 68, 197

Mill, John Stuart, 53, 63, 66, 70, 74, 87, 93

Millais, Sir John, 118

Milton, John, 7, 9, 19, 30, 34, 42, 46, 49, 83, 134, 135, 137, 138, 200

Montgomery, James, 33

Moore, G. E., 164

Moore, T. Sturge, 164, 174

Moorman, Mary, 26, 240

More, Hannah, 33, 86

More, Henry, 162

Morley, John, 93

Motion, Andrew, 227, 229

Muir, Edwin, 205

Myers, F. W. H., 97

Mysticism, 182, 183, 184, 185, 189, 194, 202

Napoleon, Bonaparte, 35, 57, 59, 123

Newman, Cardinal John Henry, 36, 45, 53, 55, 69, 78, 79, 80, 81, 82, 133, 157

Newton, Isaac, 9

Niebuhr, Reinhold, 202, 203, 217, 221, 224

Niebuhr, Ursula, 202, 217, 224

Nietzsche, F. W., 112, 169, 170

O'Duffy, General Eoin, 168
Oedipus, 99
O'Leary, John, 167
Oldham, Dr. J. H., 197
Orwell, George, 209, 209

Paley, William, 50, 51, 92
Parnell, Thomas, 166
Pascal, Blaise, 152
Patten, Lewis, 240
Paul, St., 77, 81, 116, 123, 143, 195, 201, 215, 216
Pinneys, the, 8, 9
Plato, (platonic), 10, 19, 42, 49, 50, 90, 134, 143, 155, 156, 164, 165, 173, 174, 220
Plotinus, 163, 164, 165, 173, 174, 203
Poole, Thomas, 48, 49
Pope, Alexander, 137
Popper, Sir Karl, 2, 3
Pound, Ezra, 189, 190, 191
Price, Richard, 8
Priestley, Joseph, 7, 9, 118
Proust, Marcel, 73
Pusey, Edward B., 55, 68

Quakers, The, 66, 142
Quinn, John, 190

Radcliffe, Ann, 38
Renan, Ernest, 77, 153, 154
Richards, I. A., 75, 76
Rilke, Rainer Maria, 216
Robertson, William, 56
Robinson, Mary, 38
Roman Catholic Church, 79, 91, 117, 118, 149, 151, 183, 184
Royce, Josiah, 182, 184, 185, 186, 203
Ruskin, John, 55

Russell, Bertrand, 164, 192
Savonarola, Fra Girolamo, 103, 104
Schelling, Friedrich W. J., 50, 60, 73
Schleiermacher, Friedrich E. D., 18, 67
Schopenhauer, Arthur, 73, 174, 176
Scott, Sir Walter, 39
Selincourt, E. de, 240, 241
Shaftesbury, Third Earl of, 17, 33
Shaffer, Elinor, 154, 155
Shakespeare, William, 48, 52, 120, 181, 218, 219, 220
Shelley, Percy Bysshe, 89, 111
Sidney, Sir Philip, 76
Sisson, Charles, 205
Smith, Adam, 94
Socrates, 42, 43
Sophocles, 97, 99
Southey, Robert, 8, 9, 13, 19, 38, 44, 68
Spencer, Herbert, 94, 95, 96, 97, 98, 109
Spinoza, Benedict de, 18, 19, 26, 96, 97, 111, 113, 142
Stanley, Arthur Penrhyn, 78
Stephen, Leslie, 75, 85, 93, 98, 112, 114
Sterling, Edward, 66
Sterling, John, 61, 63, 64, 65, 66, 67, 69, 70, 132
Stirling, J. H., 54
Strachey, Edward, 65
Strauss, David Friedrich, 64, 66, 77, 87, 88, 89, 91, 150, 153
Swedenborg, Emanuel, 162
Swift, Jonathan, 166
Swineburne, Algernon Charles, 132, 133

Tagart, Edward, 118

Temple, Archbishop William, 155
Tennyson, Alfred, Lord, 71, 125-46, 157, 187, 238
Tennyson, Hallam, 126, 129, 130, 132, 133, 137, 139, 142
Thackeray, William Makepeace, 70, 119
Thelwall, John, 9, 14
Theresa of Avila, St., 104, 105, 106, 107, 113, 164, 184, 194
Thomas à Kempis, 100
Thomas, R. S., 205
Thorwaldsen, Bertel, 87
Tillotson, Kathleen, 132
Tolstoy, Count Lev Nikolaevich, 73, 119, 120, 121
Tractarian movement (Oxford movement), 26, 35, 78, 117
Trevelyan, Mary, 179
Trollope, Anthony, 111, 119, 123
Tulloch, John, 53
Tyndall, John, 161
Tyrrell, Father, 184

Underhill, Evelyn, 184, 185, 186, 194
Unitarianism, 7, 8, 17, 20, 27, 70, 118, 181, 183, 188

Vallon, Annette, 11, 13, 24, 27, 31
Victoria, Queen, 132, 138
Voltaire, 14, 153, 155

Walder, Dennis, 118
Warren, Austin, 2
Watts, Isaac, 31
Wedgwood, Thomas, 20
Wellek, René, 2
Wesley, John, 6, 19, 20, 21, 31, 33, 53, 68, 86
Weston, Jessie, 194
Whitehead, A. N., 164
Wilberforce, William, 6, 19, 20, 21, 33, 53, 86
Wilde, Oscar, 146
Willey, Basil, 85
Williams, Charles, 201, 202, 205, 209, 214, 215, 216, 217, 223, 224
Wilson, Angus, 119, 121
Wiseman, Cardinal, 151
Wittgenstein, Ludwig, 2
Woolf, Virginia, 115
Wordsworth, Dorothy, 9, 15, 25, 27, 30, 46, 74, 240, 241
Wordsworth, William, 1, 4, 6-54, 55, 71, 73, 74, 75, 84, 85, 108, 116, 135, 136, 175, 180, 203, 218, 225, 229, 233, 235, 240, 241

Yeats, William Butler, 146, 161-78, 190, 191, 204, 205, 211, 212, 220
Young, G. M., 78

Zunz, Leopold, 110